Mankind in Barbary

The University Press
of New England

Brandeis University

Clark University

Dartmouth College

University of New Hampshire

University of Rhode Island

University of Vermont

Stanley T. Gutman

Mankind in Barbary

The Individual and Society in

the Novels of Norman Mailer

Published for The University of Vermont by

The University Press of New England

Hanover, New Hampshire, 1975

To my parents

Ruth and Carl Gutman

Preface

What is it in Mailer's work that appeals to readers, that either stimulates and excites them, or repels them? Is Mailer the unique figure he sometimes claims to be, or is he, instead, a figure understandable in an historical and literary continuum? How do Mailer's works reflect the spirit and cultural conditions of our time? And, finally, is it possible to discover a coherent pattern in Mailer's thought and beliefs? Those are the major questions I confront.

Mailer's novels were selected as the focus of this investigation because in my opinion, and I believe Mailer's as well, it is as a craftsman and worker in fiction that his literary gifts are based. This book investigates the world of his novels and the views they offer of society and men within society; the conceptual underpinnings of Mailer's vision; and some of Mailer's formal and stylistic techniques. By concentrating on each novel, one at a time, I have sought to show both the unity and the growth of Mailer's ideas. Since one essay—"The White Negro," written in 1955— seemed indispensable to Mailer's world-view, a discussion of that is also included. *The Armies of the Night* is classified as a novel both because Mailer describes it as a hybrid between the novel and history and because it resolves many of the themes of the earlier novels.

The issues Mailer struggles with are important, even crucial, in our twentieth-century world. He tries to cope with Freud and Marx, with existentialism and the postromantic consciousness, with totalitarianism and technological society. Like many of his contemporaries, he attempts to forge an ethic that will restore the place of the individual in an era of depersonalization, alienation, and rapid change. His ethic is compounded of courage, the engagement with death, and a commitment to growth. Furthermore, his often scathing denunciation of the ills of modern society leads him into the political arena, for men must have social as well as individual patterns of action if they are to prevail and ultimately overcome the inhumane tendencies within modern society. In confronting the complex and chaotic aspects of contemporary civilization, Mailer sometimes seems outrageous and even ridiculous; yet he often comes closer to satisfying the needs of postwar Americans than others who are more deliberate and less daring. If he seems the madman at times, so at times is he the visionary.

The following abbreviations have been used to refer to Mailer's nonfiction: *AM* for *Advertisements for Myself* (New York: Putnam's, 1959); *PP* for *The Presidential Papers* (New York: Putnam's, 1963); and *C&C* for *Cannibals and Christians* (New York: The Dial Press, 1966). For permission to reprint brief extracts, I thank these publishers.

I have received generous support from Duke University, the Danforth Foundation, and the University of Vermont. At trying junctures while teaching at the University of Vermont, I found welcome support from Kenneth S. Rothwell, John G. Weiger, and William H. Macmillan.

There are many others who have helped. Richard Murphy, John Rosenwald, and Victor Strandberg stimulated my early research by their penetrating questions and suggestions. For understanding, support, and help in creating the kind of community in which intellectual investigation can flourish, I am indebted to Sture Anliot, Harry Boyte, Anthony Bradley, Arnie Katz, Gary Lepak, David Robinson, and Steven Wolinetz. I am deeply sorry James D. Mann did not live long enough to see the completion of my efforts. During the years I have worked on Mailer, the Durham, North Carolina, and Lincoln, Vermont, men's groups have provided needed self-understanding and support. Three teachers at Hamilton College, Thomas Colby, Dwight Lindley and John Morey, have given me more than they know; my understanding of the relationship between a literary work and the *Weltanschauung* of its author is the gift of their teaching.

Bernard I. Duffey, of Duke University, is responsible for many of the strongest aspects of this study. All who write should have such critics as he has been. In addition, his confidence in my work sustained me during the process of preparing the manuscript for publication. That process was made easier by the intelligent and conscientious editing of David Horne, of the University Press of New England.

My largest debt is to my wife, Buff Lindau. Her keen critical insights and her attention to matters of style have affected, all for the better, every page of this book. She has given me love and friendship, and she has given this study extensive time and effort. This is her book, as well as mine.

Burlington, Vermont   S.T.G.
March 1975

Contents

Mankind in Barbary

Chapter I

The Naked and the Dead

Violence and Power in the Military

While still a student at Harvard University, Norman Mailer decided to become a writer. He saw the Second World War as his·opportunity, for every great war requires its chroniclers. The First World War had provided the subjects of, and impetus for, the early works of Ernest Hemingway, John Dos Passos, and E. E. Cummings. Here was a new war, in need of a man who could sum it up, capture the spirit of the times, and see in the war a paradigm for human experience. Mailer decided that he would be that man, and that his war experience would make him famous and successful. After he had served in the Pacific theater, he was released from the army and went to Paris, where in a frenzy of creativity that lasted about a year and a half he wrote *The Naked and the Dead*.[1] Upon publication, the novel became a best-seller, and Mailer found himself famous.

The Naked and the Dead is set in the mid-Pacific and deals with an army campaign on the mythical island of Anopopei. Mailer concentrates on a division in the midst of a major campaign, and on a small unit within that division, the recon platoon. General Cummings, who commands the division, and Sergeant Croft, who leads the platoon, are the book's two antagonists: each seeks total mastery within the sphere of his command. Opposed to these two men are Lieutenant Hearn and Red Valsen, each of whom pursues liberal and humane values, only to end up defeated by Croft. The other men in the platoon see their lives disrupted, changed, and even destroyed by the demands made on them by both the war and Sergeant Croft.

The Naked and the Dead is a big book; it is the longest of Mailer's novels; it has the most characters and the widest sphere of action. The novel is an attempt to present a dilemma of power from a variety of perspectives: men need to control their lives and environment, but attempts to exert control lead to totalitarian structures and attitudes. Through General Cummings, who theorizes about the nature of war and the military in his frequent discussions with his aide, Lieutenant Hearn, Mailer analyzes the significance of the war to those fighting it. By splitting his focus and concentrating on both the division and the recon platoon, Mailer's vision is broad and deep, general and specific, abstract and concrete.

Mailer's primary concern is confrontation, not with the Japanese but rather within the division and the platoon as men struggle for mastery over one another and for control over their own lives. All the characters have violent relationships within the closed society of the military. One of the most important contests is that between General Cummings and Lieutenant Hearn. The General and Lieutenant are partners in a mad waltz, repelled and yet fascinated with each other, dancing in a posture created by their mutual need and the mutual contempt that holds them at arm's length. Their struggle is often over ideas but basically is an attempt by each to dominate and control the other. When Hearn tosses his cigarette on the floor of the General's tent, it is a gauntlet; the struggle, formerly held in check, erupts into open psychological confrontation, resolved only when Cummings uses his rank to put down his subordinate. Hearn, as a result of this confrontation, is transferred to the command of the recon platoon, and a similar struggle between himself and Sergeant Croft develops.

Mailer's characterizations of Croft and Cummings suggest that the need to dominate other men is an extension of the drive for self-mastery. All the characters in the novel are affected by the tensions that arise when some men seek to control others; at the same time, each of the characters is engaged in a struggle to master himself—his hopes, urges, and emotions. The men in the recon platoon are caught up by antithetical emotions such as love and hate, they are pulled toward the violent and the pacific, they want and need other members of the platoon and at the same time are threatened by them.

Mailer locates the roots of many of these contradictory urges in the warped sexual development of these men, and in the inequity of American social and economic structures. These urges control the actions of individuals, and so the characters are in continual struggle to define their needs, to determine how and when they will satisfy themselves. Mailer uses a flashback technique which he calls "The Time Machine" to investigate the sociosexual history of his characters. We discover that Croft and Cummings are driven by feelings of sexual inadequacy; Martinez, a Mexican-American who is second in command to Croft, is attracted to war because it is the only avenue toward social satisfaction available to a member of a racial minority; and Gallagher, a bigoted and disillusioned product of an Irish neighborhood in Boston, spews out bitterness because of frustrations born of the unfulfillable dreams that society has engendered in him.

War has aspects other than the search for power and mastery, and Mailer deals with them as well, particularly the brutalization of men in the recon platoon. The extreme situations into which they are pushed often deaden their feeling. At one point they come across a ghastly and nightmarish landscape strewn with limbs and burnt corpses and putrifying Japanese bodies infested with maggots. Over everything hangs the stench of death. Yet the men look for souvenirs, as if the charnel house were Coney Island. Only the frightening blast of Red's pistol, fired at a menacing snake within the confines of a small cave, moves them from mild discomfort to fear, disgust, and antipathy. Amid extremities of war, brutalization is the price the psyche pays for the continued existence of the individual. It is possible for some men to triumph over emotions that threaten to overwhelm the psyche, and thus war may result in either a disintegration or a strengthening of character. Ridges, the poor Southern farmer, is stronger at the end of the novel than before; Roth, the middle-class Jew, is stronger, in his pitiful way, just before he dies. On the other hand, Minetta, the platoon malingerer, disintegrates, as do Corporal Brown and even Red Valsen, Sergeant Croft's primary antagonist. Wilson and Red discover their insides rotting away, in one case from syphilis, in the other from nephritis. Other effects of war, also immensely powerful, are anxiety, boredom, and physical and emotional exhaustion—visible in the whole platoon—as well as a disorientation most recognizable in Gallagher's progressive inability to deal with a succession of crises, culminating in the death of his wife.

War is one of Mailer's basic metaphors for existence; throughout his work he considers all human endeavor as a martial struggle in a divided universe. His recreation of a campaign in the Pacific theater in the Second World War is in a large sense the creation of a myth that describes and perhaps explains the nature of reality. Men's individual lives, their societies, and the natural world they inhabit are all bound by the same patterns that shape the military in *The Naked and the Dead.*

Foremost in the novel is the antagonistic relationship between men and the natural world, a world Mailer consistently portrays as powerful, harsh, alien, and impenetrable. The reader's overwhelming impression is of the impotence and insignificance of human beings. Although the novel opens with a phenomenon typical of the war in the Pacific—a large-scale beach assault backed up by enormous fire-power—Mailer sees this activity in its natural perspective: "Mount Anaka rose out of a base of maroon-colored smoke. Implacably, despite the new purple robes at its feet, the mountain sat on the island, and gazed out to sea. The bombardment was insignificant before it" (20). Nature's power makes any effort of man futile and insignificant; all of the men in the platoon come to realize that there is always "the lethargic sullen power of the ocean beneath the thin metal deck" (445). Even the heroism of Goldstein and Ridges, who carry Wilson out of the jungle, pales when seen against its natural backdrop; their action has much of the significance with which Albert Camus invested Sisyphus' attempts to push his rock to the top of his hill, but it is seen from a universal as well as human scale: "They had the isolation, the insignificance of insects traversing an endless beach" (494).

If man is insignificant, human actions viewed in their natural context are useless and pointless. Two of the most important objectives of the platoon are to transport several large guns, during the night, closer to the front lines and to climb Mount Anaka. The first is only partially successful; one gun is lost merely yards away from their goal. But the whole suffering journey turns out for naught; the guns are not needed and not used; the battle they could have been used in is unimportant. The attempt to climb Mount Anaka is doubly futile: not only is it unsuccessful, but there is no reason, save human pride, to make the effort in the first place. When Polack announces, "we broke our ass for nothin'," the platoon finds it "perfectly fitting" (705). Even Cummings realizes what is clear to the reader, "that he had no more to do with the success of the attack than a man who presses a button and waits for the elevator" (560).

In the course of Mailer's fiction an aspect of the relationship between men and the natural world which receives increasing attention is mortality. Man's existence is rooted in the physical, and the realization that this physical existence must have a termination is one of the great traumas with which all human beings must cope. In *The Naked and the Dead*, Mailer traces one man's gradual recognition of mortality through Red Valsen's increasing horror as he begins to face the thought of his own eventual death. Hennessey's death, which occurs in the opening pages of the novel, gives rise to a "disquieting uncomfortable insight" for Red: death may not be "large and devastating and meaningless" (123) but personal and of ultimate significance. His reaction is to find himself "at the edge of a bottomless dread" (123), an experience that is repeated when he watches Croft prepare to kill a captured prisoner: "And yet all of this was mixed with dread, and the certainty that none of it was real. He could not believe that in a few seconds the soldier with the broad pleasant face was going to die" (189). But it remains for Red to recognize that he, too, is mortal and to confront his fear. This occurs when he comes upon a corpse after he has run from a cave filled with dead and rotting Japanese, which he and several other men had entered. He looks at the corpse, which lies naked on the ground, "its hands clenching the earth as if to ask for a last time the always futile question":

> Very deep inside of himself he was thinking that this was a man who had once wanted things, and the thought of his own death was always a little unbelievable to him. The man had had a childhood, a youth, and a young manhood, and there had been dreams and memories. Red was realizing with surprise and shock, as if he were looking at a corpse for the first time, that a man was really a very fragile thing.   (216)

Stanley Brown has a similar feeling, although for him it grows from several roots, not solely from a recognition of mortality: "Stanley felt a nameless anxiety rising in him. Dimly, he knew that part of it came from fearing death, really fearing it for the first time. . . . You look out for everything, he thought, and you still get hit from behind. It's a trap" (298). The frequent recognition of human mortality, a result of the catastrophic conditions of war and a buttress for Mailer's description of the natural world as powerful, impenetrable, and superior to the paltry efforts of men, will later become the central element in his attempt to portray and understand the human condition.

The most powerful representation of the forces of nature in *The Naked and the Dead* is Mount Anaka, which dominates both the island and the action of the novel. Sergeant Croft has an overwhelming urge to test himself against this enormous mass of rock which towers over the island that has become their home during the campaign. The mountain is his Moby Dick,[2] and Croft is another Ahab who seeks to pit himself against the forces of the natural world, to conquer the forces which threaten him, to lay bare the secrets of existence which seem hidden beneath the whiteness of Moby Dick and atop the peak of Anaka:

> The mountain attracted him, taunted and inflamed him with its size . . . feeling an instinctive desire to climb the mountain and stand on its peak, to know that all its mighty weight was beneath his feet. His emotions were intense; he knew awe and hunger and the peculiar unique ecstasy he had felt after Hennessey was dead, or when he had killed the Japanese prisoner. He gazed at it, almost hating the mountain, unconscious at first of the men about him. "That mountain's mighty old," he said at last. (447-448)

It is not only Croft who feels the mountain as the symbol of something beyond itself, some dream and ideal intimately connected with all human aspiration. Gallagher also endows the peak with human attributes: "The mountain seemed wise and powerful, and terrifying in its size . . . The idea, the vision he always held of something finer and neater and more beautiful than the moil in which he trembled now, pitched almost to a climax of words" (447). As such, it is a legitimate capstone to the tropical island itself; in a moment of shared insight the men all view Anopopei as an enchanted isle, "a vision of all the beauty for which they had ever yearned, all the ecstasy they had ever sought" (454).

But as the sun sets and the island is lit only by the waning rays of twilight, the vision of utopia changes; nature becomes harsh, threatening, an enemy to men in its implacability. "The black dead ocean looked like a mirror of the night; it was cold, implicit with dread and death. The men felt it absorb them in a silent pervasive terror" (454). It is this distant and cold look of nature that dominates the novel. Mailer does not, himself, fall into the pathetic fallacy, as his characters do; but he does realize that this very lack of concern by the natural world is a grave threat to all human beings, for it threatens all human activity with insignificance (since nature has, intrinsically, neither value nor significance). It does not so much defeat men as exist, steadily, implacably, so that men may continue to beat themselves as they try to overcome it. Throughout the novel storms rage, the jungle takes its toll, and the sea threatens whatever is upon it. Croft and his platoon are doomed to failure in their attempt to conquer Anaka. Trying to overcome nature by climbing Anaka is as futile as trying to cancel death. The same elemental physical nature of things which wiped out the farm worked by Ridges and his father is what Croft challenges when he tries to climb the mountain. Like Ahab, his effort is in many ways noble, but it cannot succeed. His failure to conquer the peak is the final statement of the power and inviolability of the natural world; it culminates the series of disasters, deaths, and unforeseen natural occurrences which Mailer has planted throughout the novel.

Allied to this assertion of the insignificance of men is the impotence and futility felt by the men in the platoon. The sense of themselves as thwarted and powerless is the most powerful emotional attitude they project—Croft being the sole exception. Throughout the novel there is a *basso continuo* of boredom, exhaustion, repetition, meaninglessness, unfulfillment. As the book opens, the platoon realizes that "there was nothing to do but go from one day into the next" (12). Their feeling of impotence is not wholly an outcome of their relationship to the natural world; it is more often a result of the military structure in which they are mired, and of those social structures in America which create not only the military but also the characters of the men themselves. To a large extent, the implacability of the social world produces the same effects and stimulates the same emotional responses from men as that of the natural world.

Because the men "knew very little about what was happening in the campaign," they find that "the days repeated themselves without incident" (252). Red Valsen, the most introspective and critical of the men in the platoon, often sums up the emotions that the other men either feel or will come to feel:

> Nobody gets what he wants, he said to himself, and this deepened his mood of pleasurable sorrow.   (140)

> Don't kid yourself, a man's no more important than a goddam cow.   (199)

> Red was feeling very drunk and very profound. "I'll tell you guys something . . . none of ya are ever gonna get anything. You're all good guys, but you're gonna get . . . the shitty end of the stick. The shitty end of the stick, that's all you're gonna get."   (202)

Although the perceived hostility of the natural world is in some part responsible for these observations, they primarily arise out of and refer to the hostility of the social world which men have created for themselves.

This is clear, for instance, in Polack's response to Wyman's question, spoken as they toil up the flanks of Anaka:

> "Listen Polack, you think there's a God?"
> Polack grinned, worked his hands under his pack straps to ease the chafing. "If there is, he sure is a sonofa-bitch." (607)

The reply neatly shifts the responsibility to God. It is General Cummings who sent the men on their mission, Croft who urges them up the mountain. Throughout the novel most of the men's suffering comes from the tyranny of the military, or because individuals use and misuse the power which the military structure has allowed them to amass. Even the opposition of the natural elements and the possibility of death—the two aspects of the natural world which men must face—are significant primarily because of the corruption of the military society they live in. The night-long struggle to move the heavy guns through the mud is a result of a military decision; so is the reconnaissance mission that leads the men to the slopes of Anaka. Roth's death, more than any other in the novel, points to the fatuous quality of death in the novel: there was no need or reason for Roth to have died. Although Mailer believes that death is the ultimate parameter of human existence and therefore essential to any process of human self-definition, he portrays the deaths of soldiers—Hearn, Wilson, Roth, and Hennessey—as pointless and wasted, a squandering of human life in the military wasteland of modern society.

The corruption of society is nowhere more evident than in the death of Gallagher's wife. His reaction to this catastrophe demonstrates a profound alienation and desensitivation of feeling; "he felt as if he were hearing a story about someone else in which he was not very interested"; "he gazed dully"; "mechanically he looked at his hands"; "when he rubbed his mouth it felt swollen and alien under his fingers"; at the sound of his cries, he "stopped, a little terrified, for they seemed so remote from him" (264). Mailer titles the flashback on Gallagher's life "The Revolutionary Reversed" (266), to emphasize that Gallagher's miseries are the result of an inequitable class structure in society, but Gallagher is not even allowed normal asocial feelings; his emotions are manipulated by petty political bosses into reactionary channels, into antisemitism, jingoism, anticommunism and eventually self-hatred. More than anything else, Gallagher is the product of the bleak social landscape in which he was raised and socialized:

> In South Boston and Dorchester and Roxbury the *gray wooden* houses parade for miles in a *file* of *drabness* and *desolation* and *waste.* The streetcars *jangle* through a *wilderness* of cobblestone and *sapless* wood; the brick is *old* and *powders* under your fingertips if you rub it vigorously. All colors are *lost* in the predominating *gray*; the faces of *the people have assumed it at last.* There are no Jews or Italians or Irish—their features have *blurred* in an anonymous *mortar* which has rendered them *homogeneous* and *dusty.* It is in their speech. They all talk with the *same depressing harsh arid tongue.*   (266, emphases mine)

Gallagher is a product of his home as well; significantly, he takes up his father's occupation and habits. But, most important, he is the offspring of a "deadening regularity and a sullen vicious temper that rides underneath the surface" of the drab physical world of his past (266–267). He has been created by social forces: he fights in gang wars against the "Yids" because he has been taught the economic and moral value of the "healthycompetitiveinstinct" (267); he is manipulated by petty political bosses caught in the grip of a corrupt and oppressive political machine. What is both sad and frightening is that Gallagher, a man full of hate and warped emotions, alienated from all feelings but that hatred and an empty and perverted political rhetoric, is at his core idealistic, chivalrous, and romantic. His aspirations have been formed by the great myth of the Arthurian romances (268, 279), but have been continually manipulated and assaulted by the society in which he lives.

Nor is Gallagher the only character who has been misshaped by his environment. All the characters described in "The Time Machine" passages are seen as products of a corrupt society, not only those who show influences and traits somewhat similar to Gallagher's—Martinez, Polack, Minetta, Brown—but also the leaders, men as different as Croft, Hearn, and Cummings. The cumulative vision of these flashbacks reflects a modern American society of repression and perversion: the destroyer of ideals, molder of the military, and originator of that totalitarian instinct which seeks power and control without restraint or responsibility.

It is this pervasive social determinism, along with Mailer's resolute effort to observe and capture the totality of military experience—the dull as well as the exciting, the routine as well as the traumatic, the tasteless as well as the esthetically pleasing—that has led almost every critic who has discussed the novel to refer to its place within the naturalistic tradition. Mailer constantly affirms Zola's observation, and follows his artistic dictum: "Man is not alone; he lives in a society, in a social milieu, and hence for us novelists the social milieu endlessly modified phenomena. Indeed our great study is there, on the reciprocal influence of society on the individual and of the individual on society."[3] The overwhelming impression given by *The Naked and the Dead* is of a universe governed by the implacable forces of society and nature; all individuals, whatever their efforts, are caught in the nexus of these forces and molded by them.

The Naked and the Dead differs from the novels which follow in that it uses naturalism to emphasize social determinism. Slowly the presence of unconquerable and omnipotent natural forces is revealed; by the Time Machine and Mailer's concentration on the daily workings of the platoon, a sense of irresistible social conditioning is established. Whereas all the later works assume, in large measure, this determinism, none emphasizes it with the style we associate with naturalism: a continuing accretion of detail which builds to a realization of the ponderous and pervasive power of circumstance in affecting human character and destiny.

In his later novels Mailer again and again stresses the force of American society, which in its sickness and greed destroys the best hopes of those who live in it. He reverts to two character types, first established in *The Naked and the Dead*, which become so important and pervasive that he uses them as archetypes in *Cannibals and Christians*. What he later calls the Cannibal and the Christian are recognizable in the motivations and actions of Croft and Cummings, on the one hand, and Hearn, on the other. One must understand these three characters in order to understand the tensions that flow and recoil beneath the surface of the novel and of most of Mailer's later work. In addition, Mailer suggests in Goldstein and Ridges that there may be a third possibility for human existence, one dominated by neither the values of the Cannibal nor those of the Christian.

Lieutenant Robert Hearn represents the bankruptcy of the liberal position. His values are humane, his politics libertarian. He is a "bourgeois liberal" (586). Hearn is a young prince who ought, by education, merit, and right, to inherit the mantle of leadership in America. But he, like Hamlet, lives in a world out of joint, and he is afflicted with the curse of having to set it right without sufficient skills and understanding to do so. When Hearn thinks about the absurdity of death, he confronts his inability to integrate the world around him: "That was the thing, that was what caused his mood. Everything was completely out of whack, none of the joints . . . None of it matched. The night had broken them into all the isolated units that actually they were" (108). His discussions and arguments with Cummings are part of Hearn's attempts to find an alternative to the General's totalitarian philosophy. Upset by the General's inhumane and insensitive concepts of power and fear, Hearn finds that the liberal philosophy he had picked up in the course of his education and socialization is as lacking in practicality as Cummings' philosophy is in ethical acceptability.

Thus Hearn regards the opportunity to lead the platoon as a reprieve from his uncertainty, a chance to return to roots and reintegrate his ideas and his life.

> But at least this was a positive action. For the first time in many months there were a few things he wanted again, simply and honestly. If he could manage it, if it turned out the way he wanted, he could establish some kind of liaison with the men. . . . The truth was, he grinned, he wasn't ready for Cummings's brand-new society in which everything was issued and never owned.   (437)

In this sense, Hearn is a potential hero. He has humane values, and occasionally, as when he accepts the leadership of the platoon or when he challenges the general, he evinces an admirable courage. What he lacks, however, is the ability to cope with the powerful social forces opposed to him and his liberal leanings, forces represented in the novel by Croft and Cummings. Whenever there is a clash between power and integrity, Hearn backs down. He picks up the cigarette he has thrown down on the spotless floor of the General's tent, subordinating his own courage and honor to the authority he has offended. Likewise, Hearn never gets through to Croft; there is a continual tension between them, a tension which can be, and is, only resolved by Hearn's death. It is not accidental that he died as a result of Croft's machinations; throughout the novel, Hearn continually vacillates, and his vacillations lead him to impotence. His indecision leaves him vulnerable to anyone who grasps power firmly.

Hearn's basic flaw, and that of the liberal philosophy he espouses, is that he is unwilling to accept the totality of his own nature; in several introspective moments, he realizes that he is motivated by forces similar to those which motivate the General and the Sergeant:

> Divorced of all the environmental trappings, all the confusing and misleading attitudes he had absorbed, he was basically like Cummings.   (392)

> He could understand Croft's staring at the mountain through the field glasses, or killing the bird. When he searched himself, he was just another Croft.
> That was it. All his life he had flirted with situations [when what he really wanted was control]. He was almost horrified with this sick, anguished knowledge of himself.   (580)

Hearn is afraid of control, afraid of power, afraid of having to make decisions. This is why he decides to resign his commission. There is much that is noble in this decision: there is a heroism to his acceptance of vulnerability; his logic, "morality against bombs" (585), has wide appeal in the modern world; the decision to join the mass of victims rather than remain one of the oppressors is both difficult and admirable.

But his fear of power is, at the same time, a way of shirking responsibility for the exercise of power. His decision to resign his commission comes about partly because Hearn does not want the responsibility incumbent on all leaders. His reaction to Mount Anaka is different from Croft's inflamed desire to conquer it. "The mountain troubled him, roused his awe and then his fear. It was too immense, too powerful" (497). Hearn thus does not give in to the emotions he shares with Cummings and Croft—he represses them. As an individual human being, this makes him incomplete and results in feelings of confusion and disintegration as he tries to deny what is evidently within him. For a person with a social responsibility, it leads to his abdication from any meaningful role in the society he inhabits. Because Hearn will not use power to combat power, because he is afraid of control, he leaves all social power in the hands of those who, less humane than he, relish it for the dominance it brings over the lives of other human beings. Mailer's view of Hearn seems clear: though his decision to resign his commission may seem noble, it is in actuality useless. Hearn ends up beyond gestures, killed by the power he mistrusted and tried to give up.

In many ways Hearn, the "bourgeois liberal" who hoped that when he returned from the reconnaissance mission "he would do that little thing" (586), represents the failure of liberalism. He attempts to make up by "style" for his failure to confront the General, deal firmly with Croft, and oppose the totalitarian structure of the military: "The only thing to do is get by on style. He had said that once, lived by it in the absence of anything else, and it had been a working guide, almost satisfactory until now" (326). What is especially interesting in Hearn's espousal of style is Mailer's complex attitude toward it. By it Hearn means integrity, and his integrity, at every juncture, is no match for Cummings' power. Power always triumphs over integrity. Yet more and more frequently in his later works Mailer will come to emphasize the importance of life style and integrity, as he comes to realize that only when specific acts and the way in which they are committed are in harmony is integration of the self possible. Hearn himself begins to recognize that style without action is impotent (327).

In the novel it is Sergeant Croft and General Cummings who accept the human motivation and experience which Hearn tries to reject; they are the pursuers of power, the seekers of control, the brutal backbone of the military. Norman Podhoretz, in the first and still one of the most fertile studies of Mailer's work, recognized that they were the "natural" heroes of the novel:

> If life is truly what *The Naked and the Dead* shows it to be—a fierce battle between the individual will and all the many things that resist it—then heroism must consist in a combination of strength, courage, drive, and stamina such as Cummings and Croft exhibit and that Hearn and Valsen conspicuously lack. Moreover, Cummings and Croft are the only characters who point to anything like an adequate response to life as we see it in the novel. They are, of course, reactionaries, but they demonstrate (as reactionaries often do) the workings of the radical spirit—which is to say that the principle of their behavior is a refusal to accept the limitations inherent in any given

> situation as final, a refusal stemming from the conviction
> that the situation itself need not be regarded as final in
> advance.[4]

It appears to Podhoretz that although the author intends the
characters to be villains, Mailer's honesty in portraying them makes
their values, despite their commitment to reactionary political
ideology, the dominant human values in the novel.

Croft, because he is less intellectual, less self-conscious, and more
natural than Cummings, is the more powerful figure. His weaknesses are all too evident: he is inhumane most of the time, he
has an immense hunger for power, and he is a man driven by
neuroses that, like those which motivate most of the other characters in the novel, are predominantly sexual in origin. Time and
again he shows no compassion for the men in his platoon, for their
weaknesses, their weariness, their anxiety, their pain. This is most
evident in his maniacal effort to push the platoon up the mountain,
as if his sheer will were enough, and in his wanton display of power
and cruelty when he crushes the bird Roth had discovered and
tried to care for. The Time Machine passage devoted to Croft emphasizes that Croft's desire for power grows out of his feeling of
sexual inferiority and impotence: "There's one thing you ain't
best in, she screams. Croft stands there trembling and then wrenches
out of the room. (Goddam whore)" (163).

But if his weaknesses are evident, as the novel progresses they
take on the aspect of strengths. Croft's desire for control may be
brutal and perverse, but it is a desire he pursues with courage,
steadfastness, and a refusal to be beaten or denied. He revels in
combat—"I tell you Croft loves combat, he loves it" (17)—
because it gives him a sense of control, over himself and the men
he commands, and the men whom he must face. "Leading the men
was a responsibility he craved; he felt powerful and certain at such
moments" (28). In addition, he sees the power that mortality
promises; in his nascent realization is to be found the seed which
Mailer will develop into Barney Kelly in *An American Dream*, a
seed which in the cases of both Croft and Kelly is at once evil and
heroic: "Hennessey's death had opened to Croft vistas of such
omnipotence that he was afraid to consider it directly. All day the
fact hovered about his head, tantalizing him with odd dreams and
portents of power" (40). After Croft realizes that warfare offers
an opportunity to exercise power, he seeks it: "He hungered for

the fast taut pulse he would feel in his throat after he killed a man" (143).

Croft seeks power because it makes him feel superior, because it gratifies his ego, because he does not like to be told what to do, but basic to this thirst is an ideal of freedom and independence. At first it seems strange to speak of this brutal and insensitive killing machine as a man with ideals, but he has them, and his need for freedom can be distinguished from Red Valsen's only by the single-minded purposefulness with which he pursues it. "There was a crude unformed vision in his soul but he was rarely conscious of it" (156); this vision determines all his actions. In a society where some men control others, only he who has power has the opportunity to be free; in a world in which natural phenomena seem to hold men in bondage, freedom can be won only by triumphing over these phenomena.

Thus Croft decides he must climb Mount Anaka. The mountain symbolizes for him the limits of the natural world and by extension all the limits that govern human existence, social and natural. In attacking the mountain, he is rebelling against the deterministic universe that the novel upholds.[5] He sees the mountain as his enemy: "He stared up at Mount Anaka as if measuring an opponent. At the moment he hated the mountain too, considered it a personal affront" (527). "The sheer mass of the mountain inflamed him" (635). Croft decides that he must attack and conquer the peak; to this end he sets up Hearn's death, allows Wilson and Roth to die in the process of his personal confrontation with the mountain, and exerts all his power and will to move the men, afflicted with the inertia and fear of all soldiers, up the steep slopes.

Mailer suggested that he had Moby Dick in mind when he wrote about the mountain. It is inaccessible, awesome, and powerful, and it dominates its natural environment. To conquer it is to gain mastery of the natural world and knowledge of the eternal mysteries of existence, and to transform through courage and will the nature and actuality of human existence. Like Ahab, Croft has a monomania: "Behind him Mount Anaka bored into his back as if it were a human thing. He turned around and stared at it soberly, feeling again the crude inarticulate thrill it always gave him. He was going to climb it; he swore to himself. . . . And they had to get up" (643). Yet this compulsion has in it much that is heroic; it reveals Croft's descent into the depths of the human soul. He flouts madness, he confronts those fearful tensions which lie buried beneath the layers of the human psyche. Hearn recognizes this but chooses to avoid the ambiguities that Croft's actions arouse: "The face was consecrated for that instant, the thin lips parted, the nostrils flared. For an instant he felt as if he had peered into Croft, looked down into an abyss. . . . You couldn't trust Croft. Somehow there was reassurance in stating it so banally" (498).

These desires—for combat, power, mastery—are, seemingly, to be rejected by the reader. But Croft does to a large extent run away, with Mailer's didactic purposes strewn in disarray around him. He is as heroic as Ahab. His brutality and seeming compact with evil are redeemed by the enormous vitality he projects. He alone, of all the characters in the novel, is not possessed by self-pity; he alone does not surrender to his weakness. What Mailer discovered in Croft he later returned to: in brutality, evil, and power can be found the dynamic that the liberal and humane of our day lack. In so doing Mailer is firmly in the American naturalistic tradition, that of Norris and Dreiser. Like Norris, he tries "to practice naturalism as a form of romance";[6] he could say with Dreiser, "For all my modest repute as a realist, I seem, to my self-analyzing eyes, somewhat more of a romanticist."[7] Cowley believes that the beast within is "a favorite theme in naturalistic fiction."[8] This theme is central to Mailer's vision; unlike his predecessors, he finds in it not perdition but deliverance, not ignominy but salvation. Podhoretz concludes: "Ultimately what Mailer was looking for—and has continued to look for—is not so much a more equitable world as a more exciting one, a world that produces men of size and a life of huge possibility."[9] Thus the raw strength, the animal nature, of Croft and men like him forces them to the forefront of all Mailer's novels.

Not only does Croft fail in his attempt to master Mount Anaka, but he is aware of the implications that failure has for his freedom. "Deep inside himself, Croft was relieved that he had not been able to climb the mountain. . . . Croft was rested by the unadmitted knowledge that he had found a limit to his hunger" (701). The essential differences between Croft and Hearn are twofold. First, Hearn, rather than admit to those drives within himself of which he does not approve, denies them. In his repression and suppression of elemental human motivations, he is dishonest to himself and cripples any possibility that he can become whole or effective. Though scarcely whole, Croft is not given to repressing the brutal and power-hungry drives within himself. Second, Hearn, Red, and all the men in the platoon are afraid of the world and of themselves. They are afraid of risk, they refuse to dare; consequently, they never stand to gain much. Croft, on the other hand, sets no limits for himself; he will brook no restrictions on his freedom. When a limit is imposed upon him after he has struggled against it—as in the case of his attempt to climb Anaka—then and only then will he accept it. But even here he cannot be content. Surely the reader expects Croft to make similar efforts to dominate both the social and natural environment in the future; he is not a beaten man, only one who is taking a rest before his next assault on all that binds him. Croft's "deep unspoken belief that whatever made things happen was on his side" (9), which is first seen at the opening of the novel, is by the close only temporarily quieted by his failure to climb the mountain. One expects that he, like Ahab, will set out again and again to destroy his adversary, gain mastery, and achieve the freedom and power that comes from dominance.

General Cummings is much like Sergeant Croft; although his range is broader, the power each wields over a number of individuals is commensurate. Because Cummings is both more introspective and more self-aware than Croft, his actions and beliefs do not project the same sense of instinctive behavior that Croft's do; and they are less forceful in their effect on the reader. While Croft acts out his beliefs and fantasies, Cummings does little but talk about his. Cummings' discussions with Hearn are regarded by Cummings himself as a weakness and a luxury; they are prompted not so much by any sense of inferiority or insecurity as by a deep-seated sense of intellectual loneliness. He succumbs to the pleasure of revealing the secret knowledge he has hidden from the world, and which the world ignores.

The major justification for his discussions with Hearn, seems, however, to be esthetic. They enable Mailer to reveal to the reader the values and machinations of another product of naturalistic logic, the totalitarian mind. Mailer sees this mentality as the controlling factor in the rigid structure of the military, in American society, and in international politics. An insight into the General's mind is an insight into the powers that threaten to control all modern society.

Cummings, like Croft, is a natural hero of the novel. Both men are, despite their insensitivity to the significance of the lives and suffering of the men under their command, men of vision. It seems clear that the "crude unformed vision in his soul" which dominated Croft's subconscious and unconscious mind is very similar to the "largest vision" in Cummings' mind:

> He can only think of the man who has ordered the attack, and he pictures him with wonder. What . . . courage. The responsibility. (For want of a richer word he picks up the military expression.)
>
> There were all those men, and there had been someone above them, ordering them, changing perhaps forever the fabric of their lives. In the darkness he looks blankly at the field, tantalized by the largest vision that has ever entered his soul.
>
> There were things one could do.
>
> To command all that. He is choked with the intensity of his emotion, the rage, the exultation, the undefined and mighty hunger.   (415)

Both men are captured by a vision of power; they realize that the man who has power has the freedom to remake the world, to control his own destiny as well as the destiny of others.

Their dreams, their fantasies, their hopes, their aspirations—all yearn for omnipotence. Cummings verbalizes what Croft only feels:

> "There's that popular misconception of man as something between a brute and an angel. Actually man is in transit between brute and God."
>
> "Man's deepest urge is omnipotence?"
>
> "Yes. . . . To achieve God. When we come kicking into the world, we are *God*, the universe is the limit of our senses. And when we get older, when we discover that the universe is not us, it's the deepest trauma of our existence."   (323)

As this discussion makes clear, Cummings' drive for power is the result of the limitations which he, like any other man, finds imposed upon him by the intractability of the natural world. It also marks him as a romantic, for he seeks redemption by reversion to the state of childhood, albeit in a complex and self-conscious way. The novel makes clear the fact that men cannot and will not triumph over nature: Croft fails to climb Anaka, Cummings is thwarted by a storm. But both men, Cummings especially, exert great control over social situations. It is this control, so pervasive and so concentrated, that Mailer chooses to investigate.

What Cumings wants—consolidation of power or what Mailer usually calls totalitarianism—is one of the constant concerns of his fiction and nonfiction. Cummings seeks this concentration of power in the military. He is driven by deep ambition; each step up the military ladder gives him more control over men and materiel. But he is far more than a simple-minded military man; he realizes that power, and the quest for power, is the most significant element in modern events. For him the Second World War is not a struggle between forces of right and wrong or even a competition between differing alien ideologies: "You're misreading history if you see this war as a grand revolution. It's a power concentration" (177). Cummings' deepest desire is to emerge from the war in a position to manipulate this immense and consolidated power; the Army is a vehicle for gaining this objective.

As we noted earlier, Cummings believes that fear is the method by which consolidation of power can be achieved. He recognizes the desirability, even the absolute need, of stimulating fear in men and then creating a hierarchy, a "fear ladder" (176); he tells Hearn, "The only way you generate the proper attitude of awe and obedience is through immense and disproportionate power" (324). Wilson, one of the soldiers in Croft's platoon, has intuited these lessons from his experiences with women: "Jus' get 'em afraid, that's only way a woman understands" (374). Wilson is just as brutal and just as successful with women as Croft and Cummings are with the men under their command.

Fear destroys the ego supports and eventually the individuality of men. It breaks down their will to resist authority; they eventually respond immediately to the stimuli applied to them. Cummings' is a behavioral view of human action; he seeks, through the conditioning of fear, to evince the appropriate response to stimuli (in the form of orders and commands). Thus Cummings can write in his notebook: "We are not so discrete from the machine any longer. I detect it in my thinking. We are no longer adding apples and horses. A machine is worth so many men" (569). He also sees the mechanization of men as a function of the age of technology, and he offers this as another justification for a society based on fear. "The machine techniques of this century demand consolidation, and with that you've got to have fear, because the majority of men must be subservient to the machine, and it's not a business they instinctively enjoy" (177).

When Hearn points out that the fear-induced social structure which Cummings is proposing will create enormous anxiety, Cummings' response indicates both the depth of his understanding and the callousness of his reaction to human suffering: "Probably. The natural role of twentieth-century man is anxiety" (177). It is evident that Cummings is dealing with his vision of society, and not solely with the most efficient and efficacious way in which to operate a military unit; the tenor of his observations always tends to go beyond the army to a general relevance toward American society and the whole of modern civilization. He recognizes fascism as a direction toward which modern history is increasingly bent: "For the past century the entire historical process has been working toward greater and greater consolidation of power. Physical power for this century, an extension of our universe, and a political power, a political organization to make it possible" (321–322). He believes that "this is going to be the reactionaries' century, perhaps their thousand-year reign. It's the one thing Hitler said which wasn't completely hysterical" (85). Far from feeling saddened by the fascist drift in modern history, and trying to oppose it as Hearn does, Cummings rejoices in it, and plans on how it can most effectively benefit him. He is not a fascist—he is too shrewd to commit himself to a specific ideology, one that may meet with failure—but he is assuredly totalitarian.

In addition to the frightening picture Mailer presents of Cummings and all he and his ideas portend for the future of society and human development, he also portrays some of the effects power has on Cummings. One of the most striking of these is doubly emphasized because it is true for Cummings as well as for Croft: power as an aspect of sexuality. Mailer sees the need to wield power as a response to a threatened and even perverse sexual appetite. Croft, as we have seen, is a cuckold; this causes him to treat his sexual partner as an object, "jus' an old fuggin machine" (163). Cummings also has an unsatisfactory sexual relationship with his wife. In addition, he has homosexual tendencies, expressed when he recounts a drunken stupor in Rome during which he followed a man who obliquely promised homosexual satisfaction to him, and when he peevishly talks of his wife as a "bitch" (182). His relationship with Hearn is marked by homosexual overtones: at times

Cummings seems like a lover, surprising in the closeness and intensity of his affection for the lieutenant.

While emphasizing the sexual nature of Cummings' and Croft's neurotic desires for power, Mailer also explicitly compares sexual fulfillment and the satisfactions which war affords the two men. In his notebook, Cummings alludes to the correspondence between artillery fire and coitus: "The phallus-shell that rides through a shining vagina of steel" (568). Even more revealing is the martial sensation which, examined and contorted, becomes the basis for Cummings' pseudo-poetic metaphor. Beholding artillery bombardment, Cummings is caught up in sexual excitement. "[War] was all covered with tedium and routine, regulations and procedure, and yet there was a naked quivering heart to it which involved you deeply when you were thrust into it" (566).

This sexual aspect of power is part of Mailer's attempt to delegitimize the effort to consolidate power which Cummings is engaged in; it makes the pursuer of power a neurotic and the desire for control a sexual perversion. But this attempt does not wholly succeed. Cummings, self-professedly, seeks omnipotence, but this does not make him a villain. While Hearn is, no doubt, sensible and humane in his condemnation of the general, it is in Cummings that we can see the heroic activity of seeking to fight and recreate one's environment, so that it is less hostile and more satisfying to one's needs.

> His voice continued on and on, its ironic sustained mockery spinning its own unique web, while all the time the tensions inside him flexed and expanded, sought their inexorable satisfactions in whatever lay between Hearn and himself, between himself and the five thousand troops against him, the terrain, and the circuits of change he would mold.
> What a monster, Hearn told himself.   (85)

Throughout the whole of his work Mailer is interested in, sometimes obsessed with, power and its manifestations. Power to him is fascinating because it is unrepressed, it is primitive, elemental, vital. It differs greatly from the mechanized, superficial and unsatisfying world that Mailer sees as our twentieth-century habitat. We shall investigate, later, the links between Mailer's fascination with power and the romantic spirit that forms and informs his unique world-view. In *The Naked and the Dead* power and violence offer an alternative to the stultifying effects of modern society. They add vitality to the world that produced Gallagher and Martinez and Polack, a world of repression, false rhetoric, and unattainable social myths, a world urbanized, mechanized, and crooked. One can see the vitality of violence in Gallagher. An uneducated, bigoted man, the perverse twists and turns of his hatred are far more real, and more human, than the obsequious ambition of a man like Stanley. In like manner, Cummings is far more vital and heroic than the blundering Major Dalleson, or Croft far more than Lieutenant Hearn.

At the end of the novel, however, both Croft and Cummings are thwarted. The Sergeant fails to reach the peak he has set out to conquer; meanwhile, Major Dalleson blunders into that victory which Cummings had hoped to win by strategic maneuvering and sophisticated planning. These personal defeats are, in some measure, required by the naturalistic viewpoint from which the novel is written. Basic to naturalism is the belief that natural circumstance is the most important determinant in human actions, and that no man can hope to overcome successfully the forces of accident and entropy which rule existence. Mailer uses these reversals to tie up his narrative, to end the novel with a temporary defeat or postponement of the totalitarian forces at work in the novel.

Here, Podhoretz offers a useful insight. He maintains that Hearn was, with Red Valsen, the planned hero of the novel, but that Mailer discovered while writing the work that "his real values tended in an anti-liberal direction."[10] Certainly Hearn is not capable of dealing with either the natural world or the distintegrating social order. For him there is only resignation, in both senses of the term. The same is true of Red Valsen, who seeks an unfettered life but finally succumbs to Croft in a showdown on the slopes of Anaka: when the crisis comes, Red's need for freedom is subordinated to his cowardice and unwillingness to confront Croft's insanity. Both Hearn and Valsen submit to the dictates of power.

But Mailer, believing that liberal values are inappropriate to modern life, was not ready to glorify Croft and Cummings: "Mailer was looking for . . . a world that produces men of size and a life of huge possibility."[11] This explains why these two men emerge as natural heroes. They possess a magnitude and grandeur that the other characters lack, a heroic size that renders them distinguishable from that overpowering sense of an inconquerable and impenetrable world which the novel engenders in the reader. Yet much as he may admire their grandeur, Mailer is not ready to glorify fascism. Croft and Cummings emerge as heroes despite their totalitarian temperaments—a contradictory situation that will be explored several times again in the course of Mailer's work. Although they are more exciting than the other characters in the novel, they are also more dangerous. Mailer, intrigued by power (not by fascism), in the end cuts down the General and the sergeant because of their totalitarian commitment. Caught in this dilemma—his intended hero a failure, his intended villains heroic—Mailer suggests another alternative: endurance. In this regard he is evocative of many modern writers; one thinks of Faulkner, who in the midst of a disintegrating world finds great promise in Dilsey's endurance.

In *The Naked and the Dead* there is no more, only less. There is either Hearn, a failure, or Cummings and Croft, both heroic but also totalitarian. Thus Mailer concentrates, in the later stages of the novel, on two ordinary human beings, Ridges and Goldstein, who respond with courage to the difficult situation that confronts them. Ridges is the son of a poor white southern farmer, and Goldstein emerged from a protected existence in an urban Jewish ghetto. What they have in common is their willingness to do what must be done, to accept suffering with courage, to endure bravely what they cannot conquer.

It is Red Valsen who most clearly realizes the value of endurance. "In the war you keep on moving. . . . But if you stop and quit moving you die" (234). Red has kept moving all his life, but in so doing he has crippled himself. He is so accustomed to moving with the current that he is unable to find the courage and stamina to resist Croft effectively. Red frames a metaphor of existence which is similar to Camus' conception of Sisyphus and his rock, but he ultimately fails to keep pushing and gives up. "You keep rolling along and you never know what the hell the score is. When you're a kid they can't tell you a damn thing, and when you ain't a kid no more there's nothing new for you. You just got to keep pushing it, you don't look back" (235).

Ridges and Goldstein, less perceptive than Red, instinctively do what he should have done: they resist the power that threatens them; they seek to endure whatever the world will bring to bear on them. Four men are picked to carry the wounded Wilson back to safety; they must carry their burden over miles of ground on a makeshift stretcher, and then plunge through almost impenetrable jungle before they can reach their destination. Brown and Stanley drop off along the way, and Ridges and Goldstein must struggle on with their burden, alone. Both men feel they have a task to perform, and despite their exhaustion and the physical obstacles which confront them, they strive to perform it. Goldstein has been prepared for this journey. When young, he had heard his grandfather tell him: "I think a Jew is a Jew because he suffers. . . . We must always journey from disaster to disaster, and it makes us stronger and weaker than other men. . . . We have suffered so much we know how to endure. We will always endure" (483)—advice greatly resembling the spirit that informs the work of Bernard Malamud, one of Mailer's contemporaries. Malamud celebrates endurance and the acceptance of suffering; his concern with Jewishness is primarily a metaphor for the human condition. Goldstein, who remembers the lesson his grandfather taught him, would be recognized as a spiritual brother by all of Malamud's protagonists:

> In the Army, in the bare alien worlds of the barracks and the bivouacs, Goldstein fumbles for a new answer, a new security. And in his misery the old habits wither away like bark in winter, and he is left without a garment. . . . *We are born to suffer.* And although he strains with the sinews of his heart and mind back toward his home, his cove, his legs are beginning to steady, his thighs to set.
> Goldstein is turning his face to the wind. (492)

This is a variety of heroism, one which Ridges, who grew up in a harsh southern environment, close to the land, also exhibits. A long and intimate association with the land has taught Ridges the same lessons it teaches many of the inhabitants of Yoknapatawpha County.

Carrying Wilson reduces life to its essentials for both Goldstein and Ridges; they are reduced to "envelopes of suffering" (658) as their single-minded effort sloughs off that "avalanche of pleasant and monotonous trivia that makes up their life" (489). They reach the point of exhaustion, their fatigue is all-encompassing: "carrying him was the only reality they knew" (644). Yet they continue. Like their dying burden—"it never occurred to him to quit" (645)—the two men refuse to give up. They realize, in their total weariness, the intractability of the natural world through which they must pass, but they are determined to resist it: "Wilson was a burden they had to carry; it would go on and on and they could never let him go. They did not understand this, but comprehension was lurking behind their fatigue" (646). In their determination they possess all the strength of Cummings or Croft; in their endurance in the face of enormous obstacles they display courage and a simple nobility and heroism.

In the end, they fail. Wilson dies, the body they have carried so diligently is lost in the river, and they stagger onto the beach exhausted and unsuccessful. Ridges, in his dejection, realizes, "What counted was that he had carried this burden through such distances of space and time, and it had washed away in the end" (681). Ridges has encountered such failure before, as when the crops he and his father had labored hard to produce were destroyed in a sudden storm. He has, more than Goldstein, become stoic about the need to continue, despite adversity and the certainty of eventual failure. But both continue. And in their continuation, in their resistance and endurance, they offer something of value: if not success, at least endurance.

This does not really solve the dilemma of power which Mailer confronts: it does not promise control over one's own life and environment, nor does it engage that inhumane totalitarianism which seems to issue from any attempt to wield such control. Mailer's protagonists, as we shall see, never win; they survive. In *The Naked and the Dead* Mailer leaves behind the liberal solution; he commits himself to exploring new dimensions of men's experience. The novels that follow also try to fathom the mysteries of power and violence, seeking greater human understanding by investigating elemental human motivations and actions. The difficulties of this investigation are compounded by the close relationship between power and violence, on the one hand, and power and fascism on the other. Considering the magnitude and pervasiveness of Mailer's search—for ways to deal effectively with the limitations on man set by nature and the malfunctionings of society— endurance alone is not a satisfactory solution. Yet there is a small core of strength and consolation to be found in men who carry their burdens, suffer with courage, and persist in their efforts to endure.

Chapter II

Barbary Shore

The Failure of the Socialist Revolution

arbary Shore, Mailer's second novel, was poorly received by both the public and the press.[1] An openly political and even polemic novel, it hides its small hope in a vast ocean of despair. Unlike *The Naked and the Dead*, it does not offer the reader relief from the totalitarian catastrophes which Mailer felt were engulfing twentieth-century men—no vast panoply of interesting characters, no change of scene, no characters who can enlist our conscious or unconscious sympathies as easily as the heroes of the first novel. McLeod, the closest Mailer comes to creating a heroic figure in *Barbary Shore*, has wallowed in violent corruption that would frighten even Cummings and Croft.

Like its predecessor, *Barbary Shore* is a novel about the oppressiveness of American politics and society. In it Mailer again portrays an encroaching totalitarian menace which, hydra-headed, appears in the guise of both the right and the left. Anticapitalist, anti-Stalinist, and antibureaucratic, the novel tentatively offers a loosely defined humanistic socialism as the sole alternative to the forces which threaten to take over American society.

The setting is a rooming house in Brooklyn. With a few slight exceptions, every moment is spent inside this old walkup, and the entire novel becomes enclosed, caught within these narrow, dirty walls, reminiscent of the Offices of the Law in Kafka's *The Trial*. *The Naked and the Dead* was concerned with the sweep and expanse and totality of modern war; *Barbary Shore* is concerned with the same totality and its oppressiveness within a tight, closed, little society. In fact, Mailer tried to capture an intensity that cannot be conveyed by great scope nearly as well as it can by an enclosed atmosphere of imprisonment and suffocation.

Michael Lovett, the first person narrator, must live entirely in the present and so live outside of history. As the result of a head wound suffered in the war, Lovett is an amnesiac. Having no memory of the past, he feels he has no future and thus is doomed to live in an eternal present. For some reason unexplained to the reader, Lovett has decided to write a novel. In order to live cheaply while he embraces this project, he moves into a small and stuffy attic room in the house described above.

The landlady is Mrs. Beverly Guinevere, an overweight, exotically dressed, ex-burlesque star of twenty-eight. She has a daughter, Monina, who is spoiled and pampered and is kept a baby by her mother in the hope that she will someday become a child star in the movies. Mrs. Guinevere, who is appropriately named, has sexual relations with all the characters in the novel except for Lovett.

McLeod, the central figure in the book, is a man of fifty, a thin, hard figure who affects an Irish brogue and wears steel spectacles. He quickly becomes Lovett's mentor and confidant. In the middle of the novel Hollingsworth, another lodger, reveals that McLeod is also Guinevere's husband. Hollingsworth is short, blond, and muscular; he exudes a simplistic, small-town attitude and manner that contrast sharply with McLeod's intellectuality and sophistication.

The fourth character, Lannie Madison, moves into the rooming house and signals the start of what action there is in the novel. Lannie is mentally unbalanced; a thin, frenetic girl, she constantly drops cigarette ashes all over the purple suit she always wears. The suit clashes with her mouse-colored hair; her small prettiness is hidden behind an unconcern for her looks.

The first half of the novel prepares the reader for the confrontation and political rhetoric of the second half. It creates a Kafkaesque world in which fear, guilt, and desire are mingled and forced to breed upon themselves in a closed universe that has all the reality and intensity of a neurotic nightmare. Like Kafka, Mailer succeeds in objectifying the fears of the unconscious, embodying them in an oppressive and threatening sense of place. The boarding house is a microcosm of the world, a world in which "the blind lead the blind and the deaf shout warnings to one another until their voices are lost" (7).

The second half of the novel is taken up by the confrontation between Hollingsworth, who reveals himself as an agent of something like the CIA, and McLeod, who is gradually shown to be an ex-Bolshevist who eventually became known as the "hangman of the Left Opposition" (130). Lannie is an aide to Hollingsworth, while Lovett becomes involved as McLeod's witness and conscience during the nightly cross-examination of McLeod. It seems that McLeod had left the Bolshevists after the nonaggression pact between Stalin and Hitler and had reacted to the loss of his political identity by joining an arm of the American government, for which he worked until he became disenchanted with that too and disappeared. Before he dropped out of sight, however, he stole a "little object" (133) from the agency for which he worked. Since the value of this little object is immense, Hollingsworth has been ordered to retrieve it. He interrogates McLeod, who finally says he will give it to Hollingsworth if he is allowed to make a final speech—a speech apparently aimed at Lovett. After he makes it, he has one further day to find and turn over the precious object his antagonist is seeking. Lannie, who up till now has hated McLeod, suddenly urges him not to give up the object; and when Lovett agrees to continue to hide it, even though this means great responsibility, loneliness, and an uncertain future, McLeod gives it to him. Thus foiled in his quest for the object, Hollingsworth struggles with McLeod, shoots him, and runs off with Beverly Guinevere. The police arrive and capture Lannie, while Lovett goes off into the night.

Mailer has written an allegory of modern political life, one which reinforces the direction the novel itself takes when read without resort to the allegory. We will deal first with the allegory. Hollingsworth is an agent of monopoly capitalism, of the United States, of the "free world." McLeod—at least McLeod's past— is the Marxist-Leninist tradition as it has been perverted and corrupted into Stalinism, or state capitalism. Lannie represents the other offshoot of the tradition, originally powerful but which degenerated into the small band of followers who clustered around and worshiped Leon Trotsky. She constantly evinces admiration for Trotsky. It is important to note here a distinction that will be of crucial importance in the analysis that follows: although Lannie represents the followers of Trotsky, perhaps even some of Trotsky's ambitions, her insanity at the close of the novel does not reflect Trotsky's theoretical writings and his ideas. Trotsky's political perspective is consonant with Mailer's ultimate conclusions. Lannie's combination of insight and insanity represents Trotskyism as a political force in the world today, and is not a judgment on the merit of Trotsky's ideas.

Mrs. Beverly Guinevere—the ex-burlesque star who is always in an eclectic state of dress that barely covers her nudity, who is alluring and grasping, and who is unable to cope with the people around her save through self-admiration and physical desire—is the modern proletariat. She is crass and mercurial, with no firm allegiance save to herself, her pleasure, and her vanity. Unsatisfied by her husband, whom she sees only secretly, she finds excitement in the arms of Hollingsworth, who beats and abuses her but satisfies some of the needs of her ego. Beverly is even attracted by Lannie and excuses the unnatural nature of this partnership by remarking, "If we had a good time once, well I can always say I tried everything" (188). Her daughter, Monina, represents the proletariat of the future: forced into a continued infancy, self-centered, temperamental, sexually attractive and even obscene, she, like her mother, is bound to nothing but the needs of her own ego. Although Beverly is her mother, her father is not necessarily McLeod; hence, Stalinism is only a probable, but not certain, sire of future society.

The position of each of the characters at the end of the novel represents Mailer's view of the American political scene during the early fifties: monopoly capitalism (Hollingsworth) has the temporary favor of the public (Guinevere) and the future generations of mankind (Monina). Trotskyism (Lannie) is out of touch with reality and in the hands of the police. Stalinism is officially dead, but the bureaucratic and totalitarian methods of monopoly and state capitalism are so similar that it lives on under a different name. The Bolshevist McLeod and the capitalist Hollingsworth are similar: the latter respects the former for his abilities and powers, and follows in his footsteps. Hollingsworth tells McLeod, "I can't express the admiration I feel for a gentleman like yourself. I think if conditions had been more, so to speak, propitious, we could have been dear friends. . . . I've always liked your type" (217). McLeod recognizes as well that "there are deep compacts between Leroy and myself, you might almost say we are sympathetic to each other" (172).

As for Lovett, he represents that part of man which is outside of history. "I recovered nothing except to learn that I had no past and was therefore without a future. . . . It was natural, even obligatory, that the present should possess the stage" (6). Lovett can be seen as existential man, the man for whom the present is the defining and overriding reality. Unable to flee from the present through the escapes of either past or future, Lovett has the opportunity and the need to create his world continually from an existential reality. His personal history is the history of the modern world, and so he becomes a battleground on which the forces active in the world can meet and struggle. He brings nothing of his own to the struggle but his will, the determination that ultimately he must create his own destiny. When he asks McLeod to entrust the "little object" to him, Lovett says, " 'I'm not a brave man, I know that.' It was expressed at last. 'I have no future anyway. At least I can elect to have a future. If it's short, small matter' " (218). But Lovett has little importance in the allegory within the novel. Appropriately, he ends by disappearing into the night, faced with innumerable dangers, carrying an object that will probably be of little value to him.

When Mailer decided to entrust the narrative to Lovett, who relates the action in the first person, he made a decision that had major consequences for his artistic career. Abandoning the device of an omniscient third-person narrator, Mailer discovered a mode central to all his succeeding work, one which, he has declared, is the only possible narrative mode in which he can write. Indeed, Lovett, the war-wounded amnesiac, has served as the prototype for all of Mailer's later fictional narrators. O'Shaugnessy in *The Deer Park* and Rojack in *An American Dream* also were wounded during recent wars, and D.J. in *Why Are We in Vietnam?* is psychologically, though not physically, injured on a hunt in Alaska. Furthermore, like Lovett, these other narrator-protagonists are forced to live in a continuous present. The device of amnesia necessitates a narrative that describes the present and at the same time creates, without historical reference, the present it is describing.

Lovett and Mailer's other narrators, whether in fiction or nonfiction, are archetypal artists. Out of the chaotic country which is their experience, they seek to form a landscape that can be approached, understood, and enjoyed. Lovett, in the act of telling his story, must also make up his story. The fact that he has no past, save for several dreamlike memories, forces him to depend even more fully on his own resources, to decipher the present in the light of that present itself.

This, of course, poses a large question for the reader. Does the reliability of the narrator (insofar as he *is* reliable) rest on his skill as an observer and commentator, or does it rest on his imaginative powers, his creative skill? Is *Barbary Shore* a novel about several people who interact among each other, one of whom is the narrator; or is it a novel about an artist engaged in his own creative process? The soundest answer is, perhaps, that it is about both social context and the person who imagines that context. Yet this solution has limitations in that it ignores the tension between the two opposing possibilities: that the novel is concerned with portraying objective reality, and that it is concerned with portraying subjective reality.

In his later works, the relationship between Mailer and his narrator becomes problematical. Lovett, however, is a *tabula rasa* upon which is written what Mailer wants to write. Lovett's perversity, manifest in his embrace of socialism in a society that is at once monopoly capitalistic and apolitical, has its parallel in Mailer's own perversity. Mailer himself had worked in a hopeless political cause, the Progressive candidacy of Henry Wallace, shortly before the book's publication, and the book, a plea for humanistic socialism, was sharply at variance with the prevailing anticommunism and studied blandness of the early 1950's. Thus the novel, far from being solely a political and historical allegory, is an inquiry into the political, social, and historical meaning of Marxism in the twentieth century.

McLeod's long polemic near the end of the novel is largely Mailer's own view, as of 1951, of the political situation in the world and the probable future of mankind. McLeod sees the modern world divided into two societies, one he calls Monopoly Capitalism and one he calls State Capitalism. The difference between the two, once an observer penetrates beneath rhetoric and nationalism, is negligible: both concentrate power in the grasp of a small totalitarian elite connected with, in one case, the political-military-industrial complex, and in the other, the bureaucratic state. Both systems operate under bureaucratic control, so that even persons near the top of the political structures have no control over the direction their countries take. Each form of capitalism is oriented toward war, for "The factor never to be forgotten is that the economic crisis is now permanent" (22). As Lovett's catechism indicates, war is the temporary resolution: "What were the phenomena of the world today? If I knew little else, I knew the answer—war, and the preparations for new war" (116). But the resolution is only temporary, so newer and larger wars must continually be waged.

McLeod states that only in gearing itself up for war can a modern capitalist economy keep up the high level of production needed for its economic health, for only in war is the need for production an endless upward spiral. Ultimately, McLeod believes, monopoly capitalism and state capitalism will engage in a final battle, and one side will emerge the victor. The victory will be pyrrhic, however, for the winning side will still be faced with economic crisis and will resolve this situation only by declaring war on itself, thus continuing the production necessary to the temporary economic stability of the society. The victor, encumbered with a war economy, will continue to wage war:

> His demands must be so great in relation to what is left that the new military situation develops before the last has ceased. The war begins again with a new alignment of forces, and to the accompaniment of famine and civil war, the deterioration continues until we are faced with mankind in barbary.[2]   (202)

Neither McLeod nor Lovett plumbs the nadir of despair which modern man faces. Lannie Madison, former socialist, adherent and worshiper of Leon Trotsky, describes the world most vividly, sketching a picture of mankind so depressing that it even goes beyond conventional moral terminology, such as good and evil. In such a world terms like good and evil have no meaning. Trotsky is dead, "the mountain ax in his brain, and all the blood poured out, and he could not see the Mexican sun . . . the last blood of revolutionary mankind, his poor blood, ran into the carpet" (136). With Trotsky destroyed and Stalin ruling the hope of the world with an iron hand and calloused heart, Lannie has no hope, and she desires only a room closed off from the rest of the world. For her, Christ is not a savior but a mouse, which eventually dies when she blots out all the light in her room by painting the room black. The paradigm for modern times is the concentration camp, and for Lannie the horror of the camps went beyond that of genocide alone:

> "Yet my story is not done. The guards have one more resource. As they are about to close the door to the last room, an announcement is made. The State in its infinite mercy will allow one of them to be saved, the strongest. The one who can beat the others will be given a reprieve. This declaration, although it is worthy of the State, is due actually to the genius of a single guard who has conceived it at the very moment. And so through a window

the guards may watch while one naked pygmy tears the
hair of another, and blood runs where one thought no
blood was left, and half of them are dead and scream like
pigs with the head down and waiting for the knife, and
as they scratch and sob and bite each other's rinds, the
guards turn on the gas and roar like mad for the fools
thought one would be saved and so ate each other.

"This is the world, Mikey. If there had been one who
said, 'Let us die with dignity,' but they went choking into
the gas with the blood of a friend in their mouth."

"It was too late then," I murmured.

"Listen, my friend," she said softly, "the grass waves,
and we are lost again in childhood souvenir. It is too late
now. Do you understand? There are no solutions, there
are only exceptions, and therefore we are without good
and evil."   (153)

In a world of complete destruction, Lannie can only counsel love
of her destroyer. She follows the bidding of Hollingsworth and
even submits to sexual perversions to satisfy his needs.

Interestingly enough, it is Lannie who convinces McLeod to turn
over the "little object." McLeod's former absolute faith in the
rectitude and justice of the (Stalinist) socialist movement has been
destroyed, and he is not quite certain in his belief. Lannie's existence reminds him of the futility of belief, of effort, of hope. Thus
McLeod, who had completely submitted to the needs of the revolution, discovered that there was only one meaningful act left for
him when he lost faith in the revolution: "to save one's life" (160).
When Lannie reminds him of the inhumanity and hopelessness of
the world he has predicted, a world in continual war, McLeod,
with nothing to believe in, decides to put his own survival before
causes and ideology. He decides to surrender the little object which
Hollingsworth demands.

After this decision, Lannie remonstrates; half mad, she still has
a remnant of the hope she once had, and although she fears the
worst, she cannot allow McLeod to extinguish the last possibility
of a socialist future. But it is Lovett, with his offer to take on a
lonely responsibility for the "little object," who confirms McLeod's
new resolution to continue his resistance.

The "little object" is purposely kept ambiguous, although its
general meaning and importance are clear. The object is the revolu-

tionary spirit, the continued will to struggle with the capitalist powers and keep alive the spark of socialism, the small but potent germ of a vision of a new world, a world in which war is unnecessary and love is possible.

At the close of the novel, after McLeod has been killed, Lovett reads his friend's will: "To Michael Lovett to whom, at the end of my life and for the first time within it, I find myself capable of the rudiments of selfless friendship, I bequeath in heritage the remnants of my socialist culture. And may he be alive to see the rising of the Phoenix" (223). After a period during which McLeod had probed and tested the narrator, and Lovett had searched deeply for his own responses, the two had come to realize that they shared this socialist heritage. In the face of the nightmare world which McLeod and Lannie described, both see an alternative only in the course of revolutionary socialism.

Both Lovett and McLeod share the basic Marxist assumption that an individual man is the product of his social milieu. Lovett recalls a sentence, "Men enter into social and economic relations independent of their wills,"[3] and then asks of it, "did it not mean more than all the drums of the medicine men?" (117). And McLeod asks Hollingsworth, "What if there is no point and only a context?" (138). Both then go on to offer similar Marxist analyses of contemporary society. Man has long ago been alienated from the product of his labor. A small group of men who benefit from this alienation in the form of profits become a capitalist class, which seeks to further alienate the working class from its labor, so that their profits can increase. In order to keep the worker from rebelling, this alienation must constantly be increased. Furthermore, to ensure economic stability, there must be a continued rate of growth of both productivity and surplus value.

In the Marxist view this means that history will necessarily go through a number of stages; more specifically, the capitalism of the bourgeois state must ultimately give way to the socialism of the workers' state, and ultimately this too will wither away into a structureless society in which all men will be able to fulfill themselves. It is this historical certainty which Lovett and McLeod both reject. Their understanding of history, permeated by Trotsky's doctrine of permanent revolution, indicates that the Russian revolution has been lost, and with it the chances for a world revolution.

Trotsky propounded his theory of "permanent revolution"

shortly after the abortive Russian uprising in 1905. He and Parvus formulated the doctrine which Trotsky was to put forth continually, against all sorts of opposition, until Lenin finally accepted most of its premises a few years after the Bolshevist coup.

> The perspective of permanent revolution may be summarized in the following way: the complete victory of the democratic revolution in Russia is conceivable only in the form of the dictatorship of the proletariat, leaning on the peasantry. The dictatorship of the proletariat, which would inevitably place on the order of the day not only democratic but socialistic tasks as well, would at the same time give a powerful impetus to the international socialist revolution. Only the victory of the proletariat in the West could protect Russia from bourgeois restoration and assure it the possibility of rounding out the establishment of socialism.[4]

Basic to the concept of permanent revolution is the belief that if the socialist revolution does not spread beyond Russia to some parts of the West, the revolution is doomed. Shortly after Stalin took over the government, he propounded his idea of a one-nation revolution in which he proposed that Russia could become socialist without outside help and should concentrate on her own needs and not on the international socialist movement. In this, as in all other Stalin-Trotsky oppositions in the novel, McLeod and Lovett come out for Trotsky's point of view.

The theory of permanent revolution is central to an understanding of Mailer's view of modern man. Both McLeod and Lovett are speaking for Mailer when they analyze the historical cause of the modern catastrophe:

> And to the Socialist historian of the future the tragedy of the twentieth century will become fixed on the few years following the First World War when the revolution failed to spread to Western Europe, and the young giant of the worker's movement, mortally wounded, could only degenerate into the death agony of corruption, betrayal, and defeat. . . . By now, with the approach of the Third World War, the techniques of Barbarism are well established, and the vista of the concentration camp, the swallowing of all opposition by the secret police, and the war to be

> waged in the name of peace, comes ever into sharper
> focus. And inversely, the perspective for revolutionary
> socialism diminishes to its limit.   (160-161)

Earlier, McLeod tested Lovett's position and was answered:

> I was almost carried away. For once I grasped him by
> the shoulder. "Look, that revolution was the greatest event
> in man's history, and if it had not been confined to the
> one country, if it had spread . . ."
> "But it didn't."
> "It didn't," I agreed, "and so it died, and ever since,
> the crisis of the world has deepened until by now it's only
> your bureaucrat who can raise man as you put it, and it's
> a measure of the disaster that everywhere the bureaucrat
> has the magic power."   (89)

Underlying the whole novel is Mailer's analysis of history. The
only answer to man's needs is socialism. With the failure of the
Russian Revolution to ignite the flames of revolutionary socialism
in the West, mankind failed to grow into a new era. The social,
psychological, and physical violence of collectivity, bureaucracy,
concentration camps, and war became solidified.

McLeod's past, which often seems no more than a subject of
discussion in the novel, is important in this respect. It is the concrete demonstration of the perversion of the revolutionary spirit.
Trapped in a world which did not heed the socialist call to arms,
McLeod had to commit larger and more brutal crimes in the name
of the revolutionary dream—a dream that had already died in
the funereal coils of bureaucracy. Stalin's willingness to solidify
his personal gains and thus to neglect the world-wide cause of
socialism resulted in substituting for the tyranny of the Tsar the
dehumanizing totalitarian collectivism of the communist state.
McLeod's crimes were committed during the Spanish Revolution,
part of the European socialist struggle that Russia entered twenty
years too late.

The effects of the failure of the socialist revolution to spread
during the second and third decades of the twentieth century have
been felt on every level of contemporary life. This tragic failure, in
Mailer's view, is responsible not only for the evils of modern
society—bureaucracy, war economies, war itself, totalitarianism—
but also for the problems of the individual in modern life. With

the rise of Stalinism, there is, as Guinevere and Monina demonstrate, little for modern beings to believe in except the superficial aspects of themselves. Hollingsworth expresses something of this modern hedonistic egotism:

> You could have a good time, you could still have a good time if you'd realize that everybody is like you, and so it's pointless to work for the future. . . . More modesty. We ain't equipped to deal with big things. If this fellow came up to me and asked my advice, I would take him aside and let him know that if he gives up the pursuits of vanity, and acts like everybody else, he'd get along better. Cause we never know what's deep down inside us . . . and it plays tricks. A good-time Charley, that's myself, and that's why I'm smarter than the lot of you. You can shove theory. . . . Respect your father and mother.   (193-194)

But the most important effect the failure of socialism has had on the individual is the loss of love. Lovett spotlights this when he declares that the history of the world, up to the point of the socialist revolution, has been synonymous with the "falling rate of love" (155). But it is McLeod who enunciates the relationship between the failed revolution and the death of love. His words are given weight by the fact that although the novel gives the overwhelming impression of sexual heat and desire, there is no real fulfillment and no love. There is homosexuality between Guinevere and Lannie; Hollingsworth beats Lannie, abuses her, and forces her to "commit salacia upon him" (100); and Lovett's relations with Lannie are one-sided and make him feel like an "onanist" (100). And so McLeod:

> "Love is . . . a crutch, that's all, and there isn't a one of us that doesn't need a crutch."
> "Still, it can't be just anybody," I protested.
> "Not today, no. Existence warps us too much. But in the abstract, in essence, any two human beings can find warmth together. It's a primitive notion, and history won't set it free again until socialism is established. That's the human assumption of socialism, to find relationships with everybody."   (125)

McLeod still believes in the socialist dream. So does Lovett, and

so, as the novel implies, does Mailer. The only ladder from the
pit of despair of modern times is revolutionary socialism.

In addition to resurrecting love, socialism will bring men "two
principles, freedom and equality, and without them we are nothing" (204). Such is the dream, but it remains far distant, since the
revolution has failed. The "little object" is man's hope for salvation. McLeod passes it on to the narrator, but its future is dubious.

The "little object" has great importance to Mailer. His reading
of Marx reveals a revisionist interpretation of Marxist thought.
By accepting Trotsky's theory of permanent revolution and apply-
ing it to recent history, Mailer is led to a conclusion different from
that of Marx: socialism is not inevitable. Only if the revolution
spreads throughout the world can it be sustained. Permanent
danger from without leads, as in the case of Soviet Russia under
Stalin, to destruction of the revolution from within. McLeod
seems to be speaking directly for Mailer when he says: "We assumed for far too long that socialism was inevitable and the error
has reduced us to impotence. Socialism is inevitable only if there
will be a civilization" (203). Thus, as Mailer sees it, men must
exercise will to achieve socialism. When McLeod says that "socialism does not come about by an act of will," he is echoing the
Marxist contention that man's existence is always determined by
external reality, by the social and economic world in which he
lives. But he is not denying that the exercise of man's will is necessary for the establishment of successful socialism. Men must want
to survive, they must want peace, they must bend their thoughts
and, more important, their actions in the direction of the socialist
revolution.

Lovett's existential choice—"I have no future anyway. At least
I can elect to have a future"—has already been pointed out. Mc-
Leod makes a similar choice several times. He rejects Stalinism:
"But do you know what it means to turn back? It's the one achieve-
ment of my life" (173). He steals the "little object" as a moral act,
although it is fraught with personal danger. Finally, he refuses
Hollingsworth's offer and faces death rather than surrender that
"little object."

In the first chapter Lovett tells of a recurring dream that plagues
him. A man climbs into a taxicab and gives the driver directions.
The route he takes seems strange, but the man is too tired to tell
the taxi driver to change direction. The city becomes stranger and

stranger, but the man decides it must be a dream and does nothing about it. "I shout at him. You are wrong, I cry, although he does not hear me; this city is the real city, the material city, and your vehicle is history" (7). History is out of control, and only by an effort of will can men change its direction away from perpetual war and unfulfilled desire and toward a socialist future of equality, freedom, and love.

Unlike *The Naked and the Dead*, in which Mailer also explored the modern totalitarian trend, *Barbary Shore* goes into the specific political failure that led to the modern dilemma and suggests a political solution, although a rather unlikely one. *Barbary Shore* shares with its predecessor the criticism of liberalism, but the barbs of Mailer's wrath (especially after his futile efforts on behalf of Henry Wallace and the Progressives during the 1948 election) have now been sharpened and dipped in poison. McLeod's entire polemic near the close of the novel is directed against the modern liberal, who will compromise rather than root out all the evils of modern society, who believes in reform rather than in the complete overthrow of the established system by revolutionary socialism. It is because the liberal will not commit himself entirely that the struggle is never really won. And as the doctrine of permanent revolution indicates, unless socialism is thoroughgoing and international in scope, it is doomed to failure; it will destroy itself from within to meet the challenges from without. McLeod's final speech is a plea to Lovett to engage himself, completely, totally, in the historic struggle facing modern man.

Lovett engages himself. He accepts the responsibility and the long and lonely wait. "So the heritage passed on to me, poor hope, and the little object as well, and I went out into the world" (223). Lovett, alone, friendless, without history, is indeed a "poor hope" for the future. But at least now he has a future, and despite the paucity of the hope, it is nonetheless better than the world of war and alienation and unfulfilled desire that surrounds him. There is at least the hope that Lovett will find others, brothers in his cause, and that after the major powers have exhausted themselves in a futile way, another opportunity will arise for revolutionary socialism. The hope is small, Mailer tells us, and it demands sacrifice and will from each of us.

The novel ends where it began, with the traveler still moving through the strange world in the taxi of history. The last line of the novel is also the last line of the first chapter. It is a warning to the reader, for *Barbary Shore* is Mailer's indictment of the blindness and deafness of modern mankind:

> Meanwhile, vast armies mount themselves, the world revolves, the traveller clutches his breast. From out the unyielding contradictions of labor stolen from men, the march to the endless war forces its pace. Perhaps, as the millions will be lost, others will be created, and I shall discover brothers where I thought none had existed.
>
> But for the present the storm approaches its thunderhead, and it is apparent that the boat drifts ever closer to shore. So the blind will lead the blind, and the deaf shout warnings to one another until their voices are lost. (223)

Chapter III

The Deer Park

An Ethic of Growth

he Deer Park[1] is set in Desert D'Or, a community modeled after California's Palm Springs. Desert D'Or, like Palm Springs, is a convenient vacation spot for Hollywood's harried movie colony. All of its residents are transient except Marion Faye, a nascent hipster who supplies its populace with prostitutes, drugs, and similar illicit commodities. Desert D'Or is at once a golden locale and the entrance to the dry and arid places of the human heart. Although the resort, occupied by practically no one save those who wish to see and be seen, is a radically different setting from the wartorn jungles of the Pacific and the underground urban battlefield of modern revolutionary politics that we saw in the previous novels, the nexus of social repression, violence, and failure that are at the heart of the previous novels figures importantly in this one as well.

The Deer Park is narrated by Sergius O'Shaugnessy, who recounts a critical period in the life of his friend, Charley Eitel. Eitel, a former director of Hollywood movies, has been blacklisted by the film establishment for refusing to testify about his past associations before a congressional investigating committee. At the time O'Shaugnessy meets him, Eitel is living in Desert D'Or and is just beginning an affair with Elena Esposito, a dancer of great sensuality but little talent. As the novel progresses, the affair becomes increasingly important to Eitel, who realizes he is in the midst of a fight against not only the powers of Hollywood but also encroaching middle age. The demands he and Elena make on each other grow progressively more painful, and they finally separate. Eitel eventually agrees to testify before the congressional committee, Elena's affair with the hipster Marion Faye leaves her in a hospital, and finally, in an act of resignation, Eitel and Elena marry.

The second plot line of the novel concerns O'Shaugnessy himself, a recent hero of the Korean conflict. O'Shaugnessy, too, has an affair, with the cinematic sex queen Lulu Myers. Unlike Eitel and Elena, however, they quickly recognize they are not suited to each other and go their separate ways. As Eitel struggles with his conscience and strives to maintain his courage, O'Shaugnessy observes him and tries to figure out how he will deal with his own future. Eventually he turns down an offer to become a film actor, and at the close of the novel leaves the wasteland of Desert D'Or for the East Coast.

The Deer Park is a novel about growth and courage. When Charley Eitel, the middle-aged director, realizes near the close of the book that "there was that law of life so cruel and so just which demanded that one must grow or else pay more for remaining the same" (36), he discovers the underlying principle of the world in which he lives. More importantly, insofar as Mailer's novels delineate a coherent universe, this law governs that universe. Time and again Mailer reformulates the necessity for growth, often in the exact words of Eitel's insight.

Once again in this novel Mailer poses the problem of how a man should live in the real world, a world of suffering, cruelty, violence and death. "There was a real world as I called it, a world of wars and boxing clubs and children's homes on back streets, and this real world was a world where orphans burned orphans" (47; the last phrase is repeated on pages 231 and 374). Men must continually engage this real world, for avoiding it is avoiding growth; and embracing illusions, even minor ones, ultimately leads to spiritual death. It is as if reality and consciousness were two almost parallel rails: if consciousness does not continually change, adapting itself to the course of reality, the two will eventually spread so far apart that all travel over them must come to a halt. Reality and one's apprehension of it are never the same, and even the slightest discrepancy between them becomes, through time, an insurmountable gap. Growth, for Mailer, is the process of continual readaptation to the real world.

To live in that real world requires the courage to confront reality daily and to make the continual choice of growth over stagnation. Sergius O'Shaugnessy, the narrator of the novel, attempts to heed the demand for courage. The night following a visit from two investigators from the McCarthy-inspired "Norton Committee," at a juncture critical to his maturing psyche, O'Shaugnessy attempts to plumb his own depths: "For I touched the bottom myself, there was a bottom that time" (326). O'Shaugnessy's struggle is reminiscent of Jacob's nightlong match with the angel of God, or of that modern equivalent when Bernard wrestles through the night with his demon in Gide's *The Counterfeiters*.[2] It recalls Lovett's lonely nights, and that last night when Hearn decides to resign his commission. Mailer's heroes never quite make what Hemingway called "a separate peace,"[3] but they always fight the war which precedes it. Since one must continue to grow, there is never a peace. There is only the occasional respite which gives a man the rest he needs in order to reenlist in the wars of self and reality. By the end of the novel O'Shaugnessy has the wisdom to say, "But I would have told him that one must invariably look for a good time since a good time is what gives us the strength to try again" (374).

Although Mailer holds that men must remain in contact with reality, he does not maintain that they must accept it. The artist— Eitel tells O'Shaugnessy in an imaginary dialogue—must deal with the real world, but he must also strive to change it from a world of suffering and pain to something nobler and finer. "You must blow against the walls of every power that exists, the small trumpet of your defiance" (374). In this novel the artist and his art become the "little object" in which men may rest their hopes. Thus Mailer, in *The Deer Park*, turns from revolutionary socialism to artistic creation as a possible vehicle for human redemption.

On that night when he touches bottom, O'Shaugnessy realizes that although one must live with courage and honesty, there is no courage without weakness, that the honest pursuit of truth is wedded to error, that love and hate spring together from the same soil. O'Shaugnessy is coming, in his own fashion, to an understanding that reality is dialectical by nature. Both O'Shaugnessy's desire to be a writer and Mailer's glorification of art in this novel are prompted by the recognition that art can express that marriage of opposites which is so evident in the actual nature of things.

This dance of opposites necessitates growth. If motives are always unclear, if closeness to reality can also be distance, there is a constant need for change, so that men are not left in static and false positions.

> I thought of courage and of cowardice, and how we are all brave and all terrified each in our own way and our private changing proportion, and I thought of honesty and deception, and the dance of life they make, for it is exactly

> when we come closest to another that we are turned
> away with a lie, and blunder forward on a misconcep-
> tion, moving to understand ourselves on the platitudes
> and lies of the past. . . . I thought of such couples as love
> and hate, and victory and defeat, and what it was to feel
> warm and what it was to be cool.   (325)

Mailer regards himself as an existentialist; his understanding of
growth is existential. One must act, for action creates a new existent reality. Thus he concludes the tortured spiritual struggle described above with O'Shaugnessy's resolution: "I knew that finally
one must do, simply do, for we act in total ignorance and yet in
honest ignorance we must act, or we can never learn for we can
hardly believe what we are told, we can only measure what has
happened inside ourselves" (326). But to act honestly is not an
easy task. Eitel's rudimentary awareness of this anticipates the
intense involvement with authenticity of the later novels. "The
essence of spirit, he thought to himself, was to choose the thing
which did not better one's position but made it more perilous"
(257). Eitel's thought becomes, later in the novel, Marion Faye's
obsession.

Faye hypothesizes that God, as well as man, must struggle for
survival and mastery; furthermore, God in His conflict is dependent
upon the results of human struggles. When men grow and triumph,
God's force is enhanced; when they retreat from danger, fail to
change, and die spiritually, His power is impaired. This theme was
to be central to a vast epic of eight linked novels, of which *The
Deer Park* was envisioned as one. Although the epic was never
published, its Prologue has been printed.[4] Yet since the divine
struggle becomes a central concern of Mailer's next novel, *An
American Dream*, we will postpone a deeper investigation of it
until a later chapter.

Still, growth is not easily accomplished. Because society needs
stability to maintain itself, it seeks to repress the growth and development of the individual. If the individual is allowed to change
and grow freely, he will, as he changes, also change the society
in which he lives. Opposed to the individual's need for growth is
the need of other individuals who possess power and identify their
interests with those of the state, to ensure stability and thereby
safeguard their power. The conflict between the two needs, freedom and power, was central in *The Naked and the Dead*. In this

novel Mailer once again investigates the violence committed by institutions and the men who control them.

For the first time, however, Mailer seems to realize the need for another sort of violence. In the earlier novels he was subconsciously aware of this emergent need. Croft and Cummings are the natural heroes of the war novel precisely because they have the courage to accept and even embrace the violence that surrounds them. There is a perverse heroism in the young McLeod who, in his youthful commitment, served as the bloody executioner of the enemies of his faction of the Communist Party. In *The Deer Park* Mailer once again explores the contradictory needs to embrace and restrain violence. In *Advertisements for Myself*, Mailer explains that while writing and revising the novel, he was cultivating the experience of excess—smoking marijuana, drinking, indulging his sexual appetite (*AM*, 228–248). It is not unreasonable to suggest that this immersion in excess led Mailer to consciously explore and expand those elements of his work which had hereteofore been only suggested—the need for violence, the value of overindulgence, the necessity to make the strongest possible assertion of social identity. Thus as the novel progresses, Marion Faye becomes increasingly important to Mailer's purpose. Faye carries more and more of the freight of violence, rebellion, and outlawry that serves as the impetus for Mailer's embrace of hip philosophy in "The White Negro." At the same time, he broadens and deepens our understanding of Mailer's subconscious admiration of the violent and destructive excesses of Sergeant Croft.[5]

Faye represents, in a nascent stage, Mailer's belief in authenticity.[6] The frequent references that Mailer makes to Hemingway[7] suggest that Hemingway is the immediate source for Mailer's understanding of the place of violence in authentic existence. The authentic life is revealed, Hemingway believed, by the manifestation of grace under pressure, by "playing with death, bringing it closer, closer, closer."[8] For Mailer, this belief leads to the conclusion that violence can be the mechanism by which authenticity is achieved and salvation approached.

Although Mailer's views about violence often seem contradictory, many of the contradictions disappear if we recognize that he is usually speaking of two kinds of violence, individual and social. Mailer sees the history of modern civilization as the record of the increasing domination of men's freedom and individuality by the various forces of totalitarianism. Mailer asserts that modern men must resist this centralized social violence—of the government, industry, media, and class structure—and affirm their individuality. If violence is the only way to accomplish this affirmation, such violence is justifiable and salutary. Individual violence need not be directed against society per se, for every act of violence, save those sanctioned by society itself, is a blow against the oppressive social order. Thus, though institutional violence leads to the destruction of the individual, personal violence leads to the affirmation of the individual and is a step toward the destruction of oppressive institutions.

The novel portrays three areas of institutional control: the military, the bureaucratic state, and the mass media—this last represented by Hollywood and the film industry. The first two areas continue, respectively, the probing of the first and second novels. In *The Deer Park* Mailer explores the media for the first time, using the film capital as his focus. Hollywood allows him to point to the totalitarian tendency in all areas of modern life and moves the locus of social control away from the strict confines of the military-industrial-governmental establishment. By examining Hollywood, Mailer is also able to deal with the corruption of the modern American mythos as revealed in the celluloid dreams fabricated by Hollywood. In this sense the novel is a precursor of *An American Dream*, which explores in detail the deterioration of American myths.

The military appears in the novel only in the early pages. O'Shaugnessy has been in the Air Force, but after many bombing missions, the sight of a child with a burned arm makes him realize the horror of what he is doing. "Fighting an enemy plane was impersonal and had the nice moves of all impersonal contests" (45), but O'Shaugnessy suddenly realizes that the result of this contest is personal suffering and pain. He rebels against the impersonality of violence. Here, once again, is one of Mailer's main concerns. In the modern age violence is impersonal, detached, and petty rather than heroic; in Lannie Madison's words from *Barbary Shore*, it has a banality which is "beyond good and evil." When Hearn confronts the future that Cummings represents, and when Lovett hears of McLeod's past and watches Hollingsworth operate in the present, they prefigure O'Shaugnessy's reaction. The impersonal violence of the military forces Hearn to make the futile decision to change his life, Lovett to lose his memory, and O'Shaugnessy to become impotent. Only love can end O'Shaugnessy's condition.

Published in 1955, *The Deer Park* is a product of the McCarthy era and, more specifically, the dramatic investigation of Hollywood. Congressman Richard Selwyn Crane is a thinly veiled Joe McCarthy, and the investigation that looms so importantly in Eitel's career is a fictional example of what was, for the Hollywood of the early 1950's, a common occurrence. Eitel's antagonistic stance in his appearance before the committee caused the unemployment and poverty with which he must currently cope, and his changing relations with the committee are an accurate barometer of both the state of his soul and the weakness of liberalism in America. This committee, as Mailer portrays it, powerfully influences all aspects of American life; its interest is not in security or safety or truth, but in the suppression of the independent will of the American people. Even O'Shaugnessy, uninvolved in any of the Committee's concerns, is harassed because he is a friend of Eitel's. The fact that many modern readers may find O'Shaugnessy's fear of these men disproportionate to their actual threat is a sign not of the author's ineptitude but of the change of political climate since the novel's publication. In 1955 the overt violence of the bureaucratic state seemed a believable reality.

Hollywood is a center of the American dream. It creates our myths, and its life is the culmination of the dreams it creates. The dissonance between the myth and the reality, between the illusion of film and the reality of the film industry, has been a major theme in modern American literature. In *The Last Tycoon* Fitzgerald used Hollywood to explore many of the same problems he dealt with in *The Great Gatsby*; indeed, *Gatsby* is in some ways the first Hollywood novel, for the opulence and splendor of its façade reveal the influence of the cinema. Fitzgerald's world is one in which the standard of reality is film, and it is by this standard that all else, even the physical world, is to be judged.[9] In *The Last Tycoon* he tried to create a contemporary tragedy, in which a man of creative capacity and vision is defeated by the harsh powers that manipulate the empire behind the fantasy; Monroe Stahr's dilemma is to become Eitel's, although, as we will see, Eitel is not quite the man Stahr was. Budd Schulberg, likewise, in *What Makes Sammy Run?* creates a sociological portrait of a neurotic Hollywood mogul. The story of Sammy Glick could be that of Herman Teppis, the head of Supreme Pictures in *The Deer Park*. There can be little doubt that Mailer is indebted to Schulberg's satiric portrait of the selfishness and power that run Hollywood. Teppis and his nephew Collie Munshin are Glick's colleagues, the vultures who pick over the remains of men like Stahr.

But the Hollywood novel most important to an understanding of *The Deer Park* is Nathaniel West's *Day of the Locust*. Mailer has acknowledged his admiration for West. Their religion, social milieu, and educational background were similar. And Charley Eitel's plot for the work of art he hopes to direct is a very thinly veiled copy of West's *Miss Lonelyhearts* (the fact that Eitel's best vision is but a poor copy is a significant irony). Even if we overlook these ties, the relationship between *Day of the Locust* and *The Deer Park* is obvious. The mood of the two novels is similar. Both are obsessed with the violence of life in Hollywood and with the impossibility of love. Sexual heat and the smell of orgy inundate their settings. The society of both West and Mailer teeters on the brink of apocalypse, and the object of the narrators in each novel is to portray, and attempt to understand, this apocalyptic atmosphere. *The Deer Park*, in many respects, is a panel from the painting that Nathaniel West's Tod Hackett creates out of his stay in Hollywood: a canvas of violence, lust, and greed, with flames of incipient destruction swirling around the contorted faces of the inhabitants of the mythic land of film. Both West and Mailer focus on the fringes of the film industry, concentrating on the no man's land where the illusion of Hollywood and the corruption behind it intersect with the common life of America. Both portraits are bitter commentaries on the unheroic and perverted quality of that life. Hollywood, if one examines it as a whole and not just its cinematic products, is America in microcosm: it manifests the competition, violence, and chaos of American society.

Mailer's representation of Hollywood is most brutal in his savagely satiric portraits of Herman Teppis, the head of a major studio, and Collie Munshin, the producer who is also Teppis' son-in-law and prospective successor. The two are among Mailer's most vivid comic creations. Though Teppis has no redeeming characteristics, Munshin's ambition and rapacity are offset by more endearing traits. Munshin, a fusion of egoism and concern, hatred and love, comedy and threat, is a caricature made human by Mailer's sensitivity to the depths and contradictions in his nature. The reader finds himself laughing at Munshin's mannerisms, feeling with and for him, and even growing fond of him; but beneath this acceptance is the reader's realization that Munshin is indeed a terrible figure, one who will lie, pander, and sacrifice anyone in order to achieve power and success.

Munshin's friendship with Eitel, which sometimes appears so generous, is actually a devilish contract which causes Eitel to lose his soul. One of the reasons Munshin is so often comic when he appears with Eitel is that the reader cannot quite believe that his manipulating and scheming are real. But despite Munshin's protestations, they are an integral part of his nature.

Though Munshin is an important part of the novel from start to finish, his father-in-law has only one major scene. Herman Teppis' hypocritical attitude toward his employees and toward his professed morality is revealed with comic brilliance as he tries to force a marriage between Teddy Pope, a homosexual, and an equally unwilling partner, Lulu Myers. The beneficent father turns into a savage autocrat when he encounters resistance. The scene culminates when he calls in a secretary to do him service:

> "Don't you worry, sweetie," he said, and down he looked at that frightened female mouth, facsimile of all those smiling lips he had seen so ready to serve at the thumb of power, and with a cough, he started to talk. "That's a good girlie, that's a good girlie, that's a good girlie, that's a good girlie . . ."   (284)

It is, after all, the perverse nature of Teppis which rules Hollywood. Those who oppose him, he crushes. For Mailer the catastrophe of modern society is that Teppis is right. The methods of power, of psychological, financial, and physical violence, are frighteningly successful, and ensure that all those smiling lips are ready to serve.

Both Teppis and Munshin are will to use others to further their own ends even if they use them up in the process. Their personalities are not to blame; conditions are scarcely better in any of the other studios. The apparatus of power is present in the institutional framework, and those who rise toward power must take on the characteristics that the movie industry demands. The measure of this power is that the industry—in the persons of Teppis and Munshin—always wins.

If the industry does not triumph over O'Shaugnessy, it is because O'Shaugnessy chooses to leave Desert D'Or and the opulent Hollywood community. O'Shaugnessy narrates the actions the novel embraces, and in a sense it is his novel. He is an aspiring writer, and his function within the novel is to be a participant, a historian, and an imaginative artist—overlapping roles that remind the reader of the narrator of Gide's *The Counterfeiters*, who serves as both storyteller and creator of part of the story he is telling. He is not only an observer and reflector; this is *his* story, the world presented as he has decided we should see it. He reports on the actions of himself and others; he also consciously invents the novel as it proceeds.

Unfortunately, Mailer is not entirely successful in this attempt to inject depth and irony into his narrative. O'Shaugnessy is a weak, uninteresting, and eventually boring character. Despite Mailer's efforts, he comes across in much the way a lesser matinee idol does—a flat character, formed with a certain image of the popular hero in mind, attractive but with neither intensity nor unique qualities. Richard Poirier maintains,[10] with Mailer, that when Mailer revised the manuscript and enlarged O'Shaugnessy's role and complexity, he strengthened the novel. That is a comparative judgment. *The Deer Park* is Mailer's weakest novel, and O'Shaugnessy is primarily, like Lovett, a *tabula rasa* upon which certain lessons are written. He is the battleground upon which conflicting forces meet, and a rather unexciting battleground at that.

As the novel opens, O'Shaugnessy reveals that he has left the Air Force with a mental discharge, and that owing to his vivid memory of the brutality of war, he is impotent. Shortly after his arrival in Desert D'Or he meets Lulu Myers, the girlish-featured beauty who is the queen of Supreme Pictures and a Betty Grable to the troops with whom O'Shaugnessy has served. Lulu's charms, and the knowledge that the dreams of millions of men ride with him, stimulate O'Shaugnessy. The past is dispelled, he regains his potency, and the two begin a love affair. O'Shaugnessy falls deeply in love, but Lulu remains a Hollywood creation, "never so happy as when we acted at theater and did the mime on clouds of myth" (138). For Lulu, acting is reality and life is the illusion that takes up the time between acts. Her favorite joy is to exhibit herself in little roles; she makes a continuous attempt to turn life into a variety of cinematic experiences. To O'Shaugnessy, their love is a competition in which he strives to do well; to Lulu, it is an emotion she feels when she sees herself as a dramatic character in an intimate position with a handsome young soldier just returned from heroic duty defending his country.

Not very long after the relation has begun, Lulu breaks it off. O'Shaugnessy has the courage to accept this rupture rather than debase his integrity in an attempt to reestablish it. Yet all the while their relationship has served as a counterpoint to that between Eitel and Elena, Collie Munshin's ex-mistress. Although superficially the two affairs are different, both begin at the same time, develop along similar lines, and finally disintegrate. And both loves are played out in the illumination of the klieg lights of Hollywood. Lulu belongs to that movie world to which Eitel longs to return. She breaks off her affair with O'Shaugnessy because she hears her Hollywood family, which he has just rejected, calling. She also ends it because she must always flee reality; on their last night together O'Shaugnessy tells her of his experiences during the war and she glimpses that "real world where orphans burned orphans." Finally, the overwhelming needs of her ego, kept in an infantile stage by the unreality and perversity of Hollywood, add an additional stress to their affair and bring about its demise. Eitel's reasons for breaking with Elena, though more complex and ambiguous than Lulu's, are similar.

While O'Shaugnessy is probably less successful in his love affair with Lulu than the other characters are in their relationships— he never becomes as deeply and totally involved as Eitel, Faye, and Elena do—he ultimately gains some small understanding of what it is to be human and of the part love plays in man's humanity. The novel is permeated by sex, a fact that led many readers to disparage Mailer's seriousness and dismiss the book as an attempted best-seller. Though Mailer was, and is, involved with the need to be successful, sex was not merely an incidental included to further the book's sales; it is close to the heart of the novel. At the end, O'Shaugnessy realizes what no other character can quite grasp: sex is not identical with love, nor is it a replacement for love; it is nevertheless essential to not only love but life. It is fundamental to the process of growth.

> There are hours when I would have the arrogance to reply to the Lord Himself, and so I ask, "Would you agree that sex is where philosophy begins?"
> But God, who is the oldest of the philosophers, answers in His weary cryptic way, "Rather think of Sex as Time, and Time as the connection of new circuits." (375)

Mailer illuminates his meaning in the play he made out of the
novel, where the lines O'Shaugnessy speaks immediately following the above are these:

> "Connection of new . . . circuits . . . ?" I say, and must
> add, "Sir, isn't Time rather the capture of conception?"
> "Connection of new circuits is good enough for an
> American with a mechanical head like yours," the Lord
> roars back in my ear.[11]

Growth is essential to life, and sex is growth in its most elemental
sense. Sex is conception, possibility; it is the heart of time. On
another level, it is the method by which an individual can connect
new circuits, can form new relationships, a new mindset, new
synapses. Such is O'Shaugnessy's eventual realization, and he alone
seems to speak for Mailer when he invents the dialogue quoted
above.

O'Shaugnessy, as well as being a lover is also a writer, and in
his insistence upon the importance of honest artistic vision he is
a fictional surrogate for Mailer. The significance of the artist's
vision is one of Mailer's central themes; and in this novel the examples of O'Shaugnessy and Eitel reveal that an artist must struggle
to remain honest and open or he will lose both his creative capacity and his potential to transform society. The artist must grapple
with the realities of the world and his existence and not shrink
from the horrors he discovers and the suffering which surrounds
him everywhere. Thus the process of artistic creation requires the
same continuous growth that life and authenticity demand. Art
requires courage as well, not only the courage to face reality but
the greater courage to risk all that one is in the creative process.
For Mailer and for O'Shaugnessy, a lie is a death, and the artist
in his reach for new truth and the new way of expressing this truth
is always skirting the edge of falsehood. By treading the narrow
verge between banality and falsehood the artist is, in a real and
not only symbolic manner, playing out the essence of the struggle
for authenticity: he is confronting death. Thus art becomes for
O'Shaugnessy a personal road to salvation, and it offers, because
of its courage, honesty, and defiance, a hope for mankind.

Although O'Shaugnessy is always present, and is at times a
spokesman for Mailer, Charley Eitel is the protagonist of the novel.
O'Shaugnessy is, finally, uninteresting; it is difficult to take his
self-conscious poses seriously. But Eitel, by the immediacy and

poignancy of his experience, holds our attention. He, as Hearn, Valsen, and McLeod before him, is a failure, despite, or perhaps because of, the core of humanism that is the armature of his being. He represents, for Mailer, the failure of the liberal spirit in the era of postindustrial, capitalist society. It is Croft, Cummings, Hollingsworth, Teppis, and Munshin who achieve success and some measure of victory in the early novels, but these men all lack the compassion and understanding that is required if one is to be fully human.

So, while Eitel makes continual efforts to fulfill his desire to be both decent and heroic, each attempt he makes is fated to be a repeat of his past failures. To some degree he is a contemporary Everyman, facing a changing world in which all human efforts, even those which are temporarily successful, eventually become defeats. Only continual growth can preserve him from complete defeat. There is an affinity between Mailer's view of the human condition here and that of Camus, as expressed in his retelling of the myth of Sisyphus: continual effort and continual defeat is the human condition. Eitel exists, however, not on a lonely hill but in a world filled with people and marshaled by institutions; he must attempt to push objects up his hill which are far more tenuous and imprecise than a rock, though no less important thereby. And Eitel is different from Sisyphus in that he is not a tragic figure, neither in the traditional nor in the existential sense. He is absurd, but the irony of his situation continually touches him with the comic.

There is a twofold cause for Eitel's failures. American society, particularly corporate capitalism and centralized power, makes individual fulfillment nearly impossible. And Eitel, while a good and decent man, nevertheless has weaknesses that sabotage his most well-intentioned efforts. O'Shaugnessy admits the first and recognizes the second when he summarizes his view of Eitel: "Yet one thing I believe can be said, I had the notion that there were few kind and honest men in the world, and the world always took care to put them down. For most of the time I knew Eitel, I suppose I saw him in this way" (23).

Mailer's profound belief that the humanistic, liberal hero will continually meet defeat through the agency of overwhelmingly hostile social institutions is similar to the vision of *spargamos* which Northrop Frye sees as the basis of the ironic *mythos:* "*Spargamos*, or the sense that heroism and effective action are absent, disorganized or foredoomed to defeat, and that confusion and anarchy reign over the world, is the archetypal theme of irony and satire."[12] All of Mailer's works portray the modern world as an arena of confusion and anarchy; history, that taxi-driver of Lovett's dream, is lost and out of control. Furthermore, Mailer sees the easiest and most widespread response to this social confusion as an embrace of totalitarianism. Superorganization and centralized power are wrongly thought to be antidotes to disorganization and defeat. The fight to remain alive and individual in an increasingly centralized and collective society is the major battle of the twentieth century. But, considering man's potential, Mailer asks us if even the victory of survival is not a defeat, in the light of what man could have been.

Society and its institutions have trapped Eitel. The Norton Committee and the shoddy standards of the film industry have ripped away all the external supports from his life. He has been a marionette so long that he is, despite himself, used to feeling Teppis pull the strings, and in his heart courage battles with his desire to return to the security of the puppet show. His talent has been prostituted, his integrity seduced, his moral nature raped, by the monster Hollywood. "I had the sensation of being a complete and total whore in the world, and I accepted every blow, every kick, and every gratuitous kindness with the inner gratitude that it could have been a great deal worse" (306).

Eitel is, in this sense, what Frye calls the *pharmakos*, who is neither innocent nor guilty. He is innocent in the sense that what happens to him is far greater than anything he has done provokes, like the mountaineer whose shout brings down an avalanche. He is guilty in the sense that he is a member of a guilty society, or living in a world where such injustices are an inescapable part of existence. The two facts do not come together; they remain ironically apart.[13] He is a born loser, for although his losses are often self-inflicted, he is part of a world that is moved by forces beyond his control. His original spurning of the investigating committee is heroic, as Marion realizes; but the reward for his heroism is the lonely, boring, and unheroic existence he is forced to live on the fringes of Desert D'Or society. As a result, he cancels his earlier heroism when he returns before the committee to answer their questions. He is caught in a dilemma: being a hero means giving up his dream of being an artist and also means thinking of himself as a failure; being a coward means exactly the same thing. The

only difference is that the former makes "his position more perilous." This, of course, is the way to growth, but Eitel is ironically
caught up in middle age. Finally, he succumbs to "the sad frustration of his new middle age" (374) and tries to maintain what
he has rather than risk it to grow into something new. His failure
to grow is the beginning of his spiritual death.

But Eitel does resist the committee; he does enter into the frightening complex of needs and emotions which result from his affair
with Elena. If his eventual backing out of the resistance and the
relationship is a failure, then his entrance into both is a mark of
heroism. Eitel is a *Mensch*, which is a distinction in this increasingly sterile modern age. He has courage and feels responsibility.
Although he hides things from himself, particularly during his
affair with Elena, he is also honest. O'Shaugnessy is drawn to Eitel
largely because of this honesty, which stands out in the hypocrisy
and play-acting of this modern Deer Park. With the possible exception of Elena, he is the most human character in the novel; he
comes alive, and his life and the reader's become intertwined.

Many of Mailer's contemporaries find in the *pharmakos* the
modern hero. Bellow, Malamud, and Updike all discover a type
for the heroic in the loser, the trapped victim. For Malamud especially, to suffer and be defeated is the definition of being human,
and those who suffer and meet defeat with courage and honesty are
the modern heroes. But Mailer rejects this belief in the heroism of
the *Mensch*. Mailer is searching for heroes, men who can still be
judged heroic on the scales of the past. Man may live in a world
of *spargamos*, indeed he must accept that he does, but he must
eventually triumph over it.

Nevertheless, the heroic is always finally lacking in Mailer's
novels, though there are transitory glimpses of it and the need for
it permeates his plots and attitudes and even controls his public
life. The modern world always triumphs, and thus Mailer's novels
are always colored with the frantic despair of his realizations that
spargamos must be (yet probably cannot be) escaped from. Thus
Eitel, who is heroic by many modern standards, is ultimately a
failure because he gives up and admits defeat. He ceases to grow.
So begins his inevitable death.

This is one side of Eitel, the modern *Mensch*. But if he is heroic
and pathetic, he is also comic. He is comic because he is beneath
us; he is a loser, and we laugh at him. Even his first name,
"Charley," satirizes his artistic pretensions. And his masterpiece,

as has been mentioned, is a sterile imitation of a creative novel. He is wrapped in the mantle of his ego and often lost in the folds of his self-pity. He is a man who has postponed middle age as long as possible and suddenly finds himself in the middle of it. A sad and human predicament, it is nevertheless humorous. The king of the boudoir is hitting the skids. Charley's strengths are offset by his weaknesses, and his virtues by his pretensions.

His weaknesses are not entirely excusable, as they might be in the world of much modern fiction. Early in the novel, O'Shaugnessy is impressed with Somerset Maugham's statement that " 'Nobody is any better than he ought to be' " (99). But he disagrees with Maugham: "some people are a little better, and some a little worse than they ought to be" (99). This, for O'Shaugnessy, is the human sphere, the small margin within which a man can make himself either better or worse than he ought to be. Eitel believes this as well. Later, O'Shaugnessy says of them both, "Each of us judged himself hard, for strong in us was the idea that we must be perfect. We felt we were better than others and therefore we should act better. It is a very great vanity" (228). It may be a great vanity, but by this standard Eitel must be judged; it is both his and Mailer's. Because Eitel capitulates, ceases to grow, and accepts his middle age, he fails to act better than he ought to act. His courage fails, and he is stranded short of the heroic.

Eitel's failure of courage is manifested in three ways, each making clear that the early triumphs of courage and integrity have now been undermined. He surrenders his integrity and principles by making a deal with the Norton Committee, rejecting his previous courageous resistance in order to gain the security he craves. He fails his art, sacrificing his vision for the power that he gains by creating tasteless and mediocre products. The transition from visionary to purveyor of products for audience consumption has been gradual; the final landslide that completes the erosion is his collaboration with Munshin and his readmission to the movie industry. This sacrifice of art for success makes Marion Faye judge Eitel bitterly, "Because you might have been an artist, and you spit on it" (184). And finally, Eitel fails in love.

When Eitel was in the first blush of love with Elena, "he had the faith these days that they would continue to change together" (123). But as the affair progresses, and Eitel's youthful spirit and dynamism return, he must also cope with encroaching middle age. He set out believing that "I could make something of this girl"

(107). And he achieves a partial transformation: "There were times like this when he felt the substance of his pride to depend upon exactly her improvement as if she were finally the only human creation in which he had taken part" (372). He has indeed helped Elena to mature, but he has also hurt her incalculably. If growth is the main function of the human organism, then prevention of growth is one of the cardinal sins. And Eitel, out of the needs of his ego, his desire for security, and his hunger for freedom, denies Elena the chance to grow. He admits this when he calls her stupid, and it is from this point on that their relationship begins to disintegrate. Eitel is afraid of age and insecurity. He who said "everything you learn is done by fighting your fear" (102) clings to Elena, as Faye perceives, "because you're scared" (186). Eitel no longer has the courage to face life; he depends upon Elena to uncover it to him. And yet he is frightened even of her, for with her animal spirit and her appetite for experience she also threatens him. This unsteady foundation of need and fear poorly supports the love Eitel feels for Elena and causes it to vacillate through jealousy and hatred.

> Because all the while he loved her he knew that he dare not love her. Young as she was, he had heard experience in her voice which was beyond his own experience, and so if he stayed with her, he would be obliged to travel in her directions, and he had been fleeing that for all of his life.   (257)

Eitel's failure arises out of his rejection of love and growth, and it is compounded by his attempt to prevent Elena's growth so that she can continue to succor him.

Because, for Mailer, sex is close to the heart of life, change, and conception, it is in the arena of sex that Eitel's struggles with life, heroism, and growth go on. An affair is what O'Shaugnessy called the "dance of opposites," for love is commingled with hate, independence with dependence, fear with courage, giving with receiving. In this milieu sex is a battleground for the deployment of domestic and personal violence. In the Time Machine portraits of Croft and Cummings in *The Naked and the Dead*, Mailer showed how sex could be an extreme, personal form of violence; with Charley and Elena, the sexual struggle is moved from the realm of the abnormal to that of the normal. Sex necessarily involves violence because, as one of the roots of life, it involves those fundamental contradictions warring in the human heart; it is the physical objectification of O'Shaugnessy's "dance of opposites." It should not be inferred, however, that because sex is violent it is necessarily destructive; on the contrary, out of this violence issues conception. And out of the sexual battle comes nobility and rejuvenation; it is as if sex were a bull fight, and the closer the matador comes to violence and death, the more courage and honesty he displays.[14] By performing well, a man may become a little better than he ought to be. Sex "was his dream of bounty, and it nourished him enough to wake up with the hope that this affair could return his energy, flesh his courage and make him the man he had once believed himself to be" (110).

For Eitel and Elena both, sex is violent because it serves as a sublimation for other drives. It is the outlet for the violence he conceals within himself, a violence growing out of his failure to become the artist he should have been, out of his wasted years, and out of his failure to find love. This violence is the manifestation of his thwarted love and his thwarted drive for creation and success.

Eitel is filled with violence which he directs against himself. He torments himself with jealousy over Elena. He hurts her so that he can hurt himself. He punishes himself by needlessly antagonizing other persons, such as Teppis and Dorothea and Munshin. And, finally, he destroys the mainstays of his life, his relationship with Elena and his own integrity and principle.

Eitel directs this violence toward himself because of the utter futility of leveling it against the institution that prostituted him, robbed him of his individuality and virility, and left him stranded on the shores of middle age with little to look back on with pride. His heroic resistance to the Committee is futile, for while a single man can stand up against the power of an immense institution, he cannot conquer it. His impotence in directing his violence against the outer world leads Eitel to direct it inward.

Eitel also feels that he was tempted and that he gave in to temptation. In order to destroy his weakness, he must destroy himself and any part of himself that he holds dear, such as Elena. He must punish himself for his sins, very much as Faye does, and so he tends to destroy himself. This self-destruction, more than any other action, reifies Eitel's dreams and ideals. His failure is that he is not consistently able to strive after them.

The reader's sympathy is engaged more by Elena than by Eitel. She seems a simple, passionate woman, much misused by the men in whom she puts her trust. The reader approaches her through this stereotype. It is significant that she is of Latin extraction, that she comes from an uncultured background, that polish, sophistication, and culture slide away from her as water from a greased pole. The fact that she fits the reader's conception of the passionate lover—all body and animalism and no intellect—is of utmost significance, for this is precisely the way Eitel approaches her. His major concern for her revolves around his desire to avoid an entangling and permanent relationship without hurting her simple, trusting, and dependent nature. The reader is carried away, as Eitel is, with her physicality, her animality, her lack of awareness of the complexity of human relationships.

Elena, however, is not simple, as her insights into Eitel, her sexual adventures with Faye and Munshin and Don Beda, and her final letter to Eitel indicate. Whereas Eitel's thinking and scheming are conscious, Elena's are unconscious; her complexity and her manipulation of others are hidden but nevertheless real and effective. This is manifested in her acts. It is she who gives both Eitel and Munshin the gate, even though both think that they are abandoning her. Although she seems to be in Faye's power, their relationship is in a perverted way reciprocal; and a summary view of their affair shows that it is Marion, and not Elena, who has been changed most, and who is in effect living the submissive role. Elena's silences, her superficial simplicity, lead the other characters (Munshin, Eitel, and Faye) to feel they are asserting their dominance. What actually happens in all three cases, however, is that all their efforts and complexity are ultimately dulled, ensnared, or disintegrated by the totally yielding but complex Elena. As in the old children's game of rock, paper, and scissors, the three men find that their sharpness must yield to her impassivity, and their strength is enveloped by her fullness.

Elena is no more ready and willing to accept love and responsibility for others than Eitel is, as her letter to him makes plain. Both wish to be independent while yet craving independence; but Eitel's complexity is of great concern to himself and to the reader, and is open to sight. Elena's complexity lies hidden from everyone, including herself, but for those rare moments in which she has the courage to face reality and manifest her desires and insights.

Like Eitel, she does violence to those she loves. She does so partly to punish herself; she too has ideals, she too feels guilty about a wasted life. Like Eitel, she hurts those she loves because she wishes to exert some sort of domination over them. Eitel's life is wrecked on the rocks of middle age when she leaves him in order to go to Faye, and she leaves Faye torn apart by the violence of their affair, facing a jail term which is his self-inflicted punishment. Elena is aware of the secret source of power. "You could eat up the whole world if only you didn't fall for all the talk that the middle-class squares give you" (315). She is Eitel's feminine parallel. She craves love and also power, and eventually gives up both for security. In the process she stops growing, becomes middle-class and middle-aged, and begins the slow slide toward spiritual death.

Faye constantly tries to resist the forces of stagnation. He expounds a theory of growth; his constant need is to push himself to and beyond new limits, thereby hoping to avoid the possibility of settling into inertia. Constantly he must muster his courage: he refuses to lock his doors; he avoids aiding a junkie in need because that would be the easy road, the route dictated by his fear; he drives Elena to the point of suicide, not out of hate but out of his cold but passionate need to plumb the depths of human experience. Much of what O'Shaugnessy learns, he learns from observing Faye. As the novel progresses, Faye looms larger and larger, until he dominates the author's concern.

There is something in Faye that Mailer senses as a key to unraveling the mysteries he has been grappling with, a potential solution to the problems of violence, of the individual in an age of increasing totalitarianism, and of an alternative to the untenable ethics of liberalism. But Faye seldom comes across as a human character. For the most part he remains either a grotesque caricature or a vehicle created to embody Mailer's nascent insights.

The Deer Park consolidates much of what the two previous novels have suggested. In the characters of Munshin and Teppis, it reexamines the corruption and hypocrisy that characterize the centralization of power which is increasingly the major phenomenon in modern American society. It examines in depth, in the character of Charley Eitel, the failure of the liberal spirit, a failure rooted in cowardice and the inability to cope with the immense powers which seek to dominate the modern world. For despite his many admirable qualities, Eitel is ultimately unable to sustain himself and his integrity in a hostile social world. And finally, *The Deer Park* suggests a new course, compounded of courage, flexibility, openness, and a commitment to growth. O'Shaugnessy, to a large extent, represents the possibilities inherent in this new course. As for Faye, everything he points to is developed more fully in the essay "The White Negro," the composition of which occupied Mailer for a full six months in the period following the completion of *The Deer Park*. If we wish to understand Faye and the developing vision of Norman Mailer, it is to this essay we must turn.

Chapter IV

"The White Negro"

Exploring the Rebellious

Imperatives of the Self

Between *The Deer Park* and Mailer's next novel, *An American Dream*, he published a collection of essays, stories, excerpts, and autobiographical commentary which engendered critical controversy. *Advertisements for Myself*, in spite of its many defects, is an important work because it contains and explores the core of Mailer's philosophy. The central expression of this philosophy is in the essay "The White Negro,"[1] which Mailer feels "is one of the best things I have done" (*AM*, Sixth Advertisement, 535). This philosophy is fleshed out by the exchange of views which follows the essay, an interview with Mailer by Richard Stern, and the "Prologue to a Novel in Progress" which closes the book.

During the revisions of *The Deer Park* Mailer expanded the role and importance of Marion Faye. Faye, a pimp, bisexual, a psychopath, and a thwarted priest, is intensely involved with his own growth; he has a constant need for new experience and new awareness. His interior voyages of self-discovery, made in the later stages of the novel, are journeys on the vessels of marijuana, sex, orgy, danger, violence, and attempted murder. His values—courage, growth, brutal honesty—and his means of achieving these values through risk, immoderation, and rebellion are the forerunners of Mailer's glorification of the American hipster[2] as the personification of a new consciousness, that of an indigenous American existentialism.

Rather than discuss Faye, who as a character is no more than a profile of Mailer's philosophic search, it will be more profitable to examine the philosophical and theological world-view of which Faye is a concrete manifestation. This view is defined most completely and clearly in "The White Negro."

Standing as it does midway in Mailer's career, this essay is a keystone to understanding his novels. It summarizes, explains, and expands the vision and world-view that the author created and developed in the first three novels. All three are savage in their condemnation of modern society and the violence it inflicts upon the individual. In each, Mailer opposes collectivity and mourns the general loss of heroism. He values courage and the willingness to face death. All involve a search for heroism in this modern age. And the first three deal with the complexity of modern existence, which cannot be defined on either the individual or the social level alone, but only by simultaneous exploration of the two. Although the human condition is continually determined by society and its institutions, society is changed by the actions of men, who live in a world of personal as well as social relations. And "The White Negro" also provides a basis for the next three works. It, taken in conjunction with the other self-explorations of *Advertisements for Myself*, provided Mailer with a fairly coherent vision which he could then enlarge—or reject—in his further attempts to create a fictional universe.

Ostensibly, "The White Negro: Superficial Reflections on the Hipster," is a meditation on the implications of the hip phenomenon. The subtitle is accurate, for the essay's analysis of the hipster is often mistaken or overdramatic. The essay is, nevertheless, more than a descriptive study of the philosophical underpinnings of a small modern subculture; it is an expression of the philosophy, theology, and vision of Norman Mailer—his credo. Although Mailer was never a hipster, he uses the first person plural ("It is we—hipsters") when discussing them in an interview (*AM*, Hip, Hell and Navigator, 383). Furthermore, Mailer's obsessive concern with the themes expressed in this essay has continued long after the hipster, as a specific type, has disappeared.

Mailer maintains that modern men, because of the fear engendered by the last war, live inauthentic lives. To open the possibility for authentic experience, which promises redemption, men must engage the realities of death. They must either grow continually or begin the long, slow slide through inauthenticity to spiritual death.

Unfortunately, in the modern era it is difficult to grow. The accelerated pace of technology and discovery supersedes almost all institutions as soon as they come into existence. To cope with this rapid rate of social change, men must cast themselves off from the outmoded structures of society and find within themselves new modes of action. This return to the self takes the form of confrontation with death, reversion to the senses, renewal in the primitive, and return to the child.

One modern example of this return to the self is the hipster. He lives on intimate terms with violence and death. He lives in a continual present, depending almost exclusively on his senses. He resolves the primitive urgings of his psyche by returning to his childhood fantasies and living them out. His major concern is with the good orgasm, which promises him growth, renewal, and authentic experience.

This glorification of the hipster implies that man is more good than evil, that barbarism is preferable to totalitarianism, and that anarchy is preferable to present American society. Mailer concludes by suggesting that the hipster, who seeks personal salvation, might yet be of social importance. Should the hipster be politicized, he might seek to change the society which so often interferes with his efforts to satisfy his emotional needs. In the absence of a serious radical political force in America, Mailer pins many of his hopes on the hipster and his lifestyle.

Mailer begins "The White Negro" with an elaboration of Lovett's catechism: "What were the phenomena of the world today? War, and the preparations for new war" (*BS*, 116). He states that the modern world is a world of war. The Second World War, almost global in extent, was of such immensity, left so many millions dead, that it and its novel horrors—the genocidal liquidation in the concentration camps and the overwhelming destructive capacity of the atomic bomb—had a profound effect on possibilities for future human existence.[3] Life in the postwar world has undergone a qualitative change.

The possibility of collective death, in particular, has had an enormous effect on modern life, according to Mailer's sense of things. Mailer is in one sense a Platonist, Hegelian, and Marxist: he believes things are defined by their contraries. The manner of one's possible death defines the meaning of his life. The authentic life, to use Heidegger's concepts, is revealed by an awareness of death, the ultimate limit to life.

Yet death, Mailer claims, is no longer meaningful. In order for it to be meaningful, it would have to follow "as a possible consequence to actions we had chosen" (338). But, Mailer points out, choice played no part in the deaths of those who perished collectively in Buchenwald or Hiroshima. His argument is of doubtful validity. Men have always lived in fear of inconsequent death; the existential awareness of death is precisely that it is a part of the human condition, not earned or chosen but the ultimate (and necessary) possibility. It can only be accepted, not avoided. Inconsequent death has always been a fearsome reality to men: death by natural disaster, at the hands of state or tribe, or an invader. Even the atomic bomb, which seems to threaten the whole of human existence, has had its baleful predecessors, such as the Black Plague.[4] But Mailer's argument can be supported on a different foundation. Whether or not the present age is different in kind from earlier ages, many people *think* it is different. This consciousness, justified or not, is a phenomenological reality.[5]

Natural and social disasters have remained common throughout human history, but the consciousness of men has changed, and so have their responses to disaster. In order to understand Mailer's position and its possible validity, one must understand the essentially romantic nature of his vision. Human consciousness has moved in the direction of an increasing stress on the individual: from a reliance on the divine as the arbiter of order, value, and identity to a reliance on society and, during the romantic period, the individual.[6]

Consider an earlier romantic, William Wordsworth. His faith in the goodness of natural man was traumatically injured when the French Revolution, which had promised so much to him and his contemporaries, turned into a bloodbath.[7] Its excesses destroyed his belief in man, and he found himself in a romantic dilemma: he realized that all value derives from the perceptions of the individual, who may perceive wrongly; that order is created by the individual, who may create an unjust order; that the individual, who must create his identity, may find this task impossible and be forced to live with his own internal chaos. Mailer believes that most Americans today face the same crisis, and that their trauma derives from the events of the Second World War. These are the dilemmas he addresses in "The White Negro."

Death is a major preoccupation of the romantic consciousness. If order, value, and identity are to be created by the individual man, then his death has enormous significance. The more important the individual becomes, the more important is his own death. For the romantic, personal death threatens every aspect of his existence.

Approaching the events of the Second World War with a romantic vision, Mailer finds his entire existence threatened by the implications of events of that war. If death is collective, it defines life as collective. If a man's death can pass entirely unnoticed in atomic conflagration or concentration camp anonymity, perhaps his life is equally insignificant. Yet Mailer cannot accept this; unlike Camus, he rejects the absurd. He wishes to do more than create a meaning for absurdity. He would make life meaningful. In order to do so, he must make death meaningful. Faced with the peculiar absurdity of death which Mailer feels is a result of the events of the last war, Mailer sees no redemption for men within society. The modern slough of despair promises to continue into the future, for Mailer sees nothing that can change the institutions, the collectivization, and the events of "war and the preparations for new war" which hold all men in thrall. Radicalism has a minor effect on the modern state and on society; there seems little hope for it to change the future. This triumph of the modern war-oriented state is what Cummings had predicted, what *Barbary Shore* made clear, and what the Hollywood investigating committee illustrated. Because so many men are afraid of the consequences of radical action, "we suffer from a collective failure of nerve" (338) and exist in a state of apathy and inaction. Norman Mailer, self-defined existentialist, social psychologist, theologian, spiritual healer, and visionary, suggests a cure for apathy and fear.

His plan is for personal salvation. All plans for social redemption are held in abeyance, except to the extent that individual salvation can be the first step toward social redemption. In *The Deer Park*, "The White Negro," *An American Dream*, and *Why Are We in Vietnam?* he makes an uneasy peace between his need for personal salvation and the quest for social redemption; in effect, he ignores the latter to concentrate on the former.

If one extends the comparison between Mailer and Wordsworth, the romantic aspects of Mailer's vision are clear. Like Wordsworth, Mailer is frequently involved in writing about himself and in finding in his unique perceptions a pattern for all human experience.[8] Like Wordsworth, he feels the need to cope with the social[9] as well as the individual side of man. The attempt to engage in social and political issues led to traumatic realizations on the part of both novelist and poet. Most important, as a result of their traumatic historical experiences, both ignore the need for social redemption in pursuit of the salvation of the individual. Their paths are basically similar: Wordsworth's toward salvation in the child and the natural world, Mailer's toward the primitive and the realm of sensory experience. And both find that salvation ultimately impossible because of the irresolvable tensions between subject and object: the self cannot be completely subsumed under the external world, nor can the external world be completely subsumed under the self. Salvation cannot be permanent, yet there are moments of grace when subject and object can be in harmony. Thus both men believe in the possibilities for salvation in time through an ethic of growth.

Mailer has no doubt that modern men need salvation. He believes:

> The Second World War presented a mirror to the human
> condition . . . no matter how crippled and perverted an
> image of man was the society he created, it was nonethe-
> less his creation . . . and if society was so murderous,
> who could ignore the most hideous questions about his
> own nature?   (338)

In an interview Mailer declared that something was drastically wrong with modern men if they "can liquidate millions of people in concentration camps by orderly process" (*AM*, Hip, 383). He diagnosed the ill in a romantic manner: many men are alienated from their environment, they are "divorced from the senses" (*AM*, Hip, 382). Wordsworth diagnosed the ills of society in a similar manner:

> The world is too much with us; late and soon,
> Getting and spending, we lay waste our powers:
> Little we see in Nature that is ours;
> We have given our hearts away, a sordid boon!
> The Sea that bares her bosom to the moon;
> The winds that will be howling at all hours,
> And are up-gathered now like sleeping flowers;
> For this, for everything, we are out of tune;
> It moves us not. —Great God! I'd rather be
> A Pagan suckled in a creed outworn;
> So might I, standing on this pleasant lea,
> Have glimpses that would make me less forlorn;
> Have sight of Proteus rising from the sea;
> Or hear old Triton blow his wreathèd horn.

Cutting oneself off from nature and the natural world was to Wordsworth what cutting oneself off from direct sensory experience is to Mailer. Wordsworth finds salvation through the primitive and pagan in this poem; Mailer finds it through the primitive instincts in man, especially the need for sex and the need to cope with death.

Thus Mailer insists that "one must be able to feel oneself . . . one must be aware of the character of one's frustration and know what would satisfy it" (341). One of the most horrifying possibilities for the romantic spirit is that he will no longer be able to feel, for it is on feeling, on the immediacy of his experience, that his sense of identity is based.[10] In order to cope with the exigencies of modern existence, men must be able to feel them. If they cannot feel, Mailer believes, they will destroy themselves "in the cold insensate expressions of due process of law and atomic radiation" (*AM*, Hip, 383).

For Wordsworth, the return to the senses involved immersing the self in nature; for Mailer, it means living with the immmediate possibilities of death. The recognition of death as the ultimate human possibility is necessary to an understanding of the human condition. In Heidegger's terms,

> Death is Dasein's *ownmost* possibility. Being towards this possibility discloses to Dasein its *ownmost* potentiality-for-Being, in which its very Being is the issue. Here it can become manifest to Dasein that in this distinctive possibility of its own self, it has been wrenched away from the "they." This means that in anticipation any Dasein can have wrenched itself away from the "they" already.[11]

Recognition of death heightens the individual's sense of his own identity and the particularity of the situation he discovers himself in.

But Mailer's contention is that the possibility of collective death, death of a whole society, or a subculture or geographical segment of that society, has prevented many modern men from wrenching themselves away from the "they." In other words, when a man finds there is a strong possibility that he will die from, let us say, a nuclear holocaust, he may find it difficult to find in his own particular death anything that distinguishes his particular existence from his neighbors'. For this individual, Mailer suggests, the way to return to the senses is to face the prospect of death in such a way that it can reveal his "*ownmost* possibility," and therefore wrench him away from the "they." His own individual death can define his individual life, even when the possibility of collective death may perhaps deny the individuality of his life to him. If men face their deaths alone, their existences will become particularized and authentic: "The only life-giving answer is to accept the terms of death, to live with death as an immediate danger, to divorce oneself from society, to exist without roots, to set out on that uncharted journey into the rebellious imperatives of the self" (339).

Mailer's central social concern is that contemporary society is slowly closing off the possibilities for authentic existence, for existence that is conscious of its own possibilities because it is conscious of death as the uttermost possibility. Mailer finds in the involvement in "getting and spending," in the centralization of power in government and industry, in the uniformity of taste fostered by advertising and the media, a diminishing emphasis on individual choice. "If I had one novel emotion it was rage against that national conformity which smothered creativity" (*AM*, Fifth Advertisement, 283). He sees most modern men as immersing themselves in the world of conformity because that allows them to escape from their dread of death and individuality. The individual, we recall, must face this dilemma central to the modern age: if death seemingly has no meaning, then neither, perhaps, has life. So Mailer believes modern men flee from the possibility of meaninglessness by allowing others to determine their choices for them; they surrender their individuality rather than have it continually threatened. His point is that men today are afraid to be romantic: "the sickness of our times for me has been just this damn thing that everything has been getting smaller and smaller and less and less important, that the romantic spirit has dried up, and that there is almost no shame today like the terror before the romantic" (*AM*, Hip, 382). The reason for this, he concludes, is that "we all live under the threat of extermination" (*AM*, Hip, 382).

He advocates that some men "Divorce themselves from society." Such men, like O'Shaugnessy and Lovett, will be rootless. Both of these characters have little in their past to help structure their experiences in the present; they are examples of the existential man, who lives in a continual present and can anticipate an open future. O'Shaugnessy and Lovett are in one sense caricatures, distorted to emphasize the importance of the present, existential moment.

Yet while Heidegger refuses to make a normative judgment about the merits of authentic and inauthentic existence, Mailer is a salvationist. One of his primary concerns is to direct his readers toward a course of action which offers the promise of redemption, even if that redemption can be only temporary. Unlike Heidegger, he asserts that authentic existence, in which an individual is aware of death as the parameter of life, is greatly to be preferred to inauthentic existence.[12]

Since he sees the modern sickness as a flight from the romantic consciousness, the obvious path to salvation is to embrace the romantic spirit, to strive to be authentic. To the hipster, the "inner experience of the possibilities within death is his logic. So, too, for the existentialist. And the psychopath. And the saint and the bullfighter and the lover. The common denominator for all of them is their burning consciousness of the present, exactly that incandescent consciousness which the possibilities within death has opened for them" (342).

This "incandescent consciousness" illumines moral choices. Mailer does not explain how this is done; overlooking the mechanism, he simply asserts that an awareness of the present and the self can enable a man to realize what will satisfy his urges. There is in this an assumption of "Hemingway's categorical imperative that what made him feel good became therefore 'The Good' " (340). Mailer seems to be begging an important question: is what is best for a single individual necessarily what is best for society or the other individuals with whom he exists in some sort of social relationship? Even further, he avoids the problem of whether an individual can trust his feelings, whether what he feels is best for himself is indeed "The Good." Whether this awareness of the senses is a moral panacea or not, it is most definitely an attempt to restore the heroic element to modern life, which Mailer feels is getting smaller and smaller. But he tells us that we may reverse this situation by recognizing that "The condition which enables one to remain in life only by engaging death" (342) is a heroic condition: a man may discover an escape from the petty and inauthentic by coming to grips with his own mortality.

A central concept in Mailer's world-view is that life is a continual struggle; the metaphor he uses is martial. He says that the Negro survives by "knowing in his cells that life was war, nothing but war" (341). To attribute this knowledge to "the Negro" seems specious, but what Mailer means is that he thinks existence is war. This explains much in both his novels and his personal life. It explains why he wanted to write a war novel so desperately. It explains the military idioms and metaphors that dot his essays and even most of his novels. It explains why he poses as the continual adversary, and why he regards himself so frequently as a pugilist. And, most important, it is basic to an understanding of why all his novels deal with violence, and why life and violence seem to be inseparable in both his novels and his views of the human condition. If life is war, men must fight or go down in defeat. Under martial conditions, it is small wonder that the price for failing to grow is death.

Mailer's God goes beyond the human realm but shares the same conditions of existence as men: war, division, victory and defeat, the possibility of death and extinction. He believes "God is in danger of dying" (*AM*, Hip, 380). He sees "man's fate tied up with God's fate" because "God is no longer all powerful" (*AM*, Hip, 380). God is in a mortal struggle with the Devil, good with evil; and the outcome is not at all certain. "He exists as a warring element in a divided universe and we are a part of . . . His great expression, His enormous destiny" (*AM*, Hip, 380).

"A warring element in a divided universe": this is Mailer's view of man as well as God. Division is, for Mailer, the nature of reality. One sees it in all the novels. In *The Naked and the Dead*, reality was set against the ideal, liberalism against fascism, society against the individual. In *Barbary Shore* there was continual tension between peace and violence, between radical and reactionary; history was conceived of as a dialectic. Throughout *The Deer Park* there is an admixture of love and hate; Sergius realizes that the relationship between Charley and Elena is, like all of existence, a "dance of opposites."

Mailer shows himself directly in the tradition of two of his most important mentors, Marx and Freud.[13] The Hegelian dialectic was based on the concept that the unity of reality is always the product of divided and opposed elements. Marx applied this to history, which he saw as class struggle; the dialectical process of history will ultimately lead to the triumph of the proletariat. Freud's emphasis on the ambivalence of the human condition (love and hate, life and death, id and superego) is likewise similar to Mailer's view of the essential duality of existence. Indeed, Freud's final formulation of this ambivalence, the competing drives of Eros and Thanatos, life instinct and death instinct, comes close to Mailer's belief that life is continually forced to choose either new life or death. Freud attributed part of this continual ambivalence to the conflict between the needs of the individual and the needs of society, but part of it he attributed, as in the case of Eros and Thanatos, to the essential nature of man.

Both Freud and Marx analyze this duality in terms of conflict. For Marx, the conflict is between the basic needs of the individual—freedom, lack of imposed suffering, and the possibility for self-development and self-fulfillment—and the institutions of society which stifle these needs in order to bring material well-being to a select class of tyrants.[14] Freud also saw a deep-seated conflict between the emotional needs of individuals and the repressive restrictions imposed on them by society.[15] The difference is that Marx is concerned with the conflict from a social point of view, and sees the struggle as the opposition of historic and economic forces, while Freud approaches the conflict from the individual point of view, and sees the struggle as the opposition of sexual and libidinal needs and social restraints. In Mailer's early novels, a semi-Marxist, institutional, and historical approach to man's conflict prevailed. During these first three novels, however, a note of sexuality and a concern with psychic reality became ever more strident. The fourth and fifth novels, *An American Dream* and *Why Are We in Vietnam?*, are imbued with sexuality and sensuality, and explore the realms of man's psychic life, his subconscious and unconscious desires and frustrations.

To return to Mailer's theology: God, like men, is at war, and He too faces the possibility of defeat. In His battle with the Devil, He needs all the help He can get. Indeed, Mailer believes men may be the crux of this struggle, the veritable balance of power. If the human struggle is lost, God will lose. This reversal of the Judeo-Christian tradition, in which men are dependent upon God, is another evidence of Mailer's romantic leanings. It reflects the important romantic belief, already noted, that the source of value, order, and identity is found within the individual human being.

This man-centered revival of Manicheism satisfies two of Mailer's deep needs. First, it explains the existence of evil in the world. He believes, as we shall shortly observe, that men are basically more good than evil, more creative than destructive. But if this is so, how can one explain such social cataclysms as the concentration camp and the bomb? To say that they result from the institutions of totalitarian society is valid, but who created these institutions? If society is so destructive, then what of men, who created society in their own image? For society to become murderous there must be murder in the hearts of men. Belief in a divided universe and a dual deity explains the undeniable triumphs of evil in the world yet also allows Mailer to claim that men are good, that through their courage and will they can grow into something more, not less. Were God omnipotent, Mailer seems to be asking, why would there be evil? Rejecting previous theological answers to this question, central to the Judeo-Christian vision, he seems to claim that there would be no evil if God were omnipotent.

Secondly, this theology satisfies Mailer's need for heroism in the modern age. Destruction and annihilation and depersonalization have reduced the scale of life in our times. But if God is involved in a struggle for His very existence, and "we are a part" of it, then "maybe we are engaged in a heroic activity, and not a mean one" (*AM*, Hip, 381). Men's lives, since they will determine the future of the cosmos, are magnified so that their actions are of universal import. In every one of Mailer's novels the author is searching for a modern hero; indeed, in both his artistic and public life, Mailer has been motivated by this need to discover or create a heroic figure to stand against the smallness and grayness of modern times. Both his glorification of the hipster and his theology about a God in conflict are part of Mailer's quest for grandeur and heroism. In heroism there is redemption.

The ruling principle in Mailer's cosmology is growth; even God must grow or submit to defeat. Mailer repeats Charley's formulation from *The Deer Park* about growing or paying more for remaining the same. This has become the central human directive in Mailer's theology, since it reflects the essential recognition that everything changes, that the universe is continual growth. If "life is a contest . . . in which one must grow or else pay more for remaining the same (pay in sickness, or depression or anguish for the lost opportunity) but pay or grow," then "movement is always to be preferred to inaction" (349–350). Every moment presents new possibilities which men must face. To accept them is to grow, to open up new realms of experience; to reject them is to fail, to thwart that principle which governs existence. Failure, then, is what Mailer means when he speaks of "paying more for remaining the same." By refusing new possibilities, men refuse life and so accept death; in addition, each new defeat conditions them to accepting future defeats. Therefore, human beings live an "existence which is forever moving forward into more or retreating into less" (352).

We discover in Mailer's emphasis on growth another instance

of his romantic vision. To find an earlier figure who expressed similar ideas, we must go to the generation that followed Wordsworth. Emerson had a basically Heraclitean vision in which everything is in flux:

> Nature ever flows; never stands still. Motion or change
> is her mode of existence. The poetic eye sees in Man
> the Brother of the River, and in Woman the Sister of the
> River. Their life is always in transition. Hard blockheads
> only drive nails all the time; forever remember; which is
> fixing. Heroes do not fix, but flow, bend forward and in-
> vent a resource for every moment.[16]

From the Wordsworthian view that the mature man must return to the child within him and be reborn, it is but a step to Emerson's view that existence is continual death, and demands continual rebirth. It is unfortunate that Mailer's partisans and his detractors both fail to see in his views, and even his rhetoric, that he is firmly rooted in the Emersonian tradition. In "Circles" Emerson wrote: "In nature every moment is new; the past is always swallowed and forgotten; the coming only is sacred. Nothing is secure but life, transition, the energizing spirit. . . . No truth so sublime but it may be trivial tomorrow in the light of new thoughts. People wish to be settled; only as far as they are unsettled is there any hope for them."[17] In his acceptance of change as a universal principle, and in his ethical injunction to men to continually change and explore ever deeper into themselves and the universe, Mailer is in complete agreement with Emerson.

The difference between the two men is also instructive. Emerson advocates, with Mailer, immersion in the present, pursuit of ecstasy, surrender to enthusiasm. But he rejects the precise realms of experience that Mailer embraces in "The White Negro," the realms of irrational fantasy, passion, and violence:

> The one thing which we seek with insatiable desire is to
> forget ourselves, to be surprised out of our propriety, to
> lose our sempiternal memory and to do something with-
> out knowing how or why. . . . Nothing great was ever
> achieved without enthusiasm. Dreams and drunkenness,
> the use of opium and alcohol are the semblance and
> counterfeit of this oracular genius, and hence their dan-
> gerous attraction for men. For the like reason, they ask

the aid of wild passions, as in gaming and war, to ape in some manner these flames and generosities of the heart.[18]

Emerson's critique is relevant to Mailer's glorification of hip. Is Mailer trying to "ape in some manner" what is best in human experience? Or is he, on the other hand, trying to plumb the depths of an irrational world which Emerson could never accept?

Hawthorne comes to mind as a rebuttal to Emerson's position. As he made clear in his fiction, fantasy, evil, and passion are often closely linked to "oracular genius." Mailer's *An American Dream* (see below) has roots in Hawthorne as well as in Emerson. A central dilemma of romanticism is now encountered. If value and order derive from each individual, and if individuality is the only route to salvation, what is to be made of the grotesque? Is the grotesque man, as Emerson proclaimed, merely a parody of the healthy individual? Or is he (as Dostoevsky later asserted in *Notes from Underground*) *homo humanus*? Mailer's espousal of the way of the psychopath is an acceptance of Dostoevsky and a rejection of Emerson.

In his growth-oriented universe Mailer finds salvation in the psychopath's way of living. The psychopath lives in direct contact with the pressures of the moment. He feels the overwhelming need for action and movement. He can be identified, according to Mailer's friend Robert Lindner,[19] by his need for immediate satisfaction. Nothing—not society, morals, or social conventions—can prevent him from trying to gratify the needs he feels. The criminal psychopath must satisfy needs that run counter to the needs of society. His desire to hurt or destroy is stronger than the restrictive prohibitions society attempts to induce to prevent such crimes. If he feels great hate, he will try to satisfy it by destroying its object. His overwhelming need may lead to murder.

In Mailer's view the psychopath is characterized by a compulsion to "create a new nervous system" for himself (345). In seeking a direct and valid response to the exigencies of the moment, he must often discard the conventions of society. And since society is inextricably bound up with its own conventions and traditions, it declares the psychopath an enemy. His actions negate the foundations of society, and his existence threatens the ordered relationships that make it up.

In his attitude toward the psychopath, Mailer seems to subscribe to the Freudian view that society exists at the expense of the individual's freedom to satisfy his needs. The pleasure principle must give way to the reality principle. In order for man to survive with other men, each individual must delay gratification of some of his impulses in order to channel all his energy (libido) into whatever modes of activity will be most productive to the group as a whole. This sublimation, according to Freud, is the foundation of civilization.[20] The psychopath finds sublimation impossible and becomes an enemy of society.

This is a crux of Mailer's argument: "Throughout most of modern history 'sublimation' was possible: at the expense of expressing only a small portion of oneself, that small portion could be expressed intensely. But sublimation depends upon a reasonable tempo to history" (345). History seems to be speeding up, perhaps going out of control. The last fifty years have seen an enormous growth of scientific and technical knowledge. An innovation is barely made before it is supplanted by an improvement or another innovation. Developments in communications and transportation have enabled many primitive countries to compress two hundred to two thousand years of Western civilization into several decades of sudden change. The growth of scientific and technical knowledge is geometric.

Sublimation depends upon a system of values. Without some hierarchy of importance, it is impossible to determine which aspects of life should be intensified and which psychic needs should be sacrificed. In a world of continual change, values must change. Mailer believes that "the stable middle-class values so prerequisite to sublimation have been virtually destroyed in our time, at least as nourishing values free of confusion or doubt" (345). Although he does not explain this statement further, one might support it by pointing to the increasing tendency toward alienation and anxiety in most modern men. As values disintegrate, sublimation becomes increasingly difficult. As sublimation becomes more difficult, Mailer suggests, the psychopathic element in human behavior will become more and more frequent.[21]

Thus the psychopath emerges as a "perverted and dangerous frontrunner of a new kind of personality" (345) which may be increasingly important to the future development of mankind. This, in turn, leads us to the hipster, the asocial type which seems to Mailer to reflect the entrance of the psychopathic personality into modern society.

The hipster is a "philosophical psychopath." The criminal psychopath, as delineated by Lindner in *Rebel without a Cause*, is a human being who cannot live with the strictures of society, usually because some traumatic experience he had during childhood has never been resolved. Therefore, he seeks continual resolution in his adult life. The aim of the criminal psychopath is to satisfy his desires, to resolve the tensions that arise from the psychic shock of his childhood. According to Mailer, the hipster also wishes immediate gratification but is distinguished from Lindner's criminal psychopath by his need for conscious exploration of "the rebellious imperatives of the self." There is thus not only a surrender to immediate desires, but also an exploration of these desires and an attempt to codify whatever knowledge is gained by new experiences into the inner structure of his life. The hipster is aware of the nuances of his needs and actions, hoping through such awareness to learn more of himself, to find the elusive key to understanding which will help him open the doors to future self-satisfaction and self-fulfillment. The hipster acts like a psychopath, but he has distanced himself from himself so that he may watch his actions. He is a conscious—self-conscious—psychopath. Like the protagonist of Lindner's study, he is a rebel—but a rebel with a cause. Hip has a sense of moral purpose, and its "ethic reduces to Know Thyself and Be Thyself" (354). It differs from past counsels of self-knowledge, like the Socratic, because it holds the path to self-knowledge to be not moderation but immoderation. The hipster might take Blake's "Proverb of Hell" as his motto: "The road of excess leads to the palace of Wisdom." His greatest fear is that he will miss the opportunity to grow and, by remaining static in a dynamic universe, die out of life rather than move deeper into it.

The hipster is created by the heightened contradictions of the present age, which cannot be resolved by sublimation. Things change so quickly that sensitive men are always out of phase with reality.

> Generally we are obliged to act with a nervous system which has been formed from infancy, and which carries in the style of its circuits the very contradictions of our parents and our early milieu. Therefore, we are obliged, most of us, to meet the tempo of the present and the future with reflexes and rhythms which come from the past. (345)

While men try to revise their values and their mode of experiencing, the world is also changing. Modern men face a dilemma: their capacity for change is outstripped by the changes in the world, so they are ever more divorced from the reality of their experience. Their only hope is to end their effort to revise their patterns of behavior and to discard their preconceived responses in order to begin anew. Salvation for modern men is to be found only in a reversion to the primitive, so that their basic psychological needs can be fulfilled.

The basic needs Mailer deals with in the essay are closely linked to Freud's formulation of the two main instinctual drives in human beings, Thanatos and Eros. The former is related to the emphasis Mailer places upon consciousness of death. Changed into Freudian terms, this argument might be that the individual can never repress Thanatos, so that in order to cope with this powerful drive he must recognize and accept it. As far as Eros is concerned, Mailer is specific. His view, at this stage of his development, is Reichian. The most powerful and most important erotic drive is the desire for orgasm. Wilhelm Reich felt that orgasm is the release of accumulated sexual tension; in "the involuntary contractions of the organism and the complete discharge of the excitation" he found "the biological primal and basic function which man has in common with all living organisms."[22] He also maintained that the etiology of neuroses is in the malfunctioning of the orgastic experience.[23] Mailer, like the hipster, accepts the idea that orgasm is the most important human activity, and that the cure for mental (and perhaps physical) ills lies in improving its quality.[24]

> At bottom, the drama of the psychopath is that he seeks love. Not love as the search for a mate, but love as the search for an orgasm more apocalyptic than the one which preceded it. Orgasm is his therapy—he knows at the seed of his being that good orgasm opens his possibilities and bad orgasm imprisons him.   (347)

The Freudian psychoanalyst, like almost anyone else, would call the psychopath misguided; the Reichian analyst would call his drama heroic.

Mailer finds a saving quality in another related area of psychopathic behavior, the retreat to childhood. He feels that when the psychopath acts out his infantile fantasies, he is trying to go back to the early days of his life, which have determined his character and course ever since, and remake the decisions that have led inexorably to the present. If, Mailer argues, the psychopath can relive the experiences that have created and often warped his psyche, perhaps he can relive these experiences in more satisfying ways. Thus the psychoanalyst, with a methodology based on developing his patient's understanding to a point where the patient can accept or reject his infantile contradictions, cannot succeed with a psychopath. The quality that best defines the psychopath is that he tries desperately to "live the infantile fantasy" (346) rather than repress it, and to resolve the infantile contractions by living through them again, dealing with them in a more satisfying manner, and eventually outgrowing them. He resolves the destructive contradictions of his personality through action, not confession.

In a manner not altogether unlike that of the psychopath, salvation for the romantic spirit is often achieved by reverting to childhood. Wordsworth may again serve as our example. In the "Intimations Ode" he finds himself in a situation very like that which Mailer predicates for most modern men: he feels cut off from feeling, burdened with his social role, unable to cope with age and death:

> Whither is fled the visionary gleam?
> Where is it now, the glory and the dream?
>
> Full soon the Soul shall have her earthly freight,
> And custom lie upon thee with a weight,
> Heavy as frost, and deep almost as life!

In this poem, in "Tintern Abbey," and in *The Prelude* Wordsworth describes the sufferings of his soul and illumines the only road to salvation from spiritual malaise: reversion to the child. He recognizes, more than Mailer, that the adult cannot become a child; but as he says in the "Ode," in the experiences of childhood he can find moments of grace and wisdom which will succor his adult life. Like Mailer, Wordsworth finds that a return to the childhood of civilization—the primitive—can also be a source of renewal. "The World is too much with us," quoted earlier as a manifestation of the romantic malaise of the alienated sensibility, has as its resolution a fervent desire to return to a more pagan age. One of the major tenets of romanticism is that it prefers to seek salvation by returning to a simpler age; it seeks to resolve alienation, confusion, and despair by immersion in the strong states of feeling that are associated with childhood or primitivism.

But Mailer's reversion to childhood and primitivism has one very important component which differentiates it from Wordsworth's: his commitment to violence as an integral element of primitivism. Since society exists on a substratum of sublimation and repression,[25] forcing the libido into socially meaningful patterns, it requires the suppression of the individual's psychic desires. The need for personal satisfaction often encounters societal resistance; like Freud, Mailer finds an irresolvable conflict between the needs of the self and the needs of society. The underlying social contract, which seeks to mediate between the individual and society, between the pleasure principle and the reality principle, is continually threatened by this conflict.

In this situation the psychopath, who is at odds with society and himself, becomes an admired model for Mailer. The psychopath acts to overcome the fear that leads to repression, "even if the fear is of himself, and the action is to murder." He murders "out of the necessity to purge his violence, for if he cannot empty his hatred then he cannot love . . . for self-hatred for his cowardice" (347). The hipster follows the psychopath, becoming a social outlaw in order to discover the secrets of his own identity. Like the psychopath, he will break any social sanction to fulfill himself (fulfillment for him is the discovery and satisfaction of his deepest psychological needs), even if he must murder. He feels that if he cannot rid himself of the frustrations and contradictions that cripple his ability to understand and satisfy himself, he will die. So his effort is one of purgation, and his hope is that through purgation he will be able to go back to his roots, and from these deepest levels remake himself into a human being who is more nearly whole—who adapts better, who has the possibility of fulfillment, who has the necessary requisite for survival, namely the ability to grow.

Mailer says that the underlying need of the hipster and the psychopath is for love. Since both seek immediate and sensory satisfaction of their needs, the quest becomes a search for the perfect orgasm. What Mailer does in this essay is to claim that the search for sexual freedom and fullfillment is, in some way, the central drama of our times, that the Negro is the guide for this search and, in the minds of hipsters, represents the divinity they are seeking. Mailer claims that the oppression of the Negro since the end of the Civil War (and to a large extent before that war) has its origins in the fear of many white men that black men are more potent than they. Since most white men still carry this fear, and since most black men have had to live on the margins of white society and have developed a hatred for white men, the superiority of black potency is now a fact: fear has whittled away the sexual prowess of whites, and hatred has honed that of blacks. This same view is forwarded and expanded by Eldridge Cleaver, in whose essays Mailer is applauded.[26] James Baldwin, on the other hand, attacks the argument.[27] The issue, it seems to me, is not so much whether Mailer is correctly assessing the Negro or the hipster, but what kind of solution to human problems he is proposing and whether this solution has credibility.

Basically, he is saying that sexual intercourse is the arena in which many of the primary modern conflicts are played out: the struggle for authenticity, the need to respond to crises with courage, the search for identity, the quest for love. Civilization, as both Marx and Freud point out, is based on contradictions. For Marx, these were economic; for Freud, instinctual. According to both, and to Mailer, man in society is anxious, alienated, and lacking fulfillment and happiness. Sex becomes an escape from this modern tyranny.[28] In the process of sublimating most of his urges, man is left free (relatively) to satisfy himself through genital experiences. But the libidinal energy diverted into genital sex cannot always be controlled, and so social revolution is often first noticed in sexual rebellion, a sign that the individual feels a need to find new patterns of behavior outside those prescribed by society. Freud pointed out that sublimation is ultimately an unstable foundation for social security:

> The sexual are amongst the most important of the instinctive forces thus utilized; they are in this way sublimated, that is to say, their energy is turned aside from its sexual goal and directed toward other ends, no longer sexual and socially more valuable. But the structure thus built up is insecure, for the sexual impulses are with difficulty controlled; in each individual who takes up his part in the work of civilization there is a danger that a rebellion of the sexual impulses may occur, against this diversion of their energy. Society can conceive of no more powerful menace to its culture than would arise from the liberation of the sexual impulses and a return of them to their original goal.[29]

Thus the hipster and his model the Negro explore "all those moral wildernesses of civilized life" (348) in search for the apocalyptic orgasm, that "sweet" of life which is in such short supply. For them "the emphasis is on energy because [they] are nothing without it" (349). Their sensitivity and courage prohibit the stale outmoded tyrannies of custom from destroying their individuality:

> What he must do . . . is find his courage at the moment in violence, or equally—make it in the act of love . . . but paramount, imperative, is the necessity to make it, because in making it, one is making the new habit, the new talent which the old frustration denied.   (350)

This emphasis on "making it" is what enables Mailer to call the hipster the American existentialist. For the hipster, life is process, a continual search for the new habit; and the new habit always becomes the old habit that must be broken. For the hipster wants nothing so much as to experience the phenomena of existence; and to do so he must continually discard the essence he has derived from experience in order to plunge back into the vibrant but chaotic sea of existence. Hip's standards are not formulated a priori but come directly out of experience and are constantly changed by experience. Every answer becomes a new question.

Thus the hipster denies "conventional moral responsibility" (353) because of the relativity and complexity of moral judgment. If everything constantly changes, then relativity quickly becomes so complex that any normative standards are obsolete and unwise. "Character being thus seen as perpetually ambivalent and dynamic enters then into an absolute relativity where there are no truths other than the isolated truths of what each observer feels at each instant of his experience" (354). Truth, then, "is no more or less than what one feels at each instant in the perpetual climax of the present" (354). "What is consequent therefore is the divorce of man from his values, the liberation of the self from the Super-Ego of society" (354). The emphasis on the self as the source of all value is the most significant aspect of romanticism. One thinks of Emerson and his self-reliance: "Trust thyself: every heart vibrates to that iron string."[30] He too finds that this self is always in process, always in a continuous present: "The one thing in the world, of value, is the active soul."[31]

Mailer's abiding faith in man is nowhere shown more clearly than in this discussion of the hipster. The enormous sense of fate, which moved like a giant hand behind the adventures of *The Naked and the Dead*, is a dominant feature of all Mailer's fiction. He is speaking more for himself than the hipster when he says, "Hip sees the context as generally dominating the man, dominating him because his character is less significant than the context in which he must function" (353). When Lovett and O'Shaugnessy and Rojack and D.J. end their narratives, we can feel a partial triumph in the mere fact of their survival. Lovett, O'Shaugnessy, and Rojack all end up plunging into the night, having found some small wisdom, ready to do battle with existence. All three are somehow stronger than they were at the start of their stories, but this frail strength can operate only during those lulls when the universe is not hostile.

Mailer does project a sense that these characters have progressed, have grown, albeit a precarious and qualified growth. And in "The White Negro," which explores modern human existence by examining the implications of the atomic bomb and the concentration camps, Mailer works his way toward an affirmation of the good in man. By blaming much of what is malignant in modern society upon the forces of social order and control, he reveals a fundamentally anarchistic viewpoint. The anarchy he advocates, here, functions in a climate of hedonism: hip's morality is to do as one wants, and one wants whatever makes him feel good.

A central passage of "The White Negro" states: "The nihilism of Hip proposes as its final tendency that every social restraint and category be removed, and the affirmation implicit in the proposal is that man would then prove to be more creative than murderous and so would not destroy himself" (354). Although the spectrum of anarchist viewpoints is broad, common to all is the belief that social structures and customs have imprisoned rather than liberated man and that, given the choice, the absence of institutions is preferable to ones that are imposed. Another common position is that if societal institutions were destroyed, men would either be able to live without them or be able to develop new and meaningful structures out of desire and necessity.

Mailer shares these assumptions. His "description" of hip is actually his own philosophical—or theological—credo. He believes in primitive urges, which perhaps explains why Croft and Cummings seem more heroic than Valsen and Hearn, why Hollingsworth in his crassness is respected by McLeod, and why Faye takes over the center of *The Deer Park* from Eitel. In man's primitive nature is the well-spring of his being, and if that center is a good one, then reversion to the primitive can be the cure for all weaknesses and social ills.

As an anarchist, Mailer lays the blame for man's predicament on society. It is society that has warped the individual. Here he breaks with Freud, who believed that man's dilemmas were largely created by his life in society, but who also felt that society and many of its incumbent ills were necessary to man's continued existence. Marx, on the other hand, could lay the blame for man's alienation on society and its economic institutions, but still find salvation for man through a (future) socialist society. Mailer believes in Marx's socialistic vision, but as we have seen in *Barbary Shore*, he feels that the fall of imperialistic capitalism and the triumph of the proletariat have failed to occur. Hip, or a philosophical primitivism, seems to him the beginning of the path by which socialism—the just and equitable and humane society— may come into being.[32]

Mailer sees a belief in society as the failure of faith in man. "What haunts the middle of the twentieth century is that faith in man has been lost, and the appeal of authority has been that it would restrain us from ourselves" (355). With good reason man is afraid of himself; the concentration camp and atomic bomb are the symbols of our times. But Mailer claims that it is society, not man, that is responsible for these horrors. The crux of the problem of destruction is that terrible implements of cruelty have been developed precisely because most men have had no faith in themselves and have put their faith in institutions and controls that supposedly protect men from other men and even themselves. Thus in the twentieth century the way to peace is war, and the road to freedom is state violence and control.

> It requires a primitive passion about human nature to believe that individual acts of violence are always to be preferred to the collective violence of the State; it takes literal faith in the creative possibilities of the human being to envisage acts of violence as the catharsis which prepares growth.   (355)

Because Mailer has this "primitive passion," he prefers the hipster to the politician or bureaucrat or middle-class American. Even murder in the most calculated and brutal fashion is to be preferred to "the collective violence of the state." The murderer

must face consequences and take responsibility, but the faceless
state can refuse both. Which is precisely what has happened, both
in the case of the concentration camps (when Eichmann refused
to admit his responsibility) and the dropping of the atomic bomb
(for whose damage the Manhattan Project scientists have refused
to take responsibility). For Mailer, social violence is always directed against individual human beings, whereas an individual's
act of violence, destructive as it may be to other individuals, is
also a way of striking out at social restrictions. Behind the individual act of violence is the need for freedom, even if that freedom
is only to gratify a wish more immediately than society allows.

Mailer has faith that the individual act of violence, by breaking down stultifying societal regulations, is an act which prepares
for growth and life. In a comment made on the hipster, he reveals
his faith in the good and constructive core of man, his disgust with
corporate violence, and his belief in the redeeming possibilties of
individual acts of violence:

> The essence of his expression, his faith if you will, is that
> the real desire to make a better world exists at the heart
> of our instinct . . . that man is therefore roughly more good
> than evil, that beneath his violence there is finally love
> and the nuances of justice, and that the removal there-
> fore of all social restraints while it would open us to an
> era of incomparable individual violence would still spare
> us the collective violence of rational totalitarian liquida-
> tions (which we must accept was grossly a psychic index
> of the buried, voiceless, and eradicable violences of whole
> nations of people), and would—and here is the differ-
> ence—by expending the violence directly, open the pos-
> sibility of working with that human creativity which is
> violence's opposite.   (*AM*, Reflections on Hip, 363).

Central to an understanding of Mailer's belief in violence is his
belief that "man is roughly more good than evil." He says of his
own and the hipster's view that "men are not seen as good or bad
(that they are good-and-bad is taken for granted) but rather each
man is glimpsed as a collection of possibilities" (353). This act
of faith, this belief in human possibility, enables Mailer to advo-
cate cutting loose from all moral strictures against violence. Men
have a "navigator at the seat of their being . . . an enormous teleo-
logical sense" (386) and can trust, in the long run, the call of
their instincts.

Trust to these instincts they must, for Mailer believes that modern men face a crisis in the development of civilization. Yet, "No matter what its horrors, the twentieth century is a vastly exciting century for its tendency to reduce all life to its ultimate alternatives" (357). These alternatives—totalitarianism or anarchy, society or the individual, nonexistence or existence—cannot be avoided. We stare into "such terrifying alternatives as totalitarianism and barbarism" (*AM*, Reflections on Hip, 364). Returning to his basic article of faith, that men are more good than evil, he declares himself willing to trust the individual in a return to barbarism. The reason we face such a terrifying alternative is that:

> The amount of collective violence buried in the people is perhaps incapable of being contained, and therefore if one wants a better world one does well to hold one's breath, for a worse world is bound to come first, and the dilemma may well be this: given such hatred, it must either vent itself nihilistically or become turned into the cold murderous liquidations of the totalitarian state.   (357)

Mailer, preferring nihilism to totalitarianism because the former offers a path to potential salvation, advocates the hipster as a model for a new consciousness. Because the hipster seeks growth at any cost, even murder, he offers hope. Totalitarianism is for Mailer a dead end; it leads to stagnation and spiritual, if not physical, death. If violence must be vented (and he assumes it must) then Mailer prefers the individual act of violence to the institutional one. He recognizes Lindner's warning:

> This is the menace of psychopathy: the psychopath is not only a criminal; he is the embryonic Storm-Trooper; he is the disinherited, betrayed antagonist whose aggressions can be mobilized on the instant at which the properly-aimed and frustration-evoking formula is communicated by that Leader under whose tinseled aegis license becomes law, secret and primitive desires become virtuous ambitions readily attained, and the compulsive behavior formerly deemed punishable becomes the order of the day.[33]

But he chooses to reject it, feeling that totalitarianism is inevitable anyway unless the psychopath points to a way out of the contemporary historical morass. He maintains, since he believes there is more good than evil in men, that the hipster, although he could

lead us deeper into totalitarianism, is more likely to lead us to freedom. By returning to direct sense experience, through the agencies
of violence and orgasm, the hipster offers a romantic hope for
salvation.

Mailer believes in the hipster for yet another reason. The hipster
is a sexual rebel. He has become a rebel because of his dissatis-
faction with an oppressive society and its mores. Since society
deals with all rebels by repressing them, the hipster not only is
bound to feel enmity for society, but will find he must destroy it
if he is to be free. His struggle will become similar to that of the
political radical. "The hipster may come to see that his condition
is no more than an exaggeration of the human condition, and
that if he would be free, then every one must be free" (355).[34]

Mailer suggested, in 1957, that the emergence of Hip and the
entrance of the Negro into the American consciousness might lead
to a sexual revolution that could challenge the totalitarian conformity of the times. That there has been some sort of sexual revolution has been apparent; what is not so apparent is that it has
challenged totalitarian conformity. Mailer prophesied a "time of
violence" (356), when society will either suppress the hip ethic
or be overcome by it. He sees so much hatred beneath the surface
of our lives—lives that are semitotalitarian in the sense that the
forms of political and social control often appear democratic, while
the actual choices we can make are far more limited than they
appear—that we must ultimately face only two choices: accept
violence and destruction now, leading to a revolution for a better
world, or postpone violence a short while longer until it becomes
the tool of society. Our age is reduced to ultimate alternatives:
either individual violence or acquiescence in the "cold murderous
liquidations of the totalitarian state" (357).

Confronting these alternatives, Mailer still sees in the radical
the only hope for mankind. But he finds that the radical has lost
touch with reality, has lost his potential for growth, has lost his
imagination. Perhaps he can learn these things—how to experience, grow, make imaginative insights—from the Negro and his
modern imitator, the hipster or White Negro. The Negro-hipster
life style, based on growth, created by alienation and rebellion,
may lend the necessary touch of reality to the radical's dreams and
visions. Although *Barbary Shore* portrayed Mailer's belief that "the
attempt [at revolution] failed in its frontal attack" "The White
Negro" presented Mailer's belief that hip might be "the first wind

of a second revolution" (*AM*, Reflections on Hip, 363). Hip moves man back into barbarism, but from there man might once again try to move forward into equity and justice. Hip forces man out of his cold rationalizations and back into the warm potency of life; it gives him a chance to grow again, to seize those magnificent opportunities lost with the failure of the socialist revolution.

As a statement of a possible route to salvation, "The White Negro" has its weaknesses. It seems to confuse personal salvation with social redemption. It tends to ignore the fact that its suggested program, that of a return to the senses through engagement with death and a search for good orgasms, may not even be good for the individual who adopts it, much less those other people he encounters in his daily life. It seems to slight, in its emphasis on ultimate alternatives, the horrifying aspects of the psychopath: his inability to love, his childishness, his criminal psyche, and his propensity to embrace the totalitarianism which Mailer so much fears. Mailer, feeling guilty about ignoring social redemption in favor of individual salvation, weakly appends political implications to his discussion of hip. But perhaps most horrifying of all is his refusal to engage the reality of the consequences of individual violence. While discussing the importance to modern men of returning to their senses so they can feel the reality of the world in which they exist, Mailer never once applies his injunction to himself. In this essay and in his novels one has the feeling that he is always aware of his own suffering, or the suffering that drives a man to commit acts of violence, but is seemingly never aware enough of the suffering he has the potential to inflict.

The essay has its strong points, however. It comes to grips with some of the problems of the day. It contains an attempt by Mailer—an attempt he makes in his novels as well—to understand existentialism in terms relevant to American life. This discussion has attempted to focus on the romantic elements of Mailer's vision because his version of existentialism emphasizes the romantic. Unlike many of his contemporaries—Bellow, Styron, Updike, Malamud—Mailer is not content to use European existential thought as the basic for his novels. His inquiry into the hipster is part of his attempt to find and create an indigenous American existentialism.

For Mailer is existential. He finds reality in the existent. He feels that man is defined by death, and that an awareness of death is necessary to live an authentic existence. He does not believe in a fixed set of values, but feels that men create their own values. He equates the personal with the universal. He believes in growth, and in the actions of men as the only reality.

If some of this sounds romantic, it should not be surprising. Existentialism is a late flowering of romanticism. What Mailer does is emphasize the romantic elements in existentialism: it is probably easier to compare him to Wordsworth or Emerson than to Heidegger or Sartre. What he develops is a unique personal vision, which combines many aspects of existentialism with the romantic emphasis on the natural goodness of men, growth, return to the feelings, and salvation through reversion to the primitive and the child.

Stated but as yet unresolved is a dilemma that Mailer grapples with in all his writings: what is the proper relationship between the radical man and society? In all his writings Mailer has a profound sense of cultural crisis: the world is falling apart; pressures are constantly building which cannot be resolved; the whole of human civilization, and even human existence, is being threatened. The radical recognizes this deterioration as the modern human condition. But what can he do about it? He has two great needs, which often seem contradictory: he must save himself and he must try to save society. The tension that is so important to the unique vision of Norman Mailer is that his historical sense of the modern human condition cries out for effective radical action to change that condition, while his sense of the role of the radical never gets beyond the radical's need to save himself from succumbing to the terrors of the condition he is trying to change.

Thus, though "The White Negro" seems to offer a path to individual salvation, there is beneath its surface an uneasy peace. Mailer seems to say, "To be a radical one must have a radical life style." But behind that is his vision of the vast panoply of the impending destruction of human civilization, a backdrop against which all individual actions must be played out; and this vision of cultural crisis cries back to Mailer's retreat to a radical life style, "More! More!" This conflict between the need for individual and social salvation continues in *An American Dream* and *Why Are We in Vietnam?* and is partially resolved in *The Armies of the Night.*

Chapter V

An American Dream

New Modes of Perception

ailer's next novel, which drew heavily on the ideas worked out in "The White Negro," was originally published serially in *Esquire*.[1] *An American Dream*, written in installments under the pressure of monthly deadlines, was revised before its publication as a novel.[2] Despite flaws that resulted from the frenzied method of its composition, the novel explores new areas of both sensibility and style and ranks as Mailer's most ambitious work since *The Naked and the Dead*. *An American Dream* is a vision of contemporary America. It is at once romance, allegory, satire, dream vision, and glorified pop art.

The novel centers on Stephen Richards Rojack, the narrator and protagonist of the novel. He tells us of three hectic days during which, on the brink of suicide, he freed himself from both his lethargy and his feeling of entrapment by murdering his wife. Rojack describes how he thereafter managed to cope with both the police and his father-in-law, the powerful, wealthy, and demonic Barney Kelly. He relates how during three days he fell in love with a nightclub singer named Cherry, engaged his deceased wife's maid in an erotic and perverse relationship, and was confronted by the sudden and violent deaths of Cherry and her former lover, Shago Martin. At the close of the novel he describes his departure from the violent and dangerous world of New York and how, passing through Las Vegas, he decided to head south to Yucatan and Guatemala in order to sort through his experiences and regain a sense of emotional composure.

Rojack, like Lovett and O'Shaugnessy, embellishes the tale he tells, so that the narrative turns back upon itself, and recounts its own coming-into-being. The story lies somewhere between reportage and fancy, recounting both the actions which we presume are occurring in an actual, objective world and the subjective imagination which plays upon those actions, orders them, charges them with meaning, and presents them to us in the form of a narrative. Rojack, who is in continual transit during the novel, voyaging simultaneously into himself and through America, is at rest only while narrating the novel, recollecting past actions in what is, we presume, some sort of tranquillity. In order to understand the book, we must understand Rojack, and in order to understand him we must understand Mailer's fascination with several of his earlier protagonists.

Something in the core of Croft, totalitarian and inhumane as he was, ignited Mailer's continuing interest and curiosity: in Croft he found the nightmare that could be America's future, and the hope that America might transcend its present wasteland. Through this character Mailer became increasingly fascinated with the violent and psychopathic elements in modern life, an interest that culminated in the writing of "The White Negro." The psychopath tries to live out his infantile fantasies and dilemmas; the hipster, by cutting himself off from society and its moral strictures, attempts to return to a more primitive and infantile level of existence and thereby resolve the social dilemmas in which he finds himself trapped.

Mailer's glorification of the hipster led to Stephen Richards Rojack, the central character of *An American Dream*. Rojack fleshes out the vision in "The White Negro," although it is interesting to note that Rojack's intellectual acuity and his concern with the upper social and economic strata of American society seem divorced from the hipster's world.[3] But it is precisely because Mailer seems more concerned with Rojack as a complex human being and less concerned with the need to create in him a reflection of a philosophic system that Rojack is a more successful characterization than his predecessor, Marion Faye. In *The Deer Park* Faye was a senseless grotesque; in this novel, however, Rojack's distorted actions and perceptions seem believable in the violently distorted world the book portrays.

The most striking achievement of the novel lies neither in its cast of characters nor in the bizarre twists of its plot but in the mode of perception that Rojack has discovered and in which he lives. As the narrator he makes his mode ours, and his manner of experiencing becomes the pathway by which we, too, experience the novel.

An American Dream is in many ways the most striking and original of Mailer's efforts. Throughout the novel, though most

notably in the first four chapters, the reader is enmeshed in a
strange and wonderful world, created by Rojack's approaches to
reality. Mailer uses Rojack to explore a new mode of perception.[4]
Throughout, the reader finds himself in a world he had not known
before; Rojack's manner of experiencing continually stretches toward and into new and heretofore hidden realms. His modes of
perception constitute a dual reversion—counseled earlier in "The
White Negro"—to the primitive and to the psychotic. In order to
understand the novel, we must understand Mailer's sense of how
Rojack's thought processes are related to magic, and how magic
and neurosis share many similar features.

I subscribe to Edward Burnett Tylor's definition of magic:

> Man, as yet in a low intellectual condition having come
> to associate in thought those things which he found by
> experience to be connected in fact, proceeded erroneous-
> ly to invert this action, and to conclude that association
> in thought must involve similar connexion in reality. . . .
> magic arts . . . have resulted from thus mistaking an ideal
> for a real connexion.[5]

Also generally accepted is Frazer's division of magic into two
branches, homeopathic or imitative, and contagious.[6] These two
result from the two major principles of the association of ideas:
similarity and contiguity. One thing is associated with another
either because the two have similar qualities or because they are
close to one another in space or time.

If one believes in magic, a clear demarcation between subjective
and objective reality disappears. Tylor tells us that association
often leads the associator to confuse an ideal connection with a
real one. In an earlier work he stated that the root of magic is that
subjective conclusions are accepted as objective realities. Freud
asserts a similar view when he states that "primitive man transferred the structural relations of his own psyche to the outer
world."[7]

The difficulties in understanding Rojack's world-view present a
situation analogous to the primitive one Freud refers to above.
Rojack believes in magic. He is a professor at a university in New
York, a "professor of existential psychology with the not incon-
siderable thesis that magic, dread, and the perception of death
were the root of motivation" (8). The return to magic—the dependence upon association of ideas for significance, and the resul-

tant erasing of the subject-object dichotomy—is one way in which Rojack follows the course laid out in "The White Negro" and returns to the primitive as a way to salvation.

Two examples show his belief in magical process; the first illustrates contagious magic. The most important event in Rojack's life prior to the opening of the novel was his wartime destruction of a German machine-gun nest. At the time of that incident, a full moon was shining. When the novel opens, Rojack is contemplating suicide on a balcony high above the street because he hears the call of the moon. And, during the next three days, he constantly feels that the full moon is exerting a powerful influence on his actions. Because of that earlier wartime moon, the moon has ever after been rich in totemic significance for him.[8] Since the full moon, trauma, and death were once linked, Rojack expects that a recurrence of the full moon will bring a recurrence of trauma and death.

An example of imitative magic is the psychic artillery battle which Rojack fights in a nightclub while listening to a song of Cherry, who is soon to be his lover. He sends mental darts and arrows at various people in the club, and feels that these have a physical effect. The homeopathic principle is evident: the thought of a bullet is like a bullet, and therefore thinking a bullet at someone can hurt him in a manner similar to shooting a real bullet at him. The parallel in primitive societies is the use of dolls or other representations to effect injury or sickness on one's enemies.

Magic operates most importantly through symbols. For the primitive, the totem was central to his world-view. And in *An American Dream* symbols figure importantly. They are unlike normal symbols in that all their secondary referents have as much validity as the primary referent. Since there is a constant correlation and interpenetration of objective and subjective levels of experience, the "symbolic" quality of actions and objects is as real as the object or action itself; in Tylor's terms, the ideal relation is taken for the real—the importance of the moon, and the psychic artillery battle. It can be seen even more clearly in the climax of the novel, when Rojack feels he must walk around the parapet of Kelly's penthouse. The action itself scarcely concerns anyone but the two individuals who are party to it, Kelly and Rojack. The walk, although difficult, is not impossible. But Rojack imbues it with symbolic value: walking the parapet is necessary to maintain himself in a state of grace and to prevent himself from dying. Yet the symbolic action of testing himself is less important than his conviction that by walking the parapet twice he can create a charm that will protect the lives of Cherry and Shago. If he does not walk it twice, he may still achieve grace, but they will not. His own symbolic act becomes essential for others as well. The normal expectation, when he does make the second journey around the parapet, would be either that nothing will happen to Cherry and Shago (since symbolic actions do not have objective significance) or that, if there is an effect, it will be because Rojack's failure will condition his future interactions with them. Tradition allows the subjective to affect the objective, but only as both meet in the mind of the individual; any relationship between both must result from a conversion from one to another within the individual. But this is not what happens in *An American Dream*. Both Shago and Cherry die, not because Rojack drives them to it, but because the subjective connection—the association that exists in Rojack's mind —becomes real.

What holds true for symbol also holds true for metaphor and simile. Mailer makes extensive use of comparison to capture the nuance and mood of the situation he is describing. In the novel these comparisons go beyond the normal illustrative purpose of metaphor. The metaphorical description becomes an essential part of the reality Mailer describes. Thus when Rojack notices "a thin high constipated smell (a smell which spoke of rocks and grease and the sewer damp of wet stones in poor European alleys)" (43) emanating from Ruta, he labels her a Nazi. And a Nazi she remains to him, for in describing her smell, in creating the metaphor, he has come upon the hidden reality of her being.

Yet what we have been calling a revelation of magical connections can also be seen as a manifestation of neurosis, psychosis, and insanity. It is not difficult to see Rojack as mentally unbalanced. Mailer has linked neurosis with dread, claiming that the neurotic is enslaved by what he feels is a magical significance of certain ritual acts, usually trivialities (*PP*, Responses and Reactions II, 152–157). The neurotic is differentiated from the psychotic in that he can know his neuroses and understand how they are deviations from the healthy norm, while the psychotic, who is entirely divorced from reality, has no norm to measure his perceptions or actions by. That he takes his apperceptions for reality is precisely what makes him a psychotic.

The possibility that Rojack is a madman immersed in a psychotic nightmare is reinforced by his own self-diagnosis. At one point he asks the reader, "Do you know psychosis? Have you explored its cave? I had gone out to the end of my string. It was stretching behind me—I could feel it ready to snap" (133). Later in the novel, he views himself in still greater extremity: "I slipped off the lip of all sanity . . . I no longer knew what I was doing, nor why I did it, I was in some deep of waters and no recourse but to keep swimming and never stop" (253). Concurrent with Rojack's emphasis on the magical, then, is his recognition of actual or impending psychosis.

Although Mailer seems to be pursuing that resemblance which Freud discovered between magic and neurosis,[9] he rejects Freud's contention that civilization has progressed from a primitive stage to one of a higher order. Mailer feels that civilization has moved into a dead end, and the only way out of the cul-de-sac in which modern men find themselves is to return to magic and psychosis, a return tentatively made by Rojack.

Rojack's perceptual world, then, is grounded in a sense of magic often indistinguishable from psychosis. All of his perceptions are ultimately ambivalent. The reader can never finally determine whether Rojack has, through magic, cut through rational conventions to a hidden significance, or whether he has entrenched himself more firmly in the illusory world of the psychotic.

This ambivalence has its roots in "The White Negro," in which Mailer glorified the concept of hip by asserting that the psychopath could serve as a paradigm for possible redemption. As previously noted, he insisted that men must return to their primitive instincts and follow the example of the psychopath: he further affirmed that the two routes—the return and the embrace of the psychotic—were one and the same. Rojack represents his attempt to create a character who embodies the vital characteristics of the hipster.

Through the ways in which he apprehends reality, particularly the reality of social and interpersonal relations, Rojack creates a world of violence and then proceeds to love and act violently as he engages this world. His return to the primitive is revealed in his reduction of the ambiguities and complexities of modern human existence to an elemental level in which force, physical violence, and libidinal desire are the major components of consciousness. The reversion is also revealed in his dependence upon thought patterns which are remarkably similar to primitive systems of magic.

Three aspects of this primitive and ambivalent vision are responsible for much of the strangeness and novelty the reader encounters in *An American Dream*. First, because subjective reality is often mistaken for objective reality by a primitive or psychotic mentality, objects and actions are imbued with a significance or power which they do not, in fact, possess. The weakness of this confusion of objective and subjective relations is obvious: it leads to useless or erroneous conclusions. But the primitive and psychotic modes of perception have corresponding strengths. In this novel, as symbolic connections become real connections, the physical world becomes imbued with significance. For Rojack objects and events that might ordinarily be commonplace, passing unnoticed or forgotten, assume great significance because they are symbolic actions or objects, and because this symbolic role is, for Rojack, indistinguishable from their actual role. The full moon and the recurrence of serpent imagery, for example, take on totemic importance. Rojack's continual need to perform ritual acts, such as walking around the parapet, climbing the stairs to Kelly's apartment, or not taking a drink, can be seen either as an elaborate system of taboo which lends order and significance to his life or as evidence of neurotic compulsion. Whichever way, we may be certain that Rojack's confusion of subjective and objective enlarges his perceptual world and imbues it with added significance, however specious it may appear to a more rational observer.

The second aspect is that neither the psychotic nor the primitive depends upon the ratiocinative processes that are the norm in civilized society. Both Tylor and Frazer emphasize a dependence upon association as the chief characteristic of magic and the thought processes of men in primitive societies. Freud's work on dreams and the etiology of neuroses emphasizes the importance of association in the subconscious and unconscious minds of human beings, and concludes that the mind and actions of a neurotic can be understood only by accepting the supremacy of association in the mental processes of the neurotic. Associative thinking has the advantage to the artist, then, of being true to that subconscious life which is so often submerged beneath superficial ratiocinative process.

Third, the actions of the psychotic and the primitive always arise out of an ambivalent nexus.[10] The wish always gives rise to the prohibition. Love is always conjoined with hate, independence with dependence. Rojack's relations with his wife, Deborah, clearly illustrate these conjunctions because he is caught up in his love for her as well as his hate; because in seeking to free himself of her he is also emphasizing his dependence on her; and because his relief is mixed with guilt, his involvement with detachment, and his joy with sorrow. This emotional ambivalence deepens and enriches Rojack's relationships and perceptions.

It is clear that Rojack's whole mode of perception—this quasi-primitive, quasi-psychotic orientation—is an outgrowth of his first encounter with death. Following his "heroic" destruction of two machine-gun nests and four German soldiers, he becomes "lost in a private kaleidoscope of death" and realizes that "death was a creation more dangerous than life" (7). In this knowledge of death, this self-conscious creation of man's mind, man is separated from all other life.

Mailer is, by his own admission, an American existentialist, and he makes his affiliation with this tradition very clear in *The Presidential Papers*,[11] the book that preceded *An American Dream*. Insofar as his work as a novelist is existential, however, it is so in light of the attitude toward death, authenticity, and dread. This area of existential thought has been most thoroughly explored by Martin Heidegger:

> This opens to me two decisively opposed modes of being: authentic being rooted in the explicit sense of my situation (*Befindlichkeit*); and inauthentic being, moving automatically in the established ruts and routes of the organized world.
>
> Dread differs from fear in seeming to have no object and no cause, and that is what makes it so profoundly disturbing.
>
> What dread reveals to me is that I am cast into the world in order to die there.
>
> I anticipate death . . . by living in the presence of death as always immediately possible and as undermining everything. This full blooded acceptance (*amor fati*) of death, lived out, is authentic personal existence.[12]

Indeed, Rojack seems, throughout the novel, to be waltzing in a solitary dance with death. He lives in its presence at all times; his "personality was built upon a void" (7). Because of this continuous awareness of death, he lives with the undirected fear that grows out of man's sense of his own mortality. He tells Cherry, "I'm always afraid" (118), and later explains to himself, "The dread had settled in on my last brave speech. To be not afraid of death, to be ready to engage it—sometimes I thought I had more of a horror of dying than anyone I knew. I was so unfit for that moment. It's going to be full moon for how many more days?" (119). This constant awareness of death is the keystone of Rojack's consciousness. It is the explanation of all of his attitudes and actions: his fight with insanity, his belief that God is courage, his need to murder, his constant urge to test and prove himself, and, as the last line above makes clear, his belief in magic. For there is an undeniable link in Rojack's thought processes between his perception of death and his acceptance of magic: magic is the power that rules what man cannot understand—death. Rojack believes his academic thesis that primitive man feared the gods, that whatever man gained or accomplished was taken from the gods by trickery, and that the theft was punished by dread (159). Thus Rojack, the civilized man, must live with dread as the price of civilization.

Significantly, the novel opens and closes with intense perceptions of death. Almost the first thing Rojack tells us—as if he must tell us quickly, so we can understand him and all his future actions— is of his encounter with the enemy during the war. He kills three soldiers; then, faced with a fourth, he loses his nerve. The soldier, mangled below the belt, faces Rojack, and in his eyes Rojack sees something, "eyes of blue, so perfectly blue and mad they go all the way in deep into celestial vaults of sky, eyes which go back all the way to God . . . and I faltered in that stare" (5). Such is the onset of dread, and though Rojack kills this fourth soldier too, his grace is shattered and he lives henceforth in dread, hanging over the abyss of death. It is noteworthy that he tells us he has seen such blue eyes another time "on an autopsy table in a small town in Missouri" (5). This autopsy turns out to be one of the last episodes which Rojack relates in his narrative, and almost immediately precedes the "present" of the novel.

Out of his wartime experience, which included both grace and dread, grows the Rojack who narrates the novel. Twenty years have passed, and he discovers himself older, without direction, without the success or fulfillment he desires. Since his life changed irreversibly on that night during the war, it is to death and murder

that he must return in order to understand his existence, purge
his soul, and grow into new life. In order to grow into his future
he must go into his past, just as he must come to grips with civilization and modern society by descending into his own primitive nature, the "rebellious imperatives of the self" (*AM*, WN, 339).

His route into the past and the self is murder. He discovers this
as he leans over a balcony at a party, and hears the call of the
moon. The moon is the dominant symbol in the novel: the first
chapter is titled "The Harbors of the Moon," the last, "The Harbors of the Moon Again." The full moon controls his first meetings
with both Deborah and Cherry, his murder of Deborah, his two
parapet experiences, his fight with the German patrol. The moon
calls him to jump off the balcony; in its subtle language it promises
him peace and grace. Thus the moon is at once the voice of extinction and the light which illumines his "raw Being" (12), a
seemingly paradoxical situation which is resolved by the realization that man's being is determined by his mortality, that it is extinction which defines existence. The moon issues a summons which,
as Rojack realizes at the close of the novel, appeals to an essential
part of his nature: "its pale call, princess of the dead, I would
never be free of her" (259).

But free he wishes to be; at his greatest crisis, when he faces
the need to walk the parapet of Kelly's apartment, he utters a
plaintive cry: "Yes God, do not make me go back and back again
to the charnel house of the moon" (162). Facing death can be ennobling; it is the only route to authentic life, in Heidegger's terms.
But precisely because it involves dread—which leads to authenticity—it is a dreadful and thereby frightening experience. Rojack
stands upon the balcony at the start of the novel and almost jumps;
he believes that he stands to lose his body but gain his soul. When
he does not yield to the moon, however, and steps back onto the
balcony, his act of self-preservation is seen as a failure. Rojack
feels an "illness . . . an extinction . . . sickness and dung" (13).
He has faced a moment in which he could have grown, and he
has not seized that opportunity. Rather, he begins to die a little,
and he feels the first flushes of cancer, that mad riot of the cells
which Mailer believes is sublimated natural self-violence, consequent to the denied growth of the soul. Henceforth, Rojack is com-
pelled to risk his life in order to recoup what he has lost on the
balcony; he possesses what Mailer has described as "the wisdom

of a man who senses death within and gambles that he can cure it by risking his life" (48).

But the drive to return to roots, to find a successful connection to reality and to the deepest needs of the psyche, need not involve suicide. Authenticity—the converse of alienation, which describes an existence separated from reality, others, and ultimately the self— results from the experience of dread. And dread is the complex of emotions felt when an individual realizes consciously that death is a process he must undergo, and that death is the ultimate existential crisis—existential because it exists. For one cannot learn about death, one cannot explain or understand it. Mailer claims elsewhere, in discussing tales of the Hasidim, that the only valid knowledge is existential, the only true learning "from situations in which the end is unknown" (*PP*, 197). Valid knowledge and authentic existence are identical. Thus death, which can never be known, is the ultimate existential experience.

One must face the extreme and the ultimate in order to find authenticity. In today's society, when the individual is dominated by the authority of stored knowledge, oppressed by a controlled environment, and reduced to social impotence, personal salvation can be found only in the extreme experience. Everything short of the extreme is programmed. Thus Mailer concludes that the experience he described in "The White Negro" is the paradigm for authenticity in the modern age:

> The logic in searching for extreme situations, in searching for one's authenticity, is that one burns out the filament of old dull habit and turns the conscious mind back upon its natural subservience to the instinct. The danger of civilization is that its leisure, its power, its insulation from nature, so alienate us from instinct that our consciousness and our habits take on an autonomy which may censor even the most necessary communication between mind and instinct.   (*PP*, 198)

Most assuredly, this concept of the authentic, heroic, modern man was the controlling factor in the creation of Stephen Rojack.

After his struggle with the suicidal impulse on the balcony, Rojack wanders away from the party. He telephones his separated wife, Deborah Caughlin Mangaravidi Kelly (Rojack) (it is significant of the domination-submission struggle which marks their relationship that she is never identified by her married name until he announces her death) and asks to see her. Deborah's veiled violence and her need for mastery and cruelty bring Rojack to a fever pitch, so that in the space of at most an hour and a half the moon guides him through a murder; a compressed orgy which involves masturbation, foot fetishism, anal and vaginal penetration; a mutilation of a dead body; and yet another sexual encounter— quite a series of "extreme situations."

Most important of these raids into the taboo and perverse is the murder of Deborah. Mailer had tried to deal with murder twice before but was not successful: Faye fails to push Elena into suicide, and the "long novel" about murder for which he published the prologue (*AM*, Prologue to a Long Novel, 512–532) was never completed. Murder seems to have been a compulsive, even obsessive, preoccupation of Mailer's during this period.[13]

What personal crises, what childhood traumas, led to this preoccupation remain hidden. What is relevant and known, however, is that this obsession meshes with Mailer's view of life, death, and authenticity as he developed it in the works discussed. Murder requires an extraordinary commitment to discover the self, since it violates the most basic mandates and taboos of society and since it involves the murderer in a confrontation with death. Certainly murder "burns out the filament of old dull habit" and forces the individual back to his instincts. His return to instinct is accomplished in several ways: first, he is caught up, as it were, in mortal combat and needs to rely on his deepest instincts for self-preservation; second, murder involves acting out one's needs and emotions rather than bottling them up by repression and sublimation; third, murder necessitates the individual's dependence upon himself and his resources and the rejection of society and its taboos; and finally, as Rojack's plight concerning the disposal of Deborah's body makes clear, it pits the individual, alone, against the society which he has rejected and which will certainly punish him for his rebelliousness if it can. In this process of death, action, rebellion, and outlawry, the murderer is forced upon himself; he must rely on his instincts and the courage he can muster.

Murder, then, involves the simultaneous confrontation of exterior and interior reality. Rojack begins his voyage without and within when he murders Deborah. As is the case with most human endeavors, his voyage within is more difficult and more important than his voyage without. He murders Deborah, ostensibly, as an act of liberation. Now he is free of her, of her malice toward him, and of his past. Their marriage is dissolved, and though Rojack believes that Deborah still maintains a magical, spiritual hold over him, the hold seems to weaken during the course of the novel. He has also won internal liberation: "Marriage to her was the armature of my ego; remove the armature and I might topple like clay" (17). He has had the courage to remove this armature, and is rewarded not by his disintegration but by the rediscovery and repossession of his own violent soul. The prospects are frightening: "I had opened a void—I was now without center. Can you understand? I did not belong to myself any longer. Deborah had occupied my center" (27). Although Rojack has been weak enough to depend upon something outside of himself for meaning, the measure of his heroism in this novel is the fact that he deliberately overthrows this external armature and seeks to find a center within himself. This process involves facing the void. And man in the void is the paradigmatic situation existentialism seeks to resolve: how does man, surrounded by nothingness, make out of his existence something meaningful or valuable? Although such a man may not be happy—indeed is not happy, being encumbered with dread—he alone leads an authentic existence.

So Rojack faces his fear and dread and commits one of the most heinous of crimes (perhaps the only other social taboo as strong as that against murder within the family is incest—a taboo broken by Kelly in a desire to discover himself, a desire in many ways comparable to Rojack's). In so doing, Rojack not only frees himself from the armature that was stifling his existence, but also wins the battle over his own fear and dread, which he had begun to lose earlier on the balcony.

Thus murder is Rojack's road to salvation. It is a journey into the deepest part of himself: "I was as far into myself as I had ever been, and universes wheeled in a dream" (31). He feels a catharsis, explicitly sexual, and then finds renewal: "I opened my eyes. I was weary with a most honorable fatigue, and my flesh seemed new. I had not felt so nice since I was twelve" (32). Or as he thinks later, "If Deborah's dying had given me a new life, I must be all of eight hours old by now" (93).

Murder, as I have said, is to Mailer sexual. Rojack finds murder more exhilarating than suicide because suicide promises no relief, "It is like carrying a two-hundred-pound safe up a cast iron hill. . . . Besides, murder offers the promise of vast relief. It is never un-

sexual" (8). Since Mailer had earlier declared that the way to
self-knowledge and the hope for the future is through a search for
the apocalyptic orgasm, it is not surprising that here he places murder close to sexual climax. Rojack describes the killing of one of
the German soldiers in explicit sexual terms: "I pulled the trigger
as if I were squeezing the softest breast of the softest pigeon which
ever flew, still a woman's breast takes me now and then to that
pigeon on the trigger . . ." (4). Sex will later be described in a
metaphor of murder: "I fired one hot fierce streak of fierce bright
murder, fierce as the demon in the eyes of a bright golden child"
(56). But the most explicit connection between sex and murder
occurs when Rojack kills his wife; he is in an orgy of violence,
first fantasizing a rare heaven within the female body, then forcing
his way in, driving, impelled by spasms; pressure and desire build
up as he imagines himself ejaculating in an unprotected woman;
and finally he explodes, hurling out what is within him in stupend-
ous array, crying "never halt now" as the orgasmic intensity over-
whelms him and he feels everything within him pass out in waves
through an open door:

> I released the pressure on her throat, and the door I had
> been opening began to close. But I had had a view of
> what was on the other side of the door, and heaven was
> there, some quiver of jeweled cities shining in the glow
> of a tropical dusk, and I thrust against the door once more
> and hardly felt her hand leave my shoulder, I was driving
> now with force against that door: spasms began to open
> in me, and my mind cried out then, "Hold back! you're
> going too far, hold back!" I could feel a series of orders
> whip like tracers of light from my head to my arm, I was
> ready to obey, I was trying to stop, but *pulse* *packed*
> behind *pulse* in a *pressure* up to thunderhead; some
> blackbiled lust, some desire to go ahead not unlike the
> instant one comes in a woman against her cry that she is
> without protection came bursting with rage from out of
> me and my mind exploded in a fireworks of *rockets, stars,*
> and *hurtling embers,* the arm about her neck leaped
> against the whisper I could still feel murmuring in her
> throat, and *crack* I choked her harder, and *crack* I gave
> her payment—never halt now—and *crack* the door flew
> open and the wire tore in her throat, and I was through

the door, hatred passing from me in wave after wave,
illness as well, rot and pestilence, nausea, a bleak string
of salts, I was floating.   (31, emphases mine)

The mounting sexual rhythm is reinforced by the use of alliteration
and repetition. Rojack has, after this action, the feeling of renewal
that has been mentioned. In the next chapter he examines this feeling in the light of what Deborah had called grace, and concludes
that the term applies to his feelings: "Speak of a state of grace—I
had never known such calm" (38).

After winning this first battle with his own fear, after embracing
his dread, Rojack finds himself, under the compulsion of three
more days of full moon, obliged to repeat this struggle again and
again. The rest of the novel is concerned with the repetition of
Rojack's confrontation with dread and death: whether to gamble
with the police, love Cherry, face Shago, see Kelly, walk the parapet; and these major confrontations are echoed and reinforced
by smaller ones: whether to take a drink, whether to face a boxer
and his gangster friends, whether to climb the stairs to Kelly's
apartment. Sometimes Rojack wins, sometimes he loses in his effort to face the compulsions and emotions deep within his soul,
to achieve in the flux of a temporal existence those rare and precious moments of authenticity. He is the finest model Mailer has
created of the dynamic individual under stress, constantly aware
of the great law of creation: "From *The Deer Park*: 'There was
that law of life, so cruel and so just, that one must grow or else
pay more for remaining the same.' I think that line is true. I think
it is biologically true" (*PP*, 104). Payment is made by dying:
either man's mood fails, or his manhood, or his potential is reduced; or, in the most serious instances, cancer sets in.

The closeness of murder and sex means that sex, too, represents
a battle of a man against himself and his fear, and that the price
for defeat in sex is as severe as such a price can be. Sex, like murder, involves courage, for the individual must face someone on a
primal battleground where all the deadening protections of civilization are stripped away and the two individuals meet each other,
both literally and figuratively, with nakedness as their only shield
and weapon. Sex becomes a major battleground of existence, on
which the individual makes himself and discovers himself. Mailer,
in this repsect, reveals one of his fundamental beliefs, that sex is
not romantic folderol or solely a drive toward libidinal satisfaction

and fulfillment, but is rather one of the few areas open to man in which he can encounter his naked desires, in which he must face up to the possibilities of mastery and subjection. In the sexual act, man is alone, and cannot put off his failures on anyone else. Mailer's short story, "The Time of Her Time" (*AM*, 478–503), emphasizes that earlier failure to achieve mutual satisfaction from the sexual act can be remedied if the male partner—in this case Sergius O'Shaugnessy again—has the sensitivity and the courage and the will to succeed.

This theme of the "heroic penis" is central to Mailer.[14] Eitel prides himself on giving Elena her first orgasm and O'Shaugnessy on giving Denise her first. In *An American Dream*, Rojack gives Cherry, veteran of a long and varied sex life, her first as well. It is in pursuing this theme that Mailer seems most shallow and allows himself the least distance from his work. It is as if he is acting out his own neuroses in discussing the male sexual power; he has never progressed beyond a stage in which "the good lay makes all ok," in which a man is a man only if he can satisfy a woman sexually. One has a feeling that Mailer must continually prove his masculinity, as if he is very dubious of it: implications can be seen in escapades in his personal life, such as acting the part of a mobster in his films (*Beyond the Law*), playing the boxer, being champion drunk, or battler, or lover; and in his fiction as a belief in the power of the penis and disgust with homosexuality.

Rojack, in accord with Mailer's own biases, is caught up in the savage world of *machismo*. He can never back down, he must always prove himself. The basis of sexual frustration which made Croft continually prove himself and his manhood over and over seems to be operative in Rojack too. Rojack *must* make it with Ruta and with Cherry, he *must* be dominant in both cases, and he *must* be successful—both women have to exclaim that he was wonderful or he can get no satisfaction. Finally, Rojack is threatened by homosexuality: one of the Germans he kills is "possessor of that overcurved mouth which only great fat sweet young faggots can have when their rectum is tuned and entertained from adolescence on" (4). The whole simplistic reaction to his threatened masculinity casts doubt on the validity of Mailer's vision, since much of his exploration of the search for meaning in the deepest levels of the psyche and the exploration of the areas beyond the fringe of morality can be seen as simple outgrowths of this insecurity. Even the necessity to grow at each instant can be interpreted as a glorification of machismo.

All of these arguments can be leveled as well at Mailer's literary (and personal) idol, Ernest Hemingway. But to say that Hemingway's ethic and style can be derived from a threatened masculinity is not to compromise the quality of his writing, nor even the incisiveness of his insight into one area of human experience. The same can be said of Mailer who, though his stylistic excellence is not as consistent as Hemingway's, has a more detailed view of a larger segment of human experience, and has an intellectual curiosity and power that Hemingway seldom revealed.

If dread is the anticipation of death and meaninglessness, then the reward for embracing dread, and acting well in the world by either confronting death or sexuality, is "grace" (38)—a temporary state that results from existence having, through action, created its own meaning. Grace is also, however, a theological concept, and Rojack/Mailer intends the theological implications. Both view the world as a battleground between God and Devil: "God's engaged in a war with the Devil, and God may lose" (236). Grace is ostensibly the reward for right actions, for having helped God in his eternal and yet unresolved war with the Devil.

But in order for Mailer to make his war between God and the Devil interesting and also plausible, he needs ambiguity. For if good and evil are clearly demarcated, then what interest is there in reading about them? And how do they relate to our experience of the world, which becomes increasingly ambivalent and indistinct the more it is subjected to consciousness? So Mailer maintains that God and the Devil are *not* distinguishable. And if the Devil were to come to man, Mailer maintains, would he not come in the guise of God? What better way to ensure that men would follow him? Or, conversely, "goodness could come on a visit to evil only in the disguise of evil" (37). Rojack, then, although he feels peace and renewal and grace, must now ask himself, "Am I now good? Am I evil forever?" (38).

Mailer lends credence to his view of man and society by tying it in with the divine: everything he describes or posits takes on richer significance if it is part of the teleology of the universe. In *An American Dream* Rojack's religion is courage. Going beyond Hemingway, who found courage the supreme value in a world untouched by the transcendent, the *nada* of "A Clean Well-Lighted

Place,"[15] Mailer elevates courage to the realm of religion. And his religion is replete with God and the Devil, Heaven and Hell, and a life after death. Just as Hemingway has a coterie of characters who know and accept the code that men must live by, so has Mailer in this novel. Rojack believes in the as yet undetermined war between God and the Devil for mastery over existence. So do the others acceptors of the code—Deborah, Cherry, Kelly, and Shago Martin. Deborah is aware of the secret of existence, that God and the Devil are in conflict and that all men are constantly helping one or the other; this knowledge is what makes her so insufferable, because like Rojack and her father, she wishes mastery for herself and for what she thinks is God. Therefore, she pushes to the extreme limits of experience, seeking in her own way for authenticity. In the process she inflicts injury on Rojack, by her sins of both commission and omission. As Faye pushed Elena in *The Deer Park*, so Deborah pushes Rojack. Indeed, he almost kills himself; but in the end, he externalizes his search and commits murder—the murder that Deborah had foreseen: "Pet, I'm not going to jump, I'm going to be murdered" (149). Rojack has been tied to her by "a devil's contract" (18) and she has taught him of "the long finger of God and the swish of the Devil" (35). And when he recalls one of her rare reflective moments, he remembers this conversation:

> "I know that I am more good and more evil than anyone alive, but which was I born with, and what came into me?"
>
> "You shift allegiance from day to day."
>
> "No. I just pretend to." She smiled. "I'm evil if truth be told. But I despise it, truly I do. It's just that evil has power." (36)

Rojack murders her not as the stronger murdering the weaker, but because he is at a crisis in his life and floundering. He, like Faye before him,

> knew that the prescription to reverse the process [of dissolution] . . . was the last of the nostrums and it had worked once before; it was murder. Brave murder. Brave murder gave the charge of the man one killed . . . it was the grand connection, and the dead man's . . . energies regenerated the dead circuits of one's own

> empty-balled time, and one moved away with greater
> strength, new nerves and a heavier burden. (*AM*, Ad-
> vertisements for Myself on the Way Out, 526)

By killing Deborah, also one of life's initiates, Rojack shores up
his failing strength with the strength of two.

Deborah has received her knowledge of good and evil from
the same sources as her father, Barney Oswald Kelly. The crux of
their relationship is revealed at the end of the novel, when Kelly
makes Rojack understand that he and his daughter had committed
incest, not once but over an extended period of time. The metaphorical way in which Kelly describes the temptation to incest
involves the same terminology and the same *Weltanschauung* that
Rojack has been acting upon. Kelly admits to Rojack that he has
been struck by the latter's idea that God and the Devil are engaged
in a heroic combat which God might lose. Then he spins a long
tale, explaining how his affair with Bess reached an incestuous
turn as he, she, and her daughter sat around, and how he had run
from the house, unable to fare further against the strength of such
a taboo as incest. He then explains how he realized that great
men, men with power and importance, "have to be ready to deal
with One or the Other, and that's too much for the average man
on his way" (246). But Kelly was bound for the top, and not ready
to give up: "I know I was ready. Incest is the gate to the worst
sort of forces" (246). His tale is full of references to "God and
the Devil" (246) and its climax is in existential terminology:

> But I was—do you know that phrase of Kierkegaard's,
> of course you do—I was in a fear and trembling. I stayed
> at that window for an hour. I was almost blubbering at
> my inability to take that simple jump. And the goat kept
> coming back. "She's down the hall," said the goat, "she's
> on her bed, it's there for you, Oswald." Then I would
> reply, "Save me Lord." Finally, I heard a voice say quite
> clearly, "Jump! That will cool your desire, fellow. Jump!"
> The Lord, you see, had a bitch of a humor about
> me. (251)

Not only is Kelly referring to Kierkegaard and his description of
a state of dread, he is also punning on the essence of Kierkegaard's
thought. The "jump" referred to his impulse to jump out of the
window—sixteen feet from the ground. The suicidal impulse is

parallel to Rojack's. But, like Rojack, he does not jump. Instead, he takes a jump much higher than sixteen feet—a leap of faith, and goes to his daughter's room to submit to his deepest desires. But he, too, like Rojack and Deborah, knows that there is an ambivalence to all things, and he might be serving God or the Devil by taking his daughter. One thing is certain: if he can break the incest taboo, he can conquer a certain part of himself, be made stronger; and he will enter into a domain of vast new powers—of magic.[16] Going beyond the normal means a possible alliance with the Devil, but it also means power. And indeed, after seducing his daughter, there is little that is denied to Kelly, who becomes one of the most powerful men in the world.

Similarly, Shago Martin and Cherry realize that there is a struggle between good and evil for mastery. Shago realizes such nuances more than Rojack; he has met Deborah only once and rejected her because of her affinity with evil powers. "And I said to myself, 'Man, you're spitting in the face of the Devil' " (189). Rojack catches whiffs of the "snake" coming off Shago (182, 183). When Cherry tells Rojack of her love with Shago, she suggests something that makes Rojack bring up the motif that is common to all those elite who understand:

> "Yes, I know," I said, "you used to think the whole country depended on you and Shago."
> "It was a crazy idea but I used to think something would get better if Shago and I could make it." She looked unhappy again. "I don't know, Steve, it's not good to think too much—at least the way I do. Cause I always end up with something like the idea that God is weaker because I didn't turn out well." (197)

It is important to note that Cherry, like the other four, has had the courage to make bargains with evil. Her subsequent success, what there is of it, is derived from her decision to be Kelly's mistress and thereby get out of the Southern life that shackles her.

Finally, Ruta, too, understands and accepts the God-Devil struggle that Rojack verbalizes. The most compelling rendering of this schema of the universe is when Rojack enters Ruta's bedroom after killing his wife and, catching her in the act of masturbation, gets into bed with her. Mailer here duplicates the driving intensity which which he described the murder of Deborah, thus underlining the close relationship between sex and murder, orgasm and death. Furthermore, the act of intercourse is described in a lyrical metaphor as yet one more competition between "der Teufel" and "God" (47). Rojack's description of the love he made to her is extremely important because it suggests the existential predicament of modern man, caught in a war between God and the Devil with both demanding his loyalty, promising renewal if he will have the strength to make the right choice:

> So that was how I finally made love to her, a minute for one, a minute for the other, a raid on the Devil and a trip back to the Lord, I was like a hound who has broken free of the pack and is going to get that fox himself. I was drunk with my choice, she was becoming mine as no woman ever had . . . a greedy mate with the taste of power in her eyes and her mouth, that woman's look that the world is theirs, and then I was traveling up again that crucial few centimeters of distance from the end to the beginning, I was again in the place where the child is made, and a little look of woe was on her face, a puckered fearful little nine-year-old afraid of her punishment, wish-to be good. (45)

Rojack mines the "canny hard packed evil in that butt" which was at first "Verboten!" (44). Then he turns to "her deserted warehouse, that empty tomb" (45), which he strokes into life, first "one poor flower growing in a gallery" (45), then "more like a chapel now, a modest decent place, but its walls were snug, its odor was green, there was a sweetness in the chapel, a muted reverential sweetness in these walls of stone." But he senses the Devil's gifts, and returns to him—"a fraction too late" (46). The choice is fateful. He, surprised, gets what he had hoped for, the "first of the gifts I'd plucked from the alley. . . . What gifts this girl had given me, what German spice!" (50, 51). He has fantasies of eating Deborah, of dismembering her and hiding the remains. Fantasies of power. And then he has the idea he will take up: he will throw her body out the window, a plan that is ruthless, bold, and promises effectiveness as a reward for courage. But he also thinks of his seed, left perhaps "perishing in the kitchens of the Devil. Was its curse on me?" (49).

This, claims Mailer, is the paradigm for all human existence. Caught in the conflict between God and the Devil, man must choose. To complicate his choice, it is thoroughly ambiguous, so that man cannot be sure if God is God or is the Devil cleverly disguised. In such a situation, man's greatest asset is courage. Mailer, I believe, would subscribe to Wallace Stevens' lines:

> The prologues are over. Now it is time
> For final belief. So, say that final belief
> Must be in a fiction. It is time to choose.

For existential man, it is always a time of final belief, it is always time to choose. The greatest evil is cowardice; only action can hope to resolve an existential situation, by making it grow into another. Inaction can only lead to stagnation, and that is death.

Three actions demand the utmost courage from Rojack: killing Deborah, loving Cherry, and going to see Kelly, the huge figure who suggests in his power and craftiness an admixture of the Devil and the heroic human. Rojack is afraid of Kelly and does not know if he should voyage to his apartment in the Waldorf Tower. Should he, as a modern Odysseus searching for home (himself), venture closer to Scylla (the whirling vortex of Harlem) or Charybdis (the rocky heights of the Tower)? Or should he avoid both in the forgetful peace of a drink and yet another and another?

> "Go to Kelly," said a voice now in mind, and it was a voice near to indistinguishable from the other voice. Which was true? When voices came, how did you make the separation? "That which you fear most is what you must do," said my mind. "Trust the authority of your senses."   (203)

Rojack's ethic is here clearly revealed: do what you most fear, for that is the way to growth. Make the leap of faith into the most perilous alternative, for these the rewards are largest. All therefore depends upon choice: whether and how to act. "It would have been better to choose" (203), says Rojack about his decision to see Kelly.

Since Mailer—and Rojack—believe existence requires continual choice, they also believe in courage. All too often growth is achieved only through confronting fear or dread. Here, too, Mailer has been heavily influenced by Hemingway. One can discover the close affinity between the need of teacher and student to glorify courage and grace under pressure; both are immersed in the compulsion of the threatened (castrated) to assert his masculinity. And both emphasize the symbolic wound (which in Mailer has always been suffered by the narrator: Lovett's head wound, Sergius' psychic wound, Rojack's injury when he cleaned out the German machine-gun nest. All of these have been sustained in war, and each wound represents a break with the past which forces the narrator to make some sense and meaning for himself out of the present so that he can have a future).

The emphasis on "magic," which is similar to *moira*, the Greek concept of fate, also links the two authors. *A Farewell to Arms* conforms to many of Aristotle's descriptions of the nature of tragedy; despite a background of the modern world in chaos and confusion, the story line is starkly tragic. And the central passage in the novel is Frederic Henry's realization:

> If people bring so much courage to this world the world has to kill them to break them, so of course it kills them. The world breaks everyone and afterward many are strong at the broken places. But those that will not break it kills. It kills the very good and the very gentle and the very brave impartially. If you are none of these you can be sure it will kill you but there will be no special hurry.[17]

The complement of this in *An American Dream* is what Rojack calls magic, which he described in a lecture he entitled "On the Primitive View of Mystery":

> In contrast to the civilized view which elevates man above the animals, the primitive had an instinctive belief that he was subservient to the primal pact between the beasts of the jungle and the beast of mystery. To the savage, dread was the natural result of any invasion of the supernatural: if man wished to steal the secrets of the gods, it was only to be supposed that the gods would defend themselves and destroy whichever man came too close.   (159)

Belief of this sort creates the tragic. Whatever a man does which elevates him above his contemporaries will be punished by the gods, who regard his achievement, his power, as a transgression. Thus to be strong or good is to dare the wrath of the gods. In this novel Cherry becomes, for Rojack, very good and Shago is his example of the very brave, bearing his defeat with honor and pride and continually coming back to the fight. And both are broken. Their deaths, especially Cherry's, seem gratuitous, the not very deft touch of Mailer the impresario. Yet the very folly of the deaths, the absurdity of death and therefore existence, is dramatically underscored when one perceives magic, or fate, as the guiding hand. The deaths of Cherry and Shago are but the fulfillment of the tragic vision operative in the novel. It is not difficult, therefore, to see why Rojack's religion is essentially tragic, why it is · compounded of anxiety and dread and death and courage: "Comfortless was my religion, anxiety of the anxieties, for I believed God was not love but courage. Love came only as a reward" (204).

Even though love is fraught with the moral ambiguity of all experience—"For how did one distinguish love from the art of the Devil" (176)—it is next in importance to courage in Mailer's view of existence. Love came as a reward for Charley Eitel's courage; when he lost his ability to take chances and tried to solidify his position with Elena, the rewards of love disappeared with his courage. In *An American Dream* Rojack's position with Cherry is analogous. Here the courage required is that he face the absurdity of magic and either go to Harlem and by some magical process save Shago and Cherry too, or engage in another absurd act, walking back along the parapet a second time so that he can save Cherry's soul—and life. But after Kelly tries to push him off the parapet, he rushes out of the suite, and when he realizes that he has not walked the return journey for Cherry, he is too drained and weak to return. So Cherry dies, like one of Hemingway's very good who cannot be broken. When Rojack says to her, " 'I think we have to be good,' by which I meant we would have to be brave" (164), he is using Hemingway's vocabulary, and Cherry's assent indicates that she has a deep similarity to Catherine Barkley (both predict, as well, the circumstances of their death, the one in the rain, the other shortly after her first orgasm). There is an "iron law to romance: one took the vow to be brave" (203). Love follows from bravery, for "love was not a gift but a vow. Only the brave could live with it for more than a little while" (165).

In order to love, one must choose; hence love is another paradigmatic existential situation, one in which the existent precedes the categorical. Love comes not by some stroke of the mystical or magical but by means of a choice in which the individual chooses to surrender a part of himself, or all of himself, to another. Rojack is faced by the possibility of love for the first time when he is in bed with Cherry; he and Deborah had always kept much of themselves back from each other. But with Cherry he can let himself go, surrender his self, in the sense not of mastery-submission, as was always the case with Deborah, but of a mutual surrender in which all defenses are let down and the two can exist together in "bliss." To do so, however, requires courage; Rojack feels a "continent of dread" surrounding him as he faces the moment of choice, knowing that the choice is irrevocable and will change his life in significant ways. In addition, his lack of defenses represents a danger, for what if Cherry does not likewise surrender? Then he would be cast in the position not of blissful lover but of dominated slave, with his vulnerability a weapon in her hands by which she might destroy him. In this instance, however, he faces his dread, summons his courage, and takes the leap into love:

> "Do you want her?" it asked. "Do you really want her, do you want to know something about love at last?" and I desired something I had never known before, and answered; it was as if my voice had reached its roots; and, "Yes," I said, "of course I do, I want love," but like an urbane old gentlemen, a dry tart portion of my mind added, "Indeed, and what has one to lose?" and then the voice in a small terror, "Oh, you have more to lose than you have lost already, fail at love and you lose more than you can know." "And if I do not fail?" I asked back. "Do not ask," said the voice, "choose now!" and some continent of dread speared wide in me, rising like a dragon, as if I knew the choice were real, and in a life of terror I opened my eyes and her face was beautiful beneath me in that rainy morning, her eyes were golden with light, and she said, "Ah, honey, sure," and I said sure to the voice in me, and felt love fly in like some great winged bird, some beating of wings at my back, and felt her will dissolve into tears, and some great deep sorrow like roses drowned in the salt of the sea came flooding from her womb and washed into me like a sweet honey of balm for all the bitter sores of my soul and for the first time in my life without passing through fire or straining the stones of my will, I came up from my body rather than down from my mind, I could not stop, some shield broke in me, bliss, and the honey she had given me I could only give back, all sweets to her womb, all come in her cunt. (128)

Rojack cannot hold on to this love, however. Part of his failure is inherent in the transitory nature of love. Bravery can sustain it, but not past its time. Like all things, man's amorous relationships must continually change and grow. "It had always been the same, love was love, one could find it with anyone, one could find it anywhere. It was just that you could never keep it. Not unless you were ready to die for it, dear friend" (165).

Finally, though, despite his many heroic characteristics, Stephen Rojack is an ambivalent character. He evidences great courage, as in his decisions to murder Deborah, to love Cherry, and to walk the parapet, but his courage is mitigated by his cowardice, as when he fails to walk it the second time, and when he resists the orgiastic invitation that charges the air of Kelly's penthouse apartment. His fear is a most understandable human frailty, but Rojack feels that his inability to face and overcome this fear at all times denotes a hint of mediocrity in his character. Seemingly, only Shago (Negro, jazz musician, issue of the violent ghetto, and paradigm for the White Negro) and Barney Oswald Kelly are thoroughly courageous. Neither ever shirks danger or refuses to grapple with the magical. Both Shago and Kelly are in a way code heroes, who show us something about what it takes to live in a nightmarish world. But the novel focuses on Rojack, and as his bravery distinguishes him, his cowardice undoes him. Shago and Cherry die through magical process because of his cowardice. He never receives Kelly's demonic powers because he never dares quite as much as Kelly. The novel begins with Rojack's failure to be brave: he refuses the call of the moon, and "on that instant when I was too fearful to jump, something had quit me forever, that ability of my soul to die in its place, take failure, go down honorably" (208). Thus, when Deirdre tells him, late in the novel, that Deborah said he was a coward, he replies, "I think I am" (213).

Another aspect of Rojack's ambivalence, one that significantly vitiates his heroic qualities, is his possible insanity. Mailer pulls the reader into the reality of a psychotic world-view by recreating in Rojack the experience of a moral and psychological outlaw. This has valuable possibilities, for it may well be that to become more than one is, "to become a saint . . . one must dare insanity" (*PP*, 28). Insanity and the insights it offers may be for some the only path to salvation, at least in Mailer's terms.

But there must always be doubt as to whether Rojack's percep-

tions are visionary or insane. There is a tension and an ambivalence built into this novel, and into Mailer's philosophy expressed
in "The White Negro": if redemption and salvation are achieved
by casting off restraint and following the inner path which leads
to madness, a voyager can find himself at any time not renewed
but merely insane. And Rojack, if he is insane, may point not to
a way out of the morass of contemporary life, but to a way deeper
into chaos and confusion.

It should be evident that, in many ways, Mailer and Rojack
are similar. Both are intellectual celebrities, both share similar beliefs about the nature of the human psyche, both consider themselves protagonists on the battleground of human existence. More
specifically, both attack their wives, and both must thereafter navi-
gate their way through that fearful territory where psychosis makes
its home.

The essential difference is that Mailer has artistic distance.
Rojack is making a desperate effort to control his world, to exert
influence over it by symbolic, magical, and artistic action. Mailer,
as novelist, is in complete control of his world (and of Rojack's).
This is to say that Mailer's role in the universe of his novel is not
that of a heroic character forging his destiny, which is what Rojack
attempts to do, but rather that of the god or omnipotent being.
It is difficult, and for the purposes of this study perhaps fruitless,
to determine Mailer's personal stake in writing the book. It is possible that he might have been trying to make coherent, through
the structure of art, events that would otherwise remain chaotic
and incoherent. Or he could have been trying to work out in the
esthetic dimension impulses that might otherwise be forced to
emerge in social dimensions. Whatever his motivation, he brings
a controlling, esthetic power to bear upon the autobiographical
content of the novel which is not paralleled by Rojack's attempts
to control his own fate nor, one presumes, by Mailer's efforts to
shape his own life outside of this esthetic dimension.

If Mailer's treatment of and relationship to his narrator is ambivalent, however, even more ambivalent is his treatment of evil.
His inquiry uses a thoroughgoing symbolism, several characters
who function allegorically, and Rojack's individualized manner of
perceiving. The symbolism is most apparent in the use of serpents
and snakes in connection with three of the characters—Deborah,
Kelly, and Shago. In every instance the serpent represents the hid-

den and evil desires that Rojack perceives in them. Its most obvious use is on the Kelly-Mangaravidi coat of arms, where we find "2, 3, sable, serpent argent, crowned azure, vorant a child proper" above the motto: "Victoria in Caelo Terraquae" (209). The child of innocence, eaten by the serpent of evil, illustrates evil's "Victory in Heaven and on Earth."

This coat of arms has other significance. *An American Dream* is partially allegory, and Kelly and his daughter Deborah are personifications of evil. Kelly's power and rapacity seem to have no bounds, and his strength and influence seem to have been rewards for his daring foray into incest. Deborah, the object of his lust, is a child of the Devil; she was conceived in some hellish miasma after Kelly entreated the Devil:

> " 'Satan, if it takes your pitchfork up my gut, let me blast a child into this bitch!' And something happened, no sulphur, no brimstone, but Leonora and I met way down there in some bog, some place awful, and I felt something take hold in her. Some sick breath came right back out of her pious little mouth. 'What in *hell* have you done?' she screamed at me. . . . That was it. Deborah was conceived." (240)

Shago recognizes that in insulting Deborah he is "spitting in the face of the Devil" (189), a recognition amended by Rojack: "He was wrong. It was the Devil's daughter" (204). And, early in his narrative, Rojack reveals that his marriage to Deborah has been "a devil's contract" (18).

Yet these allegorical figures develop an ambiguity to the evil in the novel. Both Kellys, father and daughter, seem to go beyond good and evil; they violate conventional morality, but in Mailer's antinomian world, conventional morality might well be the Devil's handiwork. And Rojack, by murdering Deborah, also seems to go beyond good and evil. All three characters have redeeming, perhaps even heroic, virtues. Deborah is "more good and evil" than anyone else, so that Rojack can only think of her paradoxically as a "ministering angel (ministering devil)" (26). Kelly has the courage all others in the novel lack, even Rojack, and in Mailer's ethic, courage is the supreme virtue. Although he seems to be a caricature of the evil which is produced by, and in turn controls, American corporate capitalism, Kelly is also a rough sketch of a man who attempts to go beyond evil, a first hint of the new man who will evolve from the very brave. If we recall Mailer's simultaneous revulsion from and attraction to Croft in *The Naked and the Dead*, this ambiguous treatment of Kelly is not altogether surprising.[18]

Despite Mailer's symbology and use of allegorical figures, his concern with evil is existential. His characters struggle with the Devil, but the struggle is not convincing, for evil as an actual force is not a significant presence in the novel. A major element, however, is Rojack's coping with the feeling of evil. For evil to be a force in the world, it needs to be existent—indeed existent in some way beyond man's control; it must at times control him. Evil need not exist at all, however, for one to feel that it does. And if one has such a feeling—as Rojack does—then evil becomes a reality because it is existential. Man creates the specter which then haunts him. Thus throughout the novel the sense of evil arises not from Mailer's characterization of the Devil but from a color, a mood, a way to look at things and discover frightening aspects and motivations.

The evil is therefore closely linked to the psychotic element. The reader perceives evil because Rojack is preoccupied with it. It is almost always linked to dread, fear, or depression and is more of an attempt to categorize his experience than an affect on his experience.[19]

This evil ambience is best viewed in his sexual congress with Ruta immediately after the murder of Deborah. The encounter is related in theological terms, as a simultaneous raid on the Devil and entrance to the Lord. Except in terms of possible procreation, however, there is no difference between the anus and the vagina; the difference is all in Rojack's act of perception of one as the chapel of the Lord and the other as the hiding place of the Devil. Rojack is projecting onto the world what he perceives as reality. The relationship to psychosis is clear: evil is the prevailing tenor of Rojack's fantasy-world; its existence is dependent upon the psychological needs of Rojack and not upon the world. Mailer investigates not the causes of evil—which would be found in some analysis of Rojack's psyche and the traumas which created its needs and wishes—but the phenomenon of the apperception of evil. He shows us evil not as a constituent element of experience but as a created ambience that colors experience. Mailer recreates a mode of perception and experience.

This discussion has dealt with the manifest content of the novel.

There are, however, several levels on which this novel may be approached. On one level *An American Dream* is an attempt to recreate the "dream life of the nation" (*PP*, 38). This level complements those of the novel we have examined above—the recreation of the perceptions of the psychotic, and the inquiry into the existential nature of evil. There is, of course, a relationship between what the theologian calls "evil" and what the psychoanalyst calls "psychotic"; for Mailer, the dream life of America is the nightmare that manifests the psychotic elements which, though repressed, nevertheless color and direct American society and culture.

In *The Presidential Papers* Mailer states that "there is a subterranean river of untapped, ferocious, lonely and romantic desires, the concentration of ecstasy and violence which is the dream life of the nation" (*PP*, 38). He could scarcely have given a more succinct explanation of the title of his next novel. *An American Dream* is not *the* American dream; it is, rather, one of the variants. Central to Mailer's beliefs is that this particular version, ferocious, lonely, and romantic, expressed in a mixture of violence and ecstasy, is the core of the contemporary American experience. He tries to tell John F. Kennedy, in his book of advice for a President, that the old frontiers have indeed disappeared, and with them the old dreams. In order to understand and cope with contemporary America, one must come to grips with the dream-turned-nightmare that is the clue to our innermost needs and desires. America, as Mailer sees it, has embodied Yeats's prediction "That twenty centuries of stony sleep / Were vexed to nightmare by a rocking cradle."

An American Dream seeks both to explore that nightmare and to discover a way of dealing with it. The world it portrays is preeminently contemporary America. Its setting is urban, ranging from concrete jungles to slum tenements to the decadent and luxurious cloisters of the rich. At the end of the novel Rojack journeys away from New York, archetypical city, and to Las Vegas, which truly symbolizes the "dream life of the nation." Built in a desert where everything is controlled, the air is filtered and refrigerated, the light synthetic, and amusement and sustenance are found only in the clicking of dice, the flick of cards, and the snickering of chips. Las Vegas is the terrestrial counterpart of the "harbors of the moon," a spiritual and cultural wasteland. It has the eerie air of destruction and desolation which pervades bomb-torn cities and a country dying of spiritual blight.

The characters of the novel are all part of the American dream as well: the powerful millionaire; the decadent socialite; cops and robbers; mafiosi; the with-it spade; the hard-assed Southern girl who, though she's been around, still has a heart of gold; the Irish policeman, hard as nails but who "knows how to cry for the dirty polluted blood of all the world" (264); the Nazi who commits the desired sexual perversions; even Rojack, ex-politico and war hero who is now professor-philosopher-psychologist and television celebrity. To cap it all, John Fitzgerald Kennedy, the cinderella President, makes a guest appearance on the first page. The roster is endless: Mailer has collected all types who people the fantasy life of America and has assembled them in the novel. There are, significantly, no janitors to clean up this world, no salesmen to keep it going, no laborers to build it or turn out its goods. From the naturalistic world of *The Naked and the Dead*, populated as it was by characters from all strata of society, Mailer has moved toward a surrealistic world, populated by only those who might appear in the fantasies of the "real" Americans who made up his first novel.

Considering the fact that the American dream life is a "concentration of ecstasy and violence," it is not surprising that the action of the novel should consist of, or culminate in, killings and sexual climaxes. Of the latter, Rojack has four and imagines several others; of the former, he experiences three and moves backward and forward in time to encompass five others. All of this occurs in the short but intense span of three days.

Mailer's attitude toward this nightmare is ambivalent. The bulk of his critical writings and the thematic direction of his novels carry a dual point: the world we live in is a nightmare, one of the most savage and suffocating cultures ever created by man; on the other hand, this is our culture and it cannot be escaped, it must be faced honestly and with courage. Our salvation from the nightmare can be achieved only by recognizing and accepting the nightmare, thereby plumbing its depths and resolving the contradictions and traumas (to mix the political and psychological points of view Mailer favors) in order to move into a new and more fulfilling life.

The hope of the novel is that Rojack has gained something from his three-day excursion into the hidden recesses of his psyche and the dream life of America. He has succeeded and he has failed in his encounters, yet during the course of the three days recounted in the novel he has grown more than he has died. As the novel ends he is about to leave Las Vegas, the nadir of American society;

its emptiness and desolation resemble the picture of Hell he envisions after choosing "the Devil" in his intercourse with Ruta:

> I had come to the Devil a fraction too late, and nothing had been there to receive me. But I had a vision immediately after of a huge city in the desert, was it a place on the moon? For the colors had the unreal pastel of a plastic and the main street was flaming with light at five a.m. A million light bulbs lit the scene.   (46)

But Rojack decides to leave, after speaking to Cherry in Heaven—an episode that reinforces the reader's conviction that Rojack may indeed have gone into the cave of the psychotic. He leaves behind not only Las Vegas–Hell–the American Dream, but also the descent he has made into his psyche and the depths of the irrational. He sets off for Yucatan and Guatemala—Wallace Stevens' line about "actual, green, and point-blank Guatemala" comes to mind—to build a new life on the ground of his past experience. "In the morning, I was something like sane again, and packed the car, and started on the long trip to Guatemala and Yucatan" (270).

With the exception of his first long work, in which a young unpublished Mailer set out to write the Great American Novel, this book is his most ambitious. If *Barbary Shore* was an inquiry into the political sickness of modern times and *The Deer Park* an exhumation of American mores and their decadence, with the hint of a possible solution, *An American Dream* is nothing less than an attempt to grapple with the sickness delineated previously and to find new perceptual and ethical possibilities for modern man. The success, as well as the failure, of Mailer's bold attempt is ultimately to be measured by examining how successfully he has developed these possibilities.

In writing this novel, Mailer drew heavily upon the perspective he had developed in "The White Negro." Men have always needed to change their thought patterns, their reflexes, the very synapses of their nervous systems. The structure of a man's internal reality, never quite coextensive with the structure of reality, requires a constant modification of thought in order for the pattern of his action to approach the pattern of reality. And the twentieth century, with its speeded-up technology and air of apocalypse, has brought to a critical stage the necessity for a radical readjustment to reality.

In order to change the actions so that they are closer to reality,

man must make two adjustments. There must be a change of perception, so that the individual can break out of the stereotyped
patterns of perception he has learned and thereby find ways of
perceiving reality freshly, and there must be a change in ethics, so
that he can react to his novel perceptions with novel patterns of
behavior. My thesis is that Mailer has succeeded in the first realm,
opening the doors of perception, and failed in the second, the creation of a new ethic.

Mailer has opened the doors of perception insofar as Rojack
experiences in new modes. Man must always experience in some
mode or category; Kant had argued that in perceiving we are always ordering experience. The problem for Mailer is not how to
avoid doing so, for order is always a necessity, but rather how to
find new orders, so that we experience reality through the mode
and not just experience a superannuated mode itself. Though we
must channel our sensations, at least we can try to develop channels
that run deep and draw experience directly from the large sea of
reality.

Mailer has maintained that his new mode of perception would
be the fruit not of cognition but of direct experience, sensual,
physical, without conscious restraints. Thus Rojack casts off the
restraints of society and the internalized social restraints of his
superego and descends into the impulses of the id. He is uncon-
sciously (although since he is a professor of existential psychology,
one might say he must be doing so consciously) following the
great Freudian dictum for health: "Where there is id, there shall
be ego." He is creating a new self out of the primal that underlies
his old, insecure, and ineffective self. Rojack is different because
he senses and interprets differently from other characters, real or
fictional.

These differences seem to fall into three nonexclusive categories:
the magical, the experiential, and the verbal. The magical has
already been dealt with. Suffice it to say that Rojack's awareness of
a conjunction or correspondence between interior and exterior
reality leads to a perception fraught with symbolic value and
significance.

Secondly, there is an experiential dimension to Rojack's new
mode of perception. Not only does he discover new correspondences
and significances, but he experiences new senses and sensations
which can thereafter be made to correspond. The most striking
example of this enlargement of the experiential real of perception

is his sense of smell. Mailer has a greater awareness of smell than any other author who comes to mind, and the significance of his enlarging perception in this particular direction will be dealt with in the next chapter. It is important to realize that he is also increasing the awareness of his readers. The novel is permeated by smells: Deborah, "like the scent of a carnivore in a zoo. This last odor was fearful—it had the breath of burning rubber" (30); "her odor, that smell (with the white gloves off) of the wild boar in full rut, that hot odor from a gallery of the zoo, no . . . she smelled like a bank" (34). And Ruta, "one full draft of a heated sex which was full of the flower, full of earth, and with suspicion of one sly mouse slipping through the garden, a bit of fish in its teeth" (42), and later, "a thin high constipated smell (a smell which spoke of rocks and grease and the sewer-damp of wet stones in poor European alleys) came needling its way out of her" (43). Or Barney Kelly:

> A deep smell came off Kelly, a hint of a big foul cat, carnal as the meat on a butcher's block, and something else, some whiff of the icy rot and iodine in a piece of marine nerve left to bleach in the sand. With it all was that congregated odor of the wealthy, a mood within the nose of face powder, of perfumes which leave the turpentine of a witch's curse, the taste of pennies in the mouth, a whiff of the tomb.   (217)

The novel is perfumed—permeated—by the smell of musk and rut, the orgy beneath the surface of things, which promise renewal but also danger, dissolution, and mortality.

Nowhere can the perception we discover in Rojack be felt so clearly as in this sense of smell. Not only is the sensation new, alien to both modern literature and consciousness—for although we smell, we usually are not aware of so doing—but it is significant. The odors Rojack recognizes hold the key to the secrets of the characters that emit them.

Finally, smell is communicated in a new and daring language that helps open the gates which hold our perceptions in check. We can be most conscious of that which we categorize verbally. Words are like clips holding our floating sensations steadily under the microscope of our intelligence while we examine them. Mailer both puts the smells into words, isolating them from the immense body of experience into the realm of consciousness, and deals with them metaphorically, so that the reader cannot say "oh, just smells" but is struck by their *haeccitas* (to borrow Scotus' term), their "thisness." The precision of his similes, recognizing not only the earthy in Ruta's sex, but also the taint of fish rotting in a rodent's furry mouth, or of Kelly's animal smell with the hint of exposed, decaying nerve—this precision is Mailer's effort not only to communicate a new realm of experience but to delineate it so clearly that it will be learned and later utilized.

There are other experiential realms that Mailer makes accessible to his readers. The psychic artillery battle in the nightclub is an example of the magical, but it is also Mailer's attempt to illuminate the psychic confrontations which so many men engage in but which so seldom consciously come to the fore. Or, to deal with a more compelling example, he deals with sex more extensively than most writers, and this concern combines a clinical realism (Mailer does not omit offensive or unacceptable details) with a metaphorical lyricism that often shows the pitch of his large poetic gift. The "entrance of love" passage quoted earlier is an example. Despite his explicit portrayal of the sex act, Mailer's essential medium is metaphor. As a lover, Rojack is a bicycle rider, a diver on a cold winter day, an undersea explorer, himself, an urbane gentleman, a joyous birdhouse, a container for a balm of roses and saltwater and honey, a defenseless warrior. The flow of images is, to use Kenneth Burke's phrase, qualitative, governed by association rather than logic. The images grow out of each other and at the same time out of the act. The two strands are united in a passage of increasing lyrical intensity as Rojack imagines himself first as an actor, then as an actor in a scene, and finally as the actor and scene merged, the self and that outside the self merged in the implosion of unity. The parallel to the act of sex and mutual orgasm is exact.

Also, this emphasis on the magical has an effect on Mailer's verbal constructions. His description is dependent largely on metaphor and simile. Since the magical erases the distinction between the ideal and the real, Mailer's metaphors often begin to take on a life of their own. What begins as a way to describe a reality in imaginative terms becomes itself a reality. Thus Rojack feels like a diver and finds that this feeling runs away with him; the "like" is forgotten, and he is engaged in the underwater exploration of a "heavenly city." Orgasm, despite the image of the bird, is primarily the sensation of drowning, as the diver submits to the underground world he has discovered, and by dying dies into new life.

The expansion of metaphor so that the metaphor takes on more importance than its referent is a mark of Mailer's mature style. Instances of it abound: the Devil-God drama that Rojack immerses himself in with Ruta becomes far more important than the act of sex. It is as if the imaginative perception becomes the perception itself.[20] Since reality is dependent upon perception, the imaginative perception becomes reality. Even so small an example as the smell of Ruta or Kelly grows into a life of its own, occupied by mice and bits of flesh in one instance, by beach and sand and salt and protoplasm in the other.

But if this foray into new modes of perception is the book's greatest achievement, its largest drawback may be its failure to create a valid ethic to accompany the new perception. Ethics should provide a normative standard by which men determine which actions they should perform, and to perceive freshly should lead to fresh standards of action. The new ethic Mailer seeks to develop is an ethic of growth. It underlies his theological view of God and the Devil, it countenances the extremes of murder and sex, it influences his constantly changing style. The ethic of change is virtually the same as the ethic of Hip which Mailer described in "The White Negro." What validity and appeal it had in the earlier work, however, is compromised in this novel. Rojack's ethics and theology are not convincing, even though his perceptions are. It is difficult to take Rojack's views as a guide to action; it is even difficult to take Rojack seriously as a moral scout, a pioneer in the wastelands that surround constrictive contemporary morality. There is a satirical element to the characterization, and his exaggerations, his hyperbole, his absurd claims in the very first paragraph indicate that Mailer is sensitive to the ridiculous in the character he has created. Paul Bunyan, although fantastic, embodies the American dream as well; Rojack, also fantastic, embodies the sickness of the American nightmare without serving as a spiritual guide, in the way that Bunyan or the Alger heroes did to earlier generations of Americans seeking to cope with their environment. Rojack's actions seem rather the embodiment of Mailer's hangups; they are supremely illustrative of those national hangups which lead to violence, alienation, confusion, and anomie without redeeming ethical value. There is no doubt that, whatever his satirical view, Mailer does want to instruct his readers in how to live the good and brave life. But Rojack is in a futile embrace with *machismo*. He must consistently prove his masculinity, which Mailer regrettably manages to confuse with humanity, as his mentor Hemingway did before him. The two are not necessarily the same. Rojack constantly proves his masculinity with women; he admires the most ridiculous stereotypes of male chauvinism, the gangster and mafioso, the cop, the spade, the boxer, the whore with the heart of gold.

Insofar as Mailer has tried to create a new ethic, he has failed. His new morality seems specious, contrived, and predominantly infantile. Although there is therapeutic value in orgasm and the expression of repressed violence, a life of orgy and murder, sex and suicide seems to offer little hope even for mankind submerged in the nightmare world Mailer has consistently striven to portray.

Chapter VI

Why Are We in Vietnam?

The Dialectic of Authentic and

Inauthentic Existence

hy Are We in Vietnam?,[1] like the novels that preceded it, is concerned with modern life on both the individual and social levels. Mailer, examining the nature of American society and its social problems, focuses on a number of individuals who live within a microcosm of that society. To some extent this fifth novel is a reversal of the growing inward focus of the others; for the first time since *The Naked and the Dead* the forces of society seem more compelling and interesting than the characters who inhabit the universe of the novel.

At the center is an investigation of violence, which Mailer feels is central to an understanding of authenticity, American society, and even the mysteries of God and His relationship with the universe. The novel deals with three major types of violence: that of nature, the natural world, and authentic man; that of American corporate life and modern socioeconomic institutions; and that implicit in American mores, especially those which repress sexual drives.

Why Are We in Vietnam? is also a novel of initiation. Recreating a strange hunting trip into the wilds of Alaska, it follows and also parodies the archetypal myth of the hunt, in which the young hunter is initiated into the mysteries of nature, of his own being, and of the universe. It is in the tradition of Ishmael and the hunt for the great white whale; of Macomber and his short but happy life; and of the great bear hunt in the swamps of Yoknapatawpha County in Faulkner's "The Bear."

Why Are We in Vietnam? is the drug-induced reverie of a young Texan who, in the midst of a dinner celebrating his impending embarcation for Vietnam, recalls an Alaskan safari made several years earlier. Memories of the hunting trip are interspersed with commentary as the narrator and protagonist, D.J., reflects on the significance of his narration. He tells us how he went on the hunt

for bear with his father, Rusty; his best friend, Tex Hyde; two sub-
ordinates of his father, Pete and Bill; and Luke Fellinka, an experienced guide. While shooting bear and caribou, D.J. sees with
great clarity the competitive and corporate spirit that motivates his
father, and he loses all respect for Rusty. Becoming disenchanted
with both their hunting companions and the mechanical aids and
comforts that protect them from the wild, D.J. and Tex set out
alone to discover whatever the Alaskan wilderness has to teach
them. With a wolf and a bear and a moose as teachers, and with
a staggering display of the Northern lights arching overhead, the
two boys feel the pulse of the wild and in the process become men.
They then return to Texas, where two years later they have rejected
the sterility of their lives by enlisting in the military.

While in Alaska, D.J. is forced into a confrontation with the
wilderness which throws into sharp relief the background in which
he was raised: the world of upper-class Texas society, of corporation executives and their psychoanalyzed wives, of intense competition and sexually charged cocktail parties. "The Alaska air is real
message—it says don't bullshit, buster" (54). D.J.'s initiation consists of a set of voyages, deeper and deeper into the primitive
Alaskan heartland, America's last frontier, and further and further
into the primitive recesses of his own consciousness and the savage dreamlife of the American continent.

The novel's greatest weakness is D.J. himself. Though an acceptable novice for the great initiation, he is an unreliable and
unbelievable narrator.[2] Mailer intends an ambiguity in the narrative voice, an unreliability which he is at pains to underline: the
narrator is either D.J. (or his inner soul); or he is "a black-ass
cripple Spade and sending from Harlem" (208); or perhaps he is
even a transistor in God's rectum. To add to the ambiguity, even
if he is indeed D.J. he is narrating the events of the hunt while
stoned on marijuana. With the exception of Rojack in *An American Dream* and Mailer's own fictional persona in his "non-fiction,"
he has never created an acceptable narrator; his handling of first-
person narrative unreliability has none of the ease which marked
the fiction of James or Conrad.

Mailer lightens the burden of dealing with this weak narrator
when he has D.J. tell the reader that there is "*no such thing as a
totally false perception*" (8). I propose that the reader follow
D.J.'s insight and accept D.J.'s perceptions as having their basis
in truth. Thus I will ignore the possible subtleties of the narrator's

role and will accept D.J. as an adequate narrator, without referring to the black double who may stand behind him. To become involved in the ambiguities of D.J.'s role is to create more confusion while failing to generate more understanding.

Although *Why Are We in Vietnam?* is a novel of initiation, it is not an ordinary one. Knowing as we do Mailer's attitude toward the war in Vietnam (he was deeply opposed to it), it is hard to understand D.J.'s final action, which is to enlist in the armed services and fight in Vietnam. Mailer is in search of a hero, and every one of his characters provokes a comparison with the heroic. Although none is completely heroic, all of Mailer's other protagonists seem more so than D.J. at the close of the novel, seated at a nouveau riche banquet in the heart of Texas, cocky, seeking to dally in sex with his parents' middle-aged friends. He is becoming a part of that America which is the object of so much of Mailer's despair. D.J.'s initiation has, in some way, failed.

In order to understand him one might see him as a character similar to Thomas Mann's Hans Castorp in *The Magic Mountain*, who is in some ways equally unheroic. Like Castorp, D.J. is outwardly an ordinary young man from the economic upper stratum of society. He, too, has an opportunity to leave his environment for a voyage into the mountains, which are beyond the reaches of civilization and consequently dangerous. Both Castorp and D.J. undergo similar experiences: out of an inner need each explores the vastness of the world about him and, more important, the world within him. In so doing, each leaves behind society, civilization, friends, and parents, so that each is without external guidance and even, at times, without reference. The result of this hermetic experience is what Mann calls *Steigerung*, or heightening. Sealed off from his daily life, each character finds his perceptions and insights heightened beyond what could normally be expected from him. This heightening enables the character to have insights which make him wise and heroic, at least as long as he remains in his hermetic environment.

Removing an ordinary person from his normal situation and setting him in an hermetic existence in which he has visions, intimations, and heroic qualities of which he ordinarily would be incapable creates a situation rich in the possibilities of irony. The protagonist may be at once dull and wise, cowardly and heroic, ordinary and vatic. So is Hans Castorp, and so, it appears, is D.J. The parallel between the two even extends to the moment at which

the hermetic experience must end, at which point both protagonists return to society and go off to one of its foolish wars. The
situation of both is ironic here too, for although their enlistment
is precisely what one would expect from a German Consul's grand-
son and a Texas executive's son, the reader can imagine deeper
motivations and insights behind the enlistment, motivations resulting from the period of *Steigerung*. The vision and heroism may be
beclouded, but they can never be forgotten.

Irony, then, is the controlling factor in the novel. Like Mann
and most other great ironists, Mailer couples his irony to its hand-
maidens, satire and paradox (for all three depend upon the simultaneous existence of more than one level of awareness). Irony has
always been important to Mailer's vision. It is the converse of the
romantic view he propounded in "The White Negro." For if Mailer
has great hopes for mankind, large dreams for the future, and a
deep belief in human goodness, he also has a clear vision of evil,
human frailty, and social injustice. He is a combination of dreamer
and realist; the clash between his romantic view of man and his
despairing and often desperate view of society makes him comfort-
able writing in the ironic mode. In *Why Are We in Vietnam?*
Mailer's usual posture is ironic, for only through irony can he reconcile the two different poles of his vision, his despair at society
and his belief in human potential. He vents his despair in many
cases by becoming satiric, ridiculing the forces that debase and destroy the humane qualities of modern existence.

D.J. must cope with two major forces, which correspond to the
two poles of Mailer's vision. One is the violence of the natural
world—a beneficial force that leads to growth and authenticity.
The second force is the violence of American civilization, which
can be broken down into the violence of American corporate life
and the violence of American mores. This violence is destructive
and malicious; it grinds down the individual, robbing him of his
individuality and freedom and denying him the possibility of satisfaction or fulfillment. The novel seeks to differentiate between
these two major forms of violence; natural violence it regards as
authentic, social violence as inauthentic.

Mailer sets the novel in Alaska to emphasize the authentic violence in nature and in natural man. The air of the last frontier,
which says "don't bullshit, buster" (54) to D.J., enables him to
face and recognize what is natural by leaving behind the distor-

tions created by society which tend to hide, pervert, and repress the primitive within men. In his hermetic environment D.J. is about to plunge into the secrets the hipster had discovered before him.

It is on the beginning of the hunt, when Tex shoots a wolf and he and D.J. drink of its blood, that D.J. realizes he is "up tight with the essential animal insanity of things" (70). The lesson is reinforced when he and Rusty must decide whether they should go down into a hollow after a wounded grizzly bear: "No man cell in him can now forget that if the center of things is insane, it is insane with force, heuuuuuu goes the bellow of the grizzer in the salt on his meat and sorrow" (143). The primitive, animal nature of things is both insane and forceful; it cannot be categorized rationally, operates under its own impulses, which cannot be organized into laws, and has its own intrinsic force as its justification.[3]

Men are animals; they too partake of the insane forces at the heart of things. D.J. feels the wolf's blood begin to rise inside him when he walks up to the bullet-ridden carcass of a bear: "some giant wolf in D.J.'s heart, some prehistoric wolf all eight feet big began to sit . . . in his blood, beasty audience, in his blood" (119). Later, D.J. kills a bear and becomes an integral part of the natural order of things. His reversion to the primitive within himself is revealed most clearly when, near the close of the novel, he and Tex fare into the wilderness unarmed and encounter a wolf. The force that emanates from the wolf and the forces that emanate from the boys engage each other in a mad, violent ballet, "Two waves of murder, human and animal, meet across the snow in a charge as fantastic and beautiful as Alexander Nevsky" (181). The newly discovered power in the boys overcomes that of the wolf, who slinks off in defeat.

If nature and men in their primal nature are violent, so is God, the transcendent yet limited being. He, too, is essentially animal, insane, and beastly:

> The lights were saying that there was something up here, and it was really here, yeah God was here, and He was real and no man was He, but a beast, some beast of a giant jaw and cavernous mouth with a full cave's breath and fangs, and secret call: come to me.   (202)

"For God was a beast, not a man, and God said, 'Go out and kill' " (203). This is D.J.'s discovery in the wilderness, and it forms a major part of his initiation. One of the great truths of existence is that every human being, every being, even God, has at the core the insanity and force of the primitive wild.

D.J. learns this again and again on the safari in Alaska. He feels the hatred of the dying wolf and the hatred of that other wolf they meet in psychic battle across the snow. He watches a fight between an eagle and a wolf, and another between a fox and a squirrel. Rusty recounts a fight he saw between an eagle and a deer. All around D.J. there is struggle and violence. That many of the characters retreat in fear and dread from the wilderness or go into it only on their own terms are signs of their moral decay.

The most shattering instance of natural violence in this violent novel is the episode in which D.J. and Tex watch in fascination as a grizzly bear kills and rips open a young caribou, not for sustenance or protection, but for the brutal joy of killing. This passage is an excellent instance of Mailer's facility for combining an almost clinical realism—the savage murder of the caribou—with a lyricism that endows events with enormous significance. The agent that makes this combination possible is Mailer's colloquial style, rooted in a language close to the reality of experience and imbued with the natural poetry of all vigorous and primitive languages:

> except for one calf who stumble in fright and griz right down on young beast and with one paw at the neck and the other on the flank, goes in with mouth open to rip her belly and get the living blood and taste of live entrail, whatever that may be, whatever taste to have fat-ass Grizzer so avid ass for it, and when calf breaks loose half for an instant, pain springing it near to free, why, Grizzer flips her down again and having had his taste of her live, kills her now by slamming his teeth through the big muscles of her back right through to the spine and vertebrae which he crunches in two closing his big mouth and she breaks like a stick of wood and is there lifeless and her death goes out over the ridge and slips into the bowl and the afternoon takes a turn and is different having just passed through one of those unseen locks of the day, everything is altered, not saying how. (192)

The violence of nature can be described in many ways. It derives from the struggle for survival, for struggle has always been a concomitant, latent or actual, of existence. It derives from the essential inhospitality, or at least lack of hospitality, of the natural world, in which all creatures must find sustenance for survival, protect themselves from destruction, and face the inevitability of death. For Mailer the violence of the natural world is a result of the basic conflict that underlies all existence. This conflict, which appears as the god-devil dichotomy of several of his earlier works— God exists "as a warring element in a divided universe" (*AM*, 380)—is the record of the growth of the human, and the divine, soul. Finally, natural violence is an authentic activity because it is the basis for existence; risk, danger, violence, and death are integral constituents of all life.

Yet while the individual must try to live authentically, he is doomed to failure by the nature of American society. Mailer believes that we must:

> rescue civilization from the pit and plague of its bedding, that gutted swinish foul old bedding on which two centuries of imperialism, high finance, moral hypocrisy and horror have lain. . . . Apocalypse or debauch is upon us. And we are close to dead. There are faces and bodies like gorged maggots on the dance floor, on the highway, in the city, in the stadium; they are a host of chemical machines who swallow the product of chemical factories, aspirin, perservatives, stimulant, relaxant, and breathe out their chemical wastes into a polluted air. The sense of a long last night over civilization is back again; it has perhaps not been here so intensely in thirty years, not since the Nazis were prospering, but it is coming back.
>
> Well, it has been the continuing obsession of this writer that the world is entering a time of plague.   (*C&C*, 2)

The bulk of Mailer's nonfiction presents the world in this light; plague, sickness and decay are the operative principles in modern society, and they can be clearly seen if only the phenomena of contemporary society are examined. America today destroys the possibility for authenticity; it is "fearful, half mad, inauthentic" (*C&C*, 143). Dread is stifled and mystery is suppressed; human needs and desires are denied; and death is carefully avoided. Caught in a network of social forces, modern men have little hope of freeing themselves to engage the mysteries of their own existences, and thereby achieve an authentic existence:

> The liver goes flat, D.J. would assure you, whenever some
> scent meets its deodorant, or an herb is fed with aspirin.
> Pretty literary for adolescent out hunting with Paw? Go
> fuck, D.J.'s got his purchase on the big thing—genius—
> and he know this: you deaden a mystery and your liver
> goes to shit.   (93-94)

Two things, above all, deaden the mysteries of life: contemporary
socioeconomic institutions, especially the giant corporation, and
the repression of natural drives, especially sexual ones, which is
demanded by American mores. The violence and sexuality that
men have in their hearts—authentic emotions which reveal their
own, human conditions—are repressed, deflected, and sublimated.
But these energies cannot be contained, and if they are not allowed
a natural expression, they will appear in the form of institution-
alized violence and a perverted sexual violence.

D.J.'s father, Rusty, whose full name is Rutherford David
Jethroe Jellicoe Jethroe, is a quintessential distillation of the corporate spirit. He has a competitive business mind and a totalitarian
spirit; he funnels all his energy into amassing of profits, thus denying himself and others the energy and concern needed for growth;
and he is a rabid nationalist and racist. Rusty and his colleagues
anxiously seek a fifty-million-dollar contract to design a waste disposal system for astronauts; they wax jubilant over cigarette filters
that cause cancer. Rusty himself belongs to dozens of clubs and
organizations, the list of which reveals his life and its limitations
just as the list of the contents of Babbitt's jumbled pockets revealed
his some four decades earlier. But Rusty, although he is far more
successful in the business world than Babbitt, appears to have sunk
deeper into the mire of American life. The freeways, ubiquitous
plastics, and fawning psychoanalysts of Dallas are a less likely
cradle for rebirth than even the crass commercialism of Zenith.
And Rusty, unlike Babbitt, is in thrall to a system which he does
not admire and which compels his respect only because he lives in
fear of it.

"Rusty's a competitive prick, you know" (39). He is competition
incarnate; his is the modern capitalistic spirit. He tells D.J., "You
got to be a nut about competition. You got to be so dominated by
a desire to win . . ." (41). Rusty's intense desire is a bastardiza-
tion of the natural urge to test oneself against the force of the
world, to build the self by engaging and even defeating the world
outside the self. Rusty is competitive, but he competes only in a

rigged game. Afraid of real struggle, terrified of defeat or death, he will not engage his enemy unless he is sure he can overwhelm him. D.J. recalls that when his father could not tackle him in a backyard football scrimmage, Rusty took advantage of a moment of compassion on his son's part to take a large bite out of his ass. The game then proceeded with Rusty tackling the formerly elusive but now crippled D.J. again and again. This is how Rusty proves his masculinity to himself and to his son. "Chap Five" (the book is divided into "Chaps," which contain the germ of the narrative, and "Intro Beeps," which attempt to reproduce D.J.'s stream of consciousness) is devoted solely to a description of the guns carried by the hunting party. It reveals that the fear at the heart of the American consciousness, a fear that requires an overabundance of firepower before it can confront the wild. Pete, in his fear, buys the biggest gun he can find and carries this weapon, entirely unsuited to the hunt, into the Alaskan wilds as his emotional crutch. Bill is interested neither in guns nor in hunting, but he is totally absorbed in the technical aspects of firepower. And Rusty enters the wilderness with five rifles, only one of which is needed. Rusty's insight into his own fear is also an insight into the fear that dictates American policy in Southeast Asia and throughout the world. Since he represents the corporate establishment, his type of hunt is the type of war favored by the military and industrial leadership in this country:

> But I like the feeling that if I miss a vital area I still can count on the big impact knocking them down, killing them by the total impact, shock! it's like aerial bombardment in the last Big War . . . you don't pinpoint vital areas in a city, you blot it all out, you bury it deep in fire, shit, and fury. (85)

Mailer is not categorically opposed to war. He feels that war can give men an opportunity to encounter a basic human condition, in which an individual must call upon his deepest resources in order to survive, and in which he is always conscious of his own death. Indeed, if we recall "The White Negro," we see that Mailer believes all life is war, and that war is *the* human condition. But the kind of war Rusty describes does not involve dread or the engagement of death; it avoids both. It is simply slaughter. Far from ennobling, it debases; and instead of leading to authenticity it denies all access to authentic existence.

Rusty exemplifies another truth about the corporate establishment: he will go to any length of dishonesty rather than reveal the unpleasant truth about his actions and motives. When Rusty and D.J. set off alone to find a bear, a feeling of love and solidarity grows between them. Together they are facing the wilderness. But this closeness is destroyed when, at the end of the hunt, Rusty claims their bagged grizzly as his own trophy. D.J.—who shot more accurately, shot twice, and showed more courage and presence than his father—actually deserved the credit for the kill. But Rusty lies about the killing in order to appear successful when he returns to the corporate world. Rusty's tendency to cover up truth when it is painful or threatening is also revealed when, during the closeness of the hunt, he recounts a terrifying scene he once witnessed. He saw an eagle wound a deer and then proceed to torture it, causing obvious pain without inflicting death. Then Rusty draws an obvious parallel:

> It got me so upset to recognize that E Pluribus Unum is in the hands of an eagle that I almost wrote an open letter to the Congress of America. Can you imagine your daddy getting that ape shit? But I think it's a secret crime that America, which is the greatest nation ever lived, better read a lot of history to see how shit-and-sure a proposition that is, is nonetheless represented, even symbolized by an eagle, the most miserable of scavengers, worse than the crow.   (133)

Rusty then avoids the obvious, which is that America's symbol is appropriate, that it accurately symbolizes a rapacious and scavenging nation.

Later in the novel the eagle theme is repeated. D.J. and Tex watch "E Pluribus, old man Eagle fuck" (182) battle a wolf. Although the fight ends unresolved, it is startlingly plain to D.J. that "death stood out in those wings" (182). Mailer emphasizes the rapacity of the American military-industrial complex and the fact that American society steadfastly closes its eyes to its own greed and violence. His criticisms go farther: contemporary American institutions, when faced with the effect of their actions, try to disclaim responsibility. Frightened of consequences, American industry, in the person of Pete, wishes to avoid taking any responsibility for the caribou it has wounded, first asking if it will be all right, then shifting the subject, and finally trying to convince Luke that the hunting party need not follow the wounded beast (95).

M.A. (for "Medium Asshole" and perhaps also Managerial Assistant) Pete and M.A. Bill reveal the lower echelons of corporate life. Frightened, fawning, they are on the make and obsessed with succeeding in the corporate game. They despair not over the states of their souls but over committing faux pas:

> Rusty's got to produce something big enough for his boys, M.A. 1 and M.A. 2, to say you're right, Rusty, and with an easy harmonious concordium of voice, a choir of Texas asspurring where the yeah boss you go right ahead and kick my Nigger ass gets a Texas hum. For then corporate power is cooking in Rusty's veins.   (53)

Pete and Bill are yes-men. Mailer implies that the American nightmare, which has led to our involvement in Vietnam, is as dependent upon their quiescent acceptance of its coming as it is upon the frightening competitive spirit represented by Rusty and the corporation for which he works.

Mailer's scorn for the corporate establishment runs deep. The hunt that dominates the novel is a time-honored activity in which a man can face himself, his world, and his god. But there is no chance that the three corporate executives, Rusty, Bill, and Pete, will face anything on this hunt. Overarmed, protected, and coddled, they find their game by helicopter and use this technological marvel to scare their prey within shooting distance. This is not an idle pursuit with little effect on the world. In their weakness these representatives of the corporate establishment manage to disrupt the entire balance of nature. Luke complains that no one can understand the bears any longer, that no one can even find them, and that the Alaskan wilderness is being polluted by gas fumes, noise, and the fearful envoys of civilization. But even Luke succumbs to Rusty's corporate magnetism, and when the two boys want to find communion with the wild, they are forced to leave behind their party, guide, and civilized trappings. Even then, in the heart of the last vast wilderness on the American continent, the sink into which all of America's primitive urges flow, they cannot escape the tawdry industrial world: "Then they hear the helicopter. Man conceived of fucking in order to get fucked. There is no doubt about that" (185). There is, of course, a parallel between this corporate invasion of the wilderness and the American military presence in Vietnam. The excesses of Rusty's safari—helicopters, superfluous firepower, lack of respect for the enemy—are precise counterparts of the excesses of the Vietnamese War.

Rusty's betrayal of his son's confidence when he in his pride lays claim to the bear they both have shot is symbolic of the heedlessness and rapacity of the corporate establishment. In *Cannibals and Christians*, the book antecedent to *Why Are We in Vietnam?*, Mailer examines the sickness at the heart of American society. In the war in Vietnam, the death of the cities, and the triumph of mediocrity in politics and the media, Mailer sees the malign tumors that herald the cancer which will destroy us. When Rusty greedily claims the bear as his, D.J. arrives at an ultimate alienation. "Whew. Final end of love of one son for one father" (147). Divorced from his progeny and his only possible hope for redemption, it is clear that Rusty's cowardice and greed have doomed him to a frustrated, inauthentic, corporate existence. He has destroyed all possibility he will ever escape from the unsatisfying corporate world of Dallas.

Mailer's concern with institutional violence has been evident in each of his novels. Concurrent with this has been his concern with the repressive nature of American mores. What cannot be controlled by the self-interested force of American institutions can be controlled by the elaborate system of taboos which has developed in conjunction with the capitalistic state. Each of Mailer's novels has made a foray into previously forbidden areas of sexuality: they have illuminated areas of human motivation and action which have in the past been left unmentioned and unexplained, they have suggested that these areas are essential to an understanding of human existence, and they have pointed out that many personal and social evils are the direct consequence of the repression of natural sexuality.

American society is repressive, as Mailer sees it. Instead of acknowledging the violent and libidinal needs of human beings, it has tended to deny these needs, forcing life into inauthentic patterns. "The White Negro" emphasized this dehumanization of modern life and suggested that redemption could be found in an embrace of the violence and sexuality which men need but society denies. Living close to death in a continual round of violence and orgasm (like Rojack in *An American Dream*) can lead to authentic experience; ignoring death, violence, and orgasm leads to the frustration of many deep human needs, to sublimation, and eventually to great cruelty and the need for self-immolation.

Owing to the oppressiveness of American mores, sexual needs are suppressed and eventually reemerge in perverse sexual desires. These perversions do not adequately fulfill sexual desires because they only displace sexual energies without satisfying deeper libidinal needs. The result of this sublimation and perversion is that the American populace is in great need of sexual fulfillment but impeded from ever achieving it. The level of frustration rises continually; this leads to more perversion, which in turn leads to more frustration. Eventually, this frustrated energy is released in a blind and unsatisfying violence that often ends in domination or destruction.

In the course of his monologue D.J. informs the reader that he has indulged in sexual perversions of all sorts—necrophilia, narcissism, masturbation (which Mailer regards as perverse); he often alludes to homosexual fantasies and discusses his heterosexual conquests. His love life is essentially unsatisfying, however, because there is no love in it, merely conquests. Perhaps the most obvious example of his frustration and lack of sexual release is in this description he gives in "Chap Nine":

> Some tooth and cunt hostesses are closet fucks. . . . Well, when fucking these mad insane ones, D.J. here to advise, get in fast, get out fast, cause they greedy fiends. This ain't young cunt from which you cop the goods—this is used cunt, burnt meat, cliff-hanging menopause types which can't get rid of the poisons by any hole but the pussy hole. And the tooth and cunters are converting their schizophrenia into cancer juice for you.   (155-156)

A lack of sufficient love and an inability to find a satisfactory release for their erotic tension is responsible for the condition of these frightening women. They use sexual intercourse as a battlefield, hoping to live with their frustrations by converting them into poisons that will destroy the enemy, their sexual partner. For them sex means neither sharing nor building love; it means momentary satisfaction and an opportunity to dominate or destroy.

The novel is a gallery of sexual freaks, all of whom receive the grotesque treatment urged by Mailer's scorn. D.J.'s mother, Hallie, leads her husband around by adroit use of her sex. As D.J. realizes when he listens to the current of her desires rather than her powdered and spiffy words, under her fine womanly façade is a love of filth, an ability to use sex for profit and degradation, and an intense urge to compete. Although Rusty is "the most competitive prick there is" (38), Hallie forces him to submit to her will. Through adroit use of threats to his masculinity, and by making him a cuckold, Hallie has struck at the weakest part of Rusty's character, his deep sense of sexual inadequacy. Superficially she seems to be an elegant lady, but D.J. penetrates her façade and in the whole of "Chap Two" presents the psychological reality that underlies appearances: "A Southern lady, she's as elegant as an oyster with powder on its ass, she don't talk that way, she just thinks that way" (22). Hallie is, beneath her polished veneer, a castrating and domineering female.

Mailer also satirizes Tex Hyde's mother, a hard, lean, joyless woman. Bred through fifty generations of dirt shacks, she is thin and stringy. Her only allure to her husband is her grasping "secret beautiful snap of a pussy" (165). Gottfried "Gutsy" Hyde is an undertaker who will "grope you silly" (164). He rubs against anything which moves and immediately ejaculates; "Gutsy has come an average of eight to ten times a day, seven days a week for forty plus years" (164). This strange pair is wed, the lean and stringy scion of the dirt who clasps tight to whatever enters her; and the energetic dynamo who stokes his fires from anything he encounters, in his enthusiasm conquering everything in sight, living or dead. Out of this marriage between the joyless tradition of the land and the unsatisfied pervert who lusts after excess issues Tex Hyde. Mailer apparently intends an allegory here, with Tex representing both Texas and its most important contemporary son, Lyndon B. Johnson (In addition, Gutsy's energetic sexuality and his wife's lean hardness seem, to me, caricatures of Johnson and his wife, Lady Bird). By extension, this son of niggardliness and rapacity represents contemporary America.

D.J. and his friend Tex are caught up in this perverse sexual world. They have intercourse with the same girl, use oral and anal entrance, make it with their parents' friends, find physical release in sixty-second intercourse and fellatio. There is no hint of the salvation sex may bring, the salvation brought to Rojack in *An American Dream* and, temporarily, to Charley Eitel in *The Deer Park*. The boys are caught up in a world as incestuous and perverse as the boarding house of *Barbary Shore*, though they live not in the crowded borough of Brooklyn but in the rich mansions of Dallas.

In "The White Negro" Mailer, discussing sublimation, alluded to Freud's hypothesis that society, which exists on the basis of repression of natural instincts, faces potential destruction as individuals who encounter heightened frustration from unsatisfactory sublimation seek to fulfill their needs in any possible way. The sexual sphere, according to Freud and to Mailer, is the one in which the top is most likely to blow off. But in the world of this novel no one ever achieves an apocalyptic orgasm; no one ever finds that society must be overthrown in order for men to achieve sexual satisfaction. Society, as the novel portrays it, is still at a stage of sickness in which perversion reigns and competition supplants love. The sexual drives of individuals are repressed, and libidinal energy is turning inward, creating a sort of cancer as the cells of the body destroy themselves.[4]

The sexuality of the novel grows out of the ubiquitous frustration of the characters. Hallie is sexually frustrated, as her session with her analyst makes clear. Rusty is frustrated with his wife, his son, and his performance as a man, both on the hunt and in the corporation. Gutsy Hyde, although supercharged, is frustrated, and so is his wife. And Medium Assholes Pete and Bill are frustrated.

> Frustration makes you more telepathic because it makes you more electric. Up to a point, Poindexter, after that dielectric, apathetic, insulated, you ass, cause to be telepathic while frustrated is to be burned on a charged wire. . . . After the bomb comes apathy.   (152-153)

Frustration eventually leads to apathy, and apathy leads men to surrender control over their lives and embrace the totalitarian horrors that threaten to inundate civilization. Apathetic men permit and demand the "cold murderous liquidations of the totalitarian state" (*AM*, 357). The ultimate end of apathy is a desire for apocalyptic destruction, in which the apathetic can destroy the agony that underlies their apathy by destroying the causes of their agony, themselves and other human beings. Because apathy will not allow *engagement*, it is identical with inauthentic experience. Apathy is a state in which experience is rigorously structured to eliminate authentic emotions and actions.

It is significant, as we have mentioned, that the central action of the novel is a hunt in the wilds of Alaska. The myth of the hunt is one of the great archetypes; it has served for many societies as the supreme rite of initiation. It is the vehicle by which the young first encounter the wild, the uncontained state of nature so different from the ordered community in which they have lived their childhood. The hunter must face a hostile environment; his prey in the hunt must be almost his equal. The hunter hopes to return with a trophy, in the process gaining knowledge, skill, and confidence. The hunt is essentially a contest for mastery between man and the forces of his environment, wherein he must conquer and kill his prey or die in the process. The hunt is an initiation not only into the world of nature, but also into the mysteries of life. It is a ritualization of the engagement with death.

Mailer uses the hunt in precisely this manner. It is an initiation for D.J. into the mysteries of life and death. Foremost, it is his first encounter with dread. "D.J. is up tight with the concept of dread" (34). The root of dread is in the consciousness of death. Death defines life, being its opposite, and so it is necessary to contemplate death in order to live an authentic life. But mortality also suspends life above an infinite void, and threatens to engulf it in meaninglessness. D.J. suggests that the possible explanation for "Herr Dread" (35) can be found in conception; if man is created, a ghost come from nothing, then he must realize that to nothing he will return.

It is on the hunt that D.J. gets his first taste of dread. He has made his first kill, a mountain goat, and lies in bed thinking about it. He feels the exploding heart of the dying goat, and "got one breath of the sense of that *force* up in the North . . . and dived back to the bed, his sixteen-year-old heart racing through the first spooks of an encounter with Herr Dread" (102). And in a central passage of the novel D.J. comes face to face with the essence of the hunt when he and Rusty follow the grizzly's trail:

> And D.J. breathes death—first time in his life—and the sides of the trail slam onto his heart like the jaws of a vise cause the grizzer could come erupting out of the brush . . . it's death D.J.'s breathing, it comes like attack of vertigo when stepping into dark and smelling pig shit, that's what death smells to him, own pig shit smell, terrible fear right out of his lungs and pores: and back of fear . . . is crazy-ass murder, cause D.J. for the first time in his life is hip to the hole of his center which is slippery desire to turn his gun and blast a shot into Rusty's fat fuck face. (136)

D.J. faces death, accepts its dangers, and overcomes his fear. He dedicates himself to the hunt.

The strange substitution of Rusty for the bear as the object of D.J.'s hunt is the resolution of the problem of natural and unnatural violence discussed earlier. Rusty and his assistants, Bill and Pete, are symbolic of unnatural violence. They refuse to face death and attack the wilderness with little sensitivity, almost no skill, and a maximum of firepower. For them, "there's just nothing to do with Mr. Anxiety but carry him around in place of Herr Dread" (92). Afraid of death and authenticity, they sublimate their primal urges along corporate paths, and live with anxiety rather than dread. Whereas dread arises out of the mysteries of life and death, anxiety arises out of the peripheral concerns that these men have made central: success, approbation, and the rewards they hope to gain from their corporate existence. D.J.'s Oedipal hate is intensified because he realizes not only that "the face of his father is a madman ass, a power which wishes to beat him to death" (137), but also that he cannot triumph simply by defeating his father and taking his place. To be like Rusty, like modern America, is to be condemned to slow meaningless spiritual death:

> If D.J. wouldn't take to pot at family dinners he might not have such a Fyodor Kierk kind of dread looking into Big Daddy's chasm and tomb. But that dread's out there, man. Because Rusty is also the highest grade of asshole made in America and so suggests D.J.'s future: success will stimulate you to suffocate.   (37)

D.J.'s hate for his father is to a large extent his rejection of the success-oriented American dream, which embodies a lust for money and power and demotes sex to necessary perversion.

This much D.J. learns on the hunt with his father and Luke. But the hunt cannot suffice for his initiation, as he and we learn. He had hoped to see "how Rusty shapes up in a contest against a man who is not an asshole—to wit, Mr. Luke Fellinka" (38). But Luke, despite his early domination of Rusty, succumbs to the corporation-dominated society of which Rusty is an envoy. It is not Rusty's superior strength or will but the unavoidable pressures of civilization which urge Luke to forget the wild and turn the safari into a helicopter derby. His fall from grace means that if D.J. is to learn what the wild has to teach, he must go into it alone, or at least with only Tex, his peer, to accompany him. So D.J. and

Tex, on their own initiative, reconstitute what has always been the
core of the hunt, the single combat between the initiate and nature, without father, guide, or even weapon.

The aim of their solitary safari is to get rid of the "general state
of mixed shit" (175). Both boys realize that they are filled with
this "mixed shit," that their lives are neither pure nor authentic.
They must purge themselves of the extraneous elements that have
crept into their natures during the years—the neuroses of their
parents, the absurd demands of their society, and the corrupting influence of their peers. Tex "gets the purification ceremony straight
in his head": they will go further into the wild with no external
aids, for "they each know . . . that this is how you get the fear,
shit, disgust, and mixed shit tapeworm out of fucked-up guts and
overcharged nerves" (175–176). Their decision resembles Ike's
decision to abandon his rifle in *The Bear*. Like him, they set off
and leave behind their provisions and rifles. "Man, they got some
of that mixed shit out of them already. About the time they cache
all belongings, they own clean fear now, cause they going to live
off the land" (176).

So they set off into the heart of "God's attic" (180). The novel
has moved slowly up to this point; suddenly, the pace quickens.
The two boys are observers of one natural phenomenon after another. They encounter the wolf discussed earlier and beat it down
in a battle of wills which flashes across the frozen tundra. They
observe an eagle and his tantalizing confrontation with the wolf.
They laugh as a squirrel escapes from a fox. They encounter a
grizzly bear, and then watch him kill and disembowel a young
caribou. And finally, just as the sun is setting, they see a moose
standing in the last light, glazed bloody on one side by the vanish-
ing sun and silver on the other by the rising moon. Watching these
manifestations of the natural world, they face dread squarely.
"Man, it's terrifying to be free of mixed shit" (184).

In this state they too become natural beings, "our two little hunt
boys, Killer I and Killer II" (186). But an interlude of boyish
horseplay is interrupted by the return of their dread; they realize
that they are in the presence of something very like God. He is the
"cannibal Emperor of Nature's Psyche," a trinity composed of
"(1) the King of the Mountain Peak M.E.F. shit, (2) Mr. Awe
and (3) Mr. Dread" (186). In the presence of this Emperor "they
alone, man, you dig? why, they just dug, they all *alone*, it's a fright
wig" (187). Alone in the wilderness these two boys confront the

dread which results from living close to death; they stand in awe of the overwhelming power and violence of the natural world; and they find themselves bombarded by an equivalent power and violence which comes from within men. The M.E.F. is "the undiscovered magnetic-electro fief of the dream" (170): it is the complex of forces and desires that have never been allowed to surface, because of suppression, and are encountered only in the deeps of dream. All the natural desires that are denied work themselves out ultimately in dreams. The Arctic Circle, the Brooks Range, turns out to be a "parabolic receptor" (117) which receives all the dreams of the American continent, the dreams of the lonely, the frustrated, the bored, the unhappy. Amid the wilds of unexplored Alaska, the boys discover that force and violence are not only around them but within them and all men. The power of these psychic vibrations is an important part of the tripartite Godhead. Thus D.J. sees the universe as Mailer does, dominated by force and death; he too sees God as similar to man, compounded of dread, awe, and force.

The boys find God in their wilderness: "He was real and no man was He, but a beast, some beast of a giant jaw and cavernous mouth with a full cave's breath and fangs, and secret call: come to me" (102).[5] D.J. and Tex are caught up in their awareness of this powerful beast-God. His forceful call urges the boys to struggle with each other, to enter into a homosexual embrace from which but one can emerge the victor. The urge is strong. The novel reaches its peak in a two-page sentence, as D.J. and Tex feel the need for buggery and mastery, each of the other; they discover that beneath their friendship lies enmity and the call of the beast-God: "Yeah, now it was there, murder between them under all friendship, for God was a beast, not a man, and God said, 'Go out and kill—fulfill my will, go and kill'" (203). Held in the grip of their lust and fear, they are saved when the Northern lights suddenly shift; some electrical charge from the M.E.F., that receiver of the psychic charges which emanate from the dream life of the frustrated continent, lights up the Arctic sky and shifts the direction of the murder in their souls: "something off in the radiance of the North went into them, and owned their fear, some communion of telepathies and new powers, and they were twins, never to be near as lovers again, but killer brothers, owned by something, prince of darkness, lord of light, they did not know" (204). Surrounded by the Northern lights and the intensity of their desires, the two complete the rite of initiation by cutting their fingers and mixing their blood. They become blood brothers, protected from their fierce desire for one another by their greater allegiance to "the deep beast whispering Fulfill my will, go forth and kill" (204).[6] Finally they return to camp and rejoin the others, who still have "the same specific mix of mixed old shit" (204).

D.J. hovers on the brink of discovery during this period. He feels he is closer to the answers of the mysteries of existence, the "center of all significant knowledge" (193), than he has ever been. He first feels this when he sees the grizzly bear massacre the young caribou; he wonders whether the look in its eyes, were it to die, would be the same as the look in the eyes of the dying bear he and Rusty shot. This second grizzly is all violence and death; he has heard the cry of the Cannibal Emperor. The first bear had a message of suffering and pain to communicate: there was a "wild wicked look of intelligence in the eye, saying something like, 'Baby, you haven't begun' " (147). Would this second bear, farther from civilization, more lordly, indifferent to the suffering and pain of the caribou, would he die in the same way?

This question is not answered, though after their adventures the boys see one final sight. A moose, a "king Moose" (197), comes to lick salt across the pond from the boys' campsite. The moose suggests a resolution to the questions D.J. has asked himself in his search for significance. These questions have to do with the tenacity of scent:

> . . . as if something in the odor of her young dead was there in the scent of the conception not ten months ago . . . some mystery then recovered now.   (193)

> D.J.'s head full spun with that for new percipience, since could it be odor died last of all when one was dead?   (194)

> . . . and D.J. could have wept for a secret was near, some mystery in the secret of things—why does odor die last and by another route?   (196)

The secret alluded to is mortality. All that continues after death is decay. One is reminded of Lear's reply to Gloucester, who wished to kiss his liege's hands: "Let me wash them first. They smell of mortality." For the moose knows death; his entrance is signaled by "some speechless electric gathering of woe" (196). He is glazed blood red on one side by the setting sun and shining platinum on the other by the rising moon. Standing thus between the two heavenly bodies, colored by each, he represents the human condition. His message is one of both violence and suffering, of the death that must be and the pain that must accompany it: he "gave a deep caw pulling in by some resonance of this grunt a herd of memories of animals at work and on the march and something gruff in the sharp wounded heart of things bleeding somewhere in the night, a sound somewhere in that voice in the North that spoke beneath all else . . ." (197).

Mailer investigates these secrets of existence through a rather complex narrative structure. There are two modes of narration, "Intro Beeps" and "Chaps." The "Chaps" recount the actions of the past (primarily those of the hunt) through D.J.'s present consciousness. The "Intro Beeps" reveal D.J.'s stream of consciousness, and since that stream shifts course from moment to moment, they are far less coherent than the "Chaps." D.J. himself tries to enlighten the reader about the form of the novel: "Form is more narrative, memory being always more narrative than the tohu-bohu of the present, which is Old Testament Hebrew, cock-sucker, for chaos and void" (60–61). The novel is indeed formally organized around its narrative; in it the only thing that vaguely makes sense is that it is a story of some sort, recollected at a banquet several years after the events described have occurred. But the past, which should be ordered in the course of the narrative and so give form to the novel, is only the "pure moment of salt forming the crystal of this narrative" (125). The past is bent and distorted by the tohu-bohu of the present, and the formal unity of the novel is always on the verge of slipping away. D.J.'s present consciousness (at the moment when he is telling the story) is chaotic. Because "the inside of the brain is always the present even if it is memory two years old" (74), what should be an orderly narrative is wrenched awry by the strange ruminations of D.J.'s marijuana-soaked brain.

Thus the novel appears to be a chaos of obscenity, filth, pretension, bad jokes, and eclectic writing. But this is merely that "tohu-bohu" which encases but does not destroy the crystal of the narrative. Furthermore, the vitality inherent in the chaotic present seems to be a countervailing force to the vision of corruption and decadence in American life which Mailer presents.

The very language of the novel, generated in the "present" of

D.J.'s brain, creates a stylistic reality at odds with the ostensible content of the novel. Depending as it does upon speech rhythms, obscenity, and physical sensations, this language has a raw appeal and power which contrast with the picture of a sick and dying society. In the opposition of content and style we can see an artistic embodiment of Mailer's despair at the social and institutional aspects of life, and his hope that within the individual is to be found the motivation to overcome his milieu. Mailer's emphasis on exploring life styles in "The White Negro" and in *An American Dream* has its effect on the attempted stylistic innovations of this novel. If a new life style can redeem an individual, perhaps a new style can redeem a novel from despair.

None of Mailer's earlier works had been as stylistically innovative and resourceful as *Why Are We in Vietnam?* His style has importance beyond the virtuosity it displays. The structure of language both mirrors and creates the structure of reality as we apprehend it. Language can communicate a vision of the structure of reality. When language is violently ripped apart, as it is in the novel before us, it is usually a sign that the author is trying to create a new way of apprehending reality, and in so doing trying to resolve the dissonance between the way society has been apprehending reality and reality itself.

It is possible that the first time a reader approaches *Why Are We in Vietnam?* he may be confused enough by the chaos of D.J.'s consciousness to miss the narrative and even the theme of the novel. But it is difficult to conjecture that a reader could not understand or feel the speech rhythms created by the flow of words and how they emanate from the words and sounds he hears every day. Each phrase, each sentence, paragraph, and chapter flows on in the rhythms to which our ears have become accustomed. In order to emphasize these rhythms, Mailer allows his sentences to stretch on for pages, much as conversational monologues do. D.J. is, after all, delivering a monologue. And his language captures the broad range of contemporary idiom and jargon. Among other things, "D.J." stands for disc jockey. Like the disc jockey, D.J. spews forth a patter that is at once so much meaningless rhetoric and the key to America's secret fantasies. In the novel the range is wider than on the airwaves. We discover obscenity; the idioms and rhythms of the black subculture and the white hipster subculture which seeks the black experience; the argot of the junkie; the patter of the broadcaster; the catchy phrases of advertisers;

the journalese of the newspapers; and the lyricism of poets. Mailer captures the eclectic variety of language any American encounters in his daily experiences; his is a world where *Field and Stream*, psychoanalysis, the ghetto, and nuclear physics intersect. He uses the language of the country and he captures the way the country speaks. In a hundred different voices he sums America up.

Mailer has consistently used the sexual sphere as a major arena for the conflicts that reveal his vision. This novel is no exception, and we would do well to look at his use of sexuality if we are to understand the style and structure of the novel. We shall deal with two noticeable sexual aspects of the novel: first with its thoroughgoing use of obscenity, and second with its use of odor and the imagery of odor.

The most immediate and obvious effect of obscenity is that it shocks. More than any other element that can be utilized in a work of art, obscenity and pornography elicit strong and violent impressions. Obscenity is obscene because it deals with an immensely powerful complex of drives and needs which society has taught us to suppress, deny or ignore. It functions as violence does, forcing us to confront the chaotic and powerful ground of existence on which we build orderly structures to secure ourselves from that chaos. Because obscenity refers to the hidden world of need and fantasy that is the core of men's subconscious and unconscious existence, it cannot be ignored. By appealing to deep urges and flouting important taboos, obscenity forces men to confront their own fantasies and needs. It is used in this novel to remind the reader of the authentic experience that is so often denied by his preoccupation with the inauthentic experiences he encounters in his daily life in modern America.

A further advantage of obscenity is that it accurately mirrors American speech patterns. Where allowed—the barracks, the ghetto, the locker room—obscene terms and references are a major vehicle to communicate feelings. Mailer has expressed the belief that the most succinct expression of existential thought is the soldier's ubiquitous use of "shit" for situation and "ass" for soul. Insofar as *Why Are We in Vietnam?* derives much of its unity from the attempted reproduction of the style of American experience, the use of obscenity is an important constituent of that unity.

Obscenity in this novel also emphasizes the pervasive sexual nature of experience. The primal animal nature of men that Mailer is dedicated to exploring is often revealed, however subconsciously and tenuously, in the steady stream of sexual reference which qualifies so much of American verbal experience. Indeed, many Americans make a conscious attempt to reestablish their contact with the more primitive modes of being by resorting to obscenity.[7]

Although obscenity reveals the tie to the primitive, it also points out the peculiarly American preoccupation with sex. The sex one perceives all about is primarily perverted—that is, twisted out of its normal channels into substitute paths. Obscenity is sublimation of natural sexual instincts that have been denied. It is a substitute for sex, a way of venting explosive libidinal desires. The unfulfilled desires of the characters in this novel are revealed in their sexual preoccupations. It is clear that Rusty's sexual prowess is threatened by his wife; therefore, he seeks to fulfill himself by dominating other men and by proving his masculinity on the hunt. Not only his words but his actions are obscene.

Mailer suggests that the American nation vents its frustrations and satisfies its repressed sexual needs by making war in Vietnam and by a host of other actions. The guns that Rusty, Pete, and Bill carry are surrogate penises; the men use them to destroy the wild as America uses its guns to destroy the world. The real obscenity, Mailer suggests, is neither the language of D.J. nor the sexuality that pervades the novel, but the destruction that results from denying legitimacy to sexuality. One of the controlling ironies of the novel is that the same mentality that judges the sexual obscene creates such overpowering obscenities as the war in Vietnam and the corporate structure.

The other aspect of sexuality which greatly influences the style is odor. The use of odor is a touchstone to Mailer's peculiar style. It is also central to his mode of perception and his vision of the modern crisis. One of the concomitants of civilization is that as it has developed it has tended to repress the need for immediate gratification and to limit the sexuality of experience. Increasingly, the sexual has been restricted to the genital, and this also in ever more confining patterns.[8] According to this view, only the child is polymorphously perverse; as he ages and becomes more civilized, his oral, anal, and genital sexuality is increasingly diminished, so that sex for the mature adult is narrowed to the act of copulation. The enormously powerful force of the libido is channeled so that it is identified with the productive act of reproduction.

This elimination of the polymorphous perverse is relevant to Mailer's use of odor because, as sexuality is limited, odor is perhaps the first sense to be repressed. This is true for two reasons: odor is associated with anal eroticism, which is threatening to most adults, and smell is the most direct of the senses. It involves a direct contact between the observer and the object he experiences. Touch, taste, and smell are direct, sound is less so, and sight is the least direct of all. Society has deemphasized the sexual base of experience by elevating sight and ignoring smell and touch; the movement toward greater suppression of the polymorphous perverse can be seen in the increasing importance of the visual in the development of western civilization. Because smell is such a direct sense, involving the actual incorporation of that which is experienced, it has been suppressed and ignored as sexuality has been limited.

Mailer's wide use of odor and the imagery of odor is therefore an attempt to escape from what he regards as the repressed and unhealthy state of modern civilization. It is another foray into the primitive, a provocative experiment that is directed at rediscovering the totality of experience, polymorphous perversity, and destroying the tendency to limit sexuality to genital experience. Even more than the use of obscenity, it is a castigation of modern society and its norms, and the first step back toward renewal and salvation.

In this novel imagery of odor is most often associated with the secrets of life and creation. The association has been emphasized in our discussion of D.J.'s explorations and his realization that the question "Why does odor die last and by another route?" is the key to "some mystery in the secret of things" (196). While in *An American Dream* specific smells were a clue for Stephen Rojack to the essential nature of individuals and to the sexuality pervading all experience, in this novel odors reveal greater mysteries. Smells are the key to the eternal mysteries, primarily those of conception, life, and death. Consider the passages on pages 9 and 120–121, or the following:

> D.J. could smell the break, gangrene in the wood, electric rot cleaner than meat and sick shit smell and red-hot blood of your flesh in putrefaction, but a confirmed wood gangrene nonetheless, Burbank, a chaos of odor on the banks of the wound. . . . Next step was into a pool of odor which came from the sweets of the earth, sweet earth smell speaking of endless noncontemplative powers, beds of rest, burgeonings, spring of life, a nectar for the

> man's muscles on the odor of that breath, yeah, D.J. was
> breathing his last, he was in the vale of breath, every
> small smell counted, it was the most fucking delicious
> moment of his life up to that point . . . (139-140)

D.J.'s investigation of the world of scent continues for twenty more
lines. It is totally new to him, holding the secrets of creation. Man
is mortal, animal, and bound to die; death is wastage and suffocation, as is inauthentic life, which is spiritual death.

Odor, for Mailer, is the language of the soul. Although one
cannot see or hear or touch spirit, one can smell it. That is why
D.J. grapples with odor when he finds himself confronting the wild
and the wilderness of his own nature. What we are is found in the
way we smell.

D.J., the narrator, realizes the importance of odor, and also the
importance of violence in the natural and human worlds. Thus, in
a way he is initiated into the mysteries of human existence. It is,
however, D.J.'s failure to make adequate use of his knowledge
that leaves the novel, a novel which in its mythic qualities summons comparison with the epic, ultimately lacking in grandeur
and heroism. The contrast between effective initiation, usual in
the hunt genre, and the ineffective initiation of D.J. and Tex is all
too clear. The authentic and heroic existence the boys seek is not
relevant to the modern world against which the novel is played
out, and the book reveals nothing so much as the triumph of modern inauthenticity. On returning from his hermetic environment,
D.J. has no choice but to revert to his previous decadence. No
longer is there a legitimate path for his violence or his sexuality;
he is allowed only "closet fucks," corporate competition, and the
war in Vietnam. These he accepts. Perhaps there is a tragedy in
his acceptance of what he knows will suffocate him. If there is, it
is an ironic tragedy, whereby the initiation that seemed so successful has ended in failure, and the attempt to become heroic has
become engulfed in the circumstantial.

Chapter VII

The Armies of the Night

Resolution in Mid-Career

he Armies of the Night[1] recounts Mailer's partici-
pation in the events surrounding the March on
Washington to protest the war in Vietnam, which occurred in October 1967. Billed as an exercise that would
"confront the warmakers," the event had been planned
to culminate in a face-to-face confrontation between
protesters and the defenders of the Pentagon, that symbolic and actual force behind the American involvement in the war.

In the course of his attempt to understand the significance of
the March, which he takes to be a possible watershed marking the
birth of a new consciousness that will radically alter the context
and quality of American life, Mailer is, successively or simultaneously, a participant, celebrity, journalist, historian, novelist, social
critic, political iconoclast, and social mythmaker. *The Armies of
the Night* is his search for "an explanation to the attack on the
Pentagon . . . somewhere in the shape of this event" (199). Mailer
seeks to discover whether the March is or will be of essential importance in the growth and development of the American republic.

In most of his work Mailer has sought to cut through the ambiguity and ambivalence of contemporary life to an ultimate alternative of our age, totalitarianism or nihilism. One can feel the tension between these two polar social attitudes in the opposition he
set up between Valsen and Croft in *The Naked and the Dead*.
"The White Negro" explicitly asserted that the major choice facing
contemporary men is between totalitarianism or anarchy. In the
two novels that followed the essay, the protagonists had to choose
whether to surrender to the powers that sought to control them
or to escape from their control by descending into the moral wilderness of the self.

Mailer particularizes this ultimate alternative in two of the social
conflicts he chronicles in *The Armies of the Night*: one pits the
young and hip against the old and established; the other, more important, pits Norman Mailer, resolute individual, against the mach-

inations of the state. In the confrontation between the young and the old, Mailer, of course, favors the exploring young over their more established and entrenched elders. But he has moved away from the total glorification of the hipster as a moral explorer; though he still finds self-destruction preferable to social annihilation, he is now more aware of the immense dangers inherent in the self-indulgent style of the hipster and his descendant, the hippie:

> The same villains who, promiscuously, wantonly, heedlessly, had gorged on LSD and consumed God knows what essential marrows of history, wearing indeed the history of all eras on their back as trophies of this gluttony, were now going forth (conscience-struck?) to make war on those other villains, corporation-land villains, who were destroying the promise of the present in their self-righteousness and greed and secret lust (often unknown to themselves) for some sexo-technological variety of neo-fascism.   (93)

Though Mailer is committed to the worth of the individual, hence prefers any alternative to totalitarianism, he seems to have turned away from an easy championship of nihilistic anarchy toward an awareness of the potential dangers of nihilism.

> Floods of totalitarian architecture, totalitarian superhighways, totalitarian smog, totalitarian food (yes, frozen), totalitarian communications—the terror to a man so conservative as Mailer, was that nihilism might be the only answer to totalitarianism. The machine would work, grinding out mass man and his surrealistic wars until the machines were broken. It would take nihilists for that. But on the other hand nothing was worse than a nihilism which failed to succeed—for totalitarianism would then be accelerated. The gloom of these alternatives . . .   (176)

The other conflict which Mailer chronicles is the one between himself and the state. Most of the first section, "Book One," of the novel-history[2] deals with Norman Mailer—a participant in the March and the events surrounding it, and an acutely self-conscious American. Mailer is aware that this concentration on himself has its dangers: "To write an intimate history of an event which places its focus on a central figure who is not central to the event, is to inspire immediate questions about the competence of the historian.

Or, indeed, his honorable motive" (53). But he offers two justifi-
cations for his stratagem of writing about himself and suggests a
third.

The first and most obvious reason is that Mailer is in many ways
a microcosm for America. In the excesses and vagaries of his
character can be seen, in miniature, many of the defining characteristics of American society; in many ways, Mailer believes, his
personal crises and conflicts mirror on an individual scale the
agonies of the American nation. Furthermore, if "the March on
the Pentagon was an ambiguous event whose essential value or
absurdity might not be established for ten or twenty years, or indeed ever" (53), it can perhaps be understood only by focusing
on an individual who is "ambiguous in his own proportions" (53).
In continuing this description of himself, Mailer asks questions that
seem relevant to an assessment of his own fictional heroes, his
public persona, and the character of those individuals who occupy
the center of the stage of contemporary American history:

> a comic hero, which is to say, one cannot happily resolve
> the emphasis of the category—is he finally comic, a ludi-
> crous figure with mock-heroic association; or is he not
> unheroic, and therefore embedded tragically in the comic?
> Or is he both at once, and all at once? These questions,
> which probably are not much more answerable than the
> very ambiguities of the event, at least help to recapture
> the precise feel of the ambiguity of the event and its
> monumental disproportions.   (53)

Second, Mailer is the lens through which the reader can examine
the event.

> (For the novel—we will permit ourselves this parenthesis
> —is, when it is good, the personification of a vision which
> will enable one to comprehend other visions better; a
> microscope—if one is exploring the pond; a telescope
> upon a tower if you are scrutinizing the forest.)   (219)

He claims that American history requires a historian who is at
once a participant and detached, one who will "look to the feel of
the phenomenon" (25). In order to do this he must be involved
in the event; in order to make sense of the feelings aroused in him,
he must be honest and detached. He believes himself to be both
involved and objective, and thus well fitted to the role of historian.

He serves simultaneously as the subject of his observations and as the sensitive observer; in fact, the use of himself as subject, Mailer claims, makes him a more reliable observer, for the reader can easily become aware of the biases and weaknesses of Mailer's vision and thus compensate for them.

He only suggests the third and most important reason for placing himself at the center of his history. He realizes that it is impossible for him, or anyone else, to understand any historical event, such as the March on the Pentagon, without first understanding himself. For the modern artist, this means that the discovery and creation of his own identity is the precondition to any future endeavor; indeed, one might say that exploration of the self becomes the major concern of all artistic creation. We can see this most clearly reflected in Wordsworth's *The Prelude*, which is one of the cornerstones of esthetic sensibility of not only the nineteenth century but our own as well. Wordsworth, we recall, felt the need to create an epic, a work which would define his nation and his time and which would create the myths that are essential to all cultures. But he found, when he tried to formulate a myth, that he could not do so.[3] Instead, he felt he must try to understand himself through a consideration of his growth and development. In choosing to recount his spiritual development, he found a subject which, though limited, promised spiritual salvation:

> One end hereby at least hath been attain'd.
> My mind hath been revived, and if this mood
> Desert me not, I will forthwith bring down,
> Through later years the story of my life.
> The road lies plain before me; 'tis a theme
> Single and of determined bounds; and hence
> I chuse it rather at this time, than work
> Of ampler or more varied argument.[4]

But Wordsworth's words were, unbeknownst to him, ironic, for the theme he thought limited and narrow expanded so that it encompassed the whole of significance and reality. Furthermore, by choosing to postpone the creation of a new myth, Wordsworth created the central mythos of modern times: the search for identity. As a precondition to understanding the world and human history, he realized he had to understand himself and his own history. He found that to discover his identity was to discover as well the significance and order that he was seeking in the natural world and in the events of history.

So once again we find Mailer's mind closely allied to the romantics.[5] When he says, "Once History inhabits a crazy house, egotism may be the last tool left to History," he is at once denying an intrinsic and comprehensible order to history and prescribing the only possible method of understanding it, one that involves an exploration of the self. In order to understand *The Armies of the Night*, we must understand that Mailer's preoccupation with himself is the central theme of the book. The novel is an attempt by Mailer to understand, define, and come to grips with his self, to describe his own human condition. His understanding of history is through the predication of the truths he learns about his own identity.

By using himself as the major subject, Mailer suggests a resolution of social problems. The solving of Mailer's individual problems has social relevance, and the only satisfactory solution to the modern problems which arise out of self-division and its incumbent antithetical tensions must grow out of a reunification of the individual and social spheres of action. (See below, page 186). For it is Mailer's wish and hope that "two very different rivers, one external, one subjective, had come together" (51). This wish, this need, determines the form of *The Armies of the Night*; it represents, as we shall see, a divergence from Mailer's previous works, in which the protagonist always explored the subjective realm against a backdrop of an alien and hostile social system.

But who is this Norman Mailer who is at the center of the book? We already know that he is an ambiguous character of misshapen proportions; we have probably assumed, from his deep involvement with the health and sickness of his country, that he has a "love affair with America" (171). Because of this love affair, because he has a schizoid personality, and because he is existential in his outlook and reactions, he effectively epitomizes much of the American spirit.

Mailer constantly refers to himself as schizophrenic, divided by antithetical urges and needs. When the March begins, he finds himself between Robert Lowell and Sidney Lens, the former an intensely private poet, jealous of his individuality, the latter a well-known radical and historian:

> If a Committee from the Feature Formers Guild of Heaven had given instructions to design a face which was halfway in appearance between Sidney Lens and Robert Lowell, they might have come up with Norman Mailer;

> stationed between Lens and Lowell he felt the separate
> halves of his nature well-represented, which gave little
> pleasure, for no American citizen likes to link arms at
> once with the two ends of his practical working-day good
> American schizophrenia.　(107)

When he describes his appearance, he resorts to the same technique, choosing as his antitheses the tragic and the comic: "Like the people's choice between Victor McLaglen and Harpo Marx" (202). And he describes his character as if it were some Gothic cathedral whose beauty results from the grotesque effects of conflicting generations of builders: "The architecture of his personality bore resemblance to some provincial cathedral which warring orders of the church might have designed separately over several centuries, the particular cathedral falling into the hands of one architect, then his enemy" (17).

The antithetical poles of Mailer's nature can also be deduced from his continual references to the beast that is at the heart of his and every civilized man's nature. Mailer, as we have demonstrated, is fascinated with the animality in man, with the need for violence. It would indeed be odd if this bestiality, which figures so importantly in his fiction, should be absent from his conception of himself. "Mailer had come to recognize over the years, the modest everyday fellow of his daily round was servant to a wildman in himself" (13). This Beast "was an absolute egomaniac . . . no recognition existed of the existence of anything beyond the range of his speech" (13). And at times the Beast in Mailer needs to come forth and "grapple with the world" (36), as he does in Mailer's drunken speech from the stage of the Ambassador Theater, or as he did when Mailer, in an incredible display of machismo, tempted Sonny Liston to fight him (*PP*, "Ten Thousand Words a Minute," 213–267). But opposed to this sense of the bestial is Mailer's self-image as an "everyday fellow," even one of the "grands conservateurs" (18). He is horrified, for instance, at the hippies' widespread use of drugs, which he fears will diminish the capacity of their brains and, worse, induce genetic damage. He feels they have no right to destroy the biological heritage of countless generations of their predecessors solely to obtain momentary satisfaction.[6] Again, while he celebrates the costumes and actions of the hippies and yippies, he also rejoices in the courtly Southern tradition which he feels is represented in the person of Commissioner Scaife, the judge before whom he must appear in order to be released from jail.

Politically, Mailer is also divided. This division has been evident since his early works, for he has always been committed to the necessity of individual freedom, and he has always been aware enough to realize that man's freedom, so often threatened by institutions and governments, can be won and defended only through some sort of social action. Calling himself a "Left Conservative" (124), he senses that he occupies a position unique in American politics: "he, Mailer, ex-revolutionary, now last of the small entrepreneurs, Left Conservative, that lonely flag—there was no one in America who had a position even remotely like his own" (181). Although he is much given to overstatement, surely we can believe he is unique, he who campaigned for Henry Wallace in 1948 after most other leftists had long given up, who cut himself off from the Old Left in his avowal that the hipster had serious political implications, who commented on the nature of political process in America while feeling totally alienated from it, who simultaneously became a hero and a severe critic of the New Left, who canceled a plan to run for Mayor of New York because he had just stabbed his wife, who wrote a sensitive book on the protestors involved in the March on the Pentagon and then skipped most of the Chicago street debacle in order to watch events on the floor of the Democratic Convention,[7] and who offered serious and imaginative proposals concerning New York's urban crises while running for Mayor[8] of a city which thought him a clown. Mailer has ample reason to maintain he is unique. He also, in his divided and contradictory life, sums America up, for America is a country of opposites, a country in which conservatives support any manipulation of individual freedom so long as it is done by an agency other than the federal government, a country in which the immigrant and urban backbone of the New Deal and liberal politics issues the loudest call for law and order to triumph over justice, a country in which a president elected on a platform of peace and noninvolvement (Johnson, or Wilson before him) sees his victory as a mandate for war.

Mailer also represents a large segment of what is often called the New Left. The New Left is distinguishable from the Old Left primarily by its emphasis on flexibility and spontaneity and by its adherence to rudimentary democracy and freedom often overlooked in rigorous Marxist analysis.[9] The strangely split political perspective which Mailer brings to bear on the March on the Pentagon allows him to be at once involved and dispassionately critical. The fact that he shares a political style with the New Left makes him an informed observer of many of their activities; his conservative dedication to the individual allows him to be objective as well as informed: "Mailer was a Left Conservative, so he had his own point of view. To himself he would suggest that he tried to think in the style of Marx in order to attain certain values suggested by Edmund Burke" (185).

Mailer sees himself also as "a simple of a hero and a marvel of a fool, with more than average gifts of objectivity" (215–216). Thus he is a wonderful protagonist for the novel, gallantly and foolishly pricking his way across the surreal American plain. As we would expect from an artist who is enmeshed in the romantic search for self and identity, "Mailer had an egotism of curious proportions" (119). This results largely from his need to test himself continually against his environment and society, to delineate through success and failure, compatibility and contrast, the outlines of his own individuality. Mailer is aware of more than the comic aspects of his oft-repeated bravura performances: the description of the drunken speech he made at the Ambassador Theater, with which the book begins, reveals a sensitive and aware exploration of his own grotesqueness. He knows most of his roles for what they are but continues to act them out in the hopes of discovering, in the process of acting, the actor who plays all the parts, dons all the masks.

> Mailer as an intellectual always had something of the usurper about him—something in his voice revealed that he likely knew less than he pretended. . . . For a warrior, presumptive general, ex-political candidate, embattled aging enfant terrible of the literary world, wise father of six children, radical intellectual, existential philosopher, hard-working author, champion of obscenity, husband of four battling sweet wives, amiable bar drinker, and much exaggerated street fighter, party giver, hostess insulter— he had on screen in this first documentary a fatal taint, a last remaining speck of the one personality he found absolutely insupportable—the nice Jewish boy from Brooklyn. Something in his adenoids gave it away— he had the softness of a man early accustomed to mother-love. (134)

It is significant that in this list of personae Mailer includes "existential philosopher." It is a role he often publicly proclaims, one which his essays frequently lift as a standard of battle. The existential nature of his thought—which is something different from his open proclamation of existential partisanship—has been discussed above in connection with most of his previous works. In *The Armies of the Night* we find an easy and sure acceptance, by Mailer, of many of the principles and perceptions he had labored strenuously to inculcate in his earlier works.

The Armies of the Night is itself existential in both purpose and form. It is an attempt to understand the modern world, and modern experience, by coming to grips with an existent situation. Mailer's hope is that if he can understand this one specific event, he can begin to understand the essential nature of America as it has been molded by the history of this republic. Furthermore, the writing of this book is in itself an existential exercise in creating meaning. The March on the Pentagon is a paradigmatic existential situation because it has no preordained conclusion or significance: "we are up, face this, all of you, against an existential situation—we do not know how it is going to turn out, and what is even more inspiring of dread is that the government doesn't either" (38). In like manner, the book he is writing is a search for the meaning of the event, a search that has no known end but only a guideline for its investigation: "Look to the feel of the phenomenon. If it feels bad, it is bad" (25).

Later in the book Mailer restates this by referring to the Hemingway statement[10] we have encountered in several other of Mailer's works: "Hemingway after all had put the key on the table. *If it made you feel good, it was good.* That, and Saint Thomas Aquinas's 'Trust to the authority of your senses,' were enough to enable a man to become a good working philosopher" (91). Thus by using experience as the matrix from which value and ultimately significance are derived, Mailer reveals his affinity with one of the basic principles of existential thought. One of the things that sets him apart from many of his contemporaries is his willingness to use the modern experience—cradled in technology, an urban environment, and a politics of powerlessness, swathed in anxiety, sexual frustration, and banal media manipulation—as the arena for his exploration of the human soul.

One of the truths he discovers about human existence is that its parameter is death, and that this final uncertainty colors the whole of human experience. This conception is familiar to any reader of

Mailer, for he has emphasized it in much of his fiction and non-fiction. We saw earlier that he believes, with Heidegger, that death not only encapsulates the uncertain quality of all existence but also creates that uncertainty by threatening all significant experience with extinction, and all existence with ultimate nonexistence. Here, though, Mailer chronicles the end of his innocence; the thought of death becomes more than a matter for philosophy, it becomes reality. The March he has joined, he realizes, can lead to jail, exile, and even death:

> Yet, there was no escape. As if some final cherished rare innocence of childhood still preserved intact in him was brought finally to the surface and there expired, so he lost at that instant the last secret delight he retained in life as a game where finally you never got hurt if you played the game well enough.   (78)

One aspect of Mailer's existential commitment is new and interesting. In earlier works, the emotion occasioned by the thought of death and the unknown was dread; and it was dread that enabled a man to experience authentically. But in *The Armies of the Night* Mailer does not stress dread as heavily, and in its stead he explores another basic emotion, guilt. It is guilt that impels him to join the March in the first place, which urges him to stand with the army of the radical and the young. Guilt, he admits, is the mainspring behind his action throughout the days preceding and during the March. It is only when he is finally in jail after the March, having gone through many changes because of this guilt, that he decides to refuse its imperatives.

To continue to surrender to guilt would be to encapsulate himself in a moral spiral which turns ever upon itself, without hope of escape or reversal. Mailer decides, in the interest of self-preservation, to step off the "ladder of moral challenges" (195). He thus escapes from the round of guilt and repentance which leads eventually to either madness or sainthood (287).

Yet guilt serves as the impetus toward that authenticity which Mailer achieves by participating in the March; it propels him on the rite of passage which will end in his sense of wholeness and integration. He realizes that there is a constructive force to guilt when he exclaims, "how much guilt lay back of a good writer!" (157). Most revealing of all is his analysis of sex, which stems from his rejection of the guilt-free sex which, he points out, is advocated by Paul Goodman. In this passage his view of guilt is analogous to his view of dread in earlier works; indeed, "dread" could be substituted for "guilt" with no change or diminution of meaning; it would then match perfectly the perceptions Rojack has about his sexual relationship with Cherry in *An American Dream*:

> For guilt was the existential edge of sex. Without guilt, sex was meaningless. One advanced into sex against one's sense of guilt, and each time guilt was successfully defied, one had learned a little more about the contractual relation of one's own existence to the unheard thunders of the deep—each time guilt herded one back with its authority, some primitive awe—hence some creative clue to the rages of the day—was left to brood about . . . one defied such a fate [as succumbing to onanism or homosexuality] by sweeping up the psychic profit derived from the existential assertion of yourself—which was a way of saying nobody was born a man; you learned manhood provided you were good enough, bold enough.   (24-25)

What Mailer calls guilt in this book, then, is often analogous to *angst* or dread. Guilt forces men toward reality and authenticity and is at times itself reality, in that it is the emotional representation of the relations between the self and things beyond the self which form so large a part of human reality. As we saw in *Why Are We in Vietnam?*, even sexual guilt can be a powerful impetus toward an engagement of social issues, such as the war in Vietnam.

But *The Armies of the Night* has a dual subject: Norman Mailer and modern America. Each serves to explain the other, and the novel-history attempts to understand the character and problems of both, as well as suggest a resolution to that self-division with which both Mailer and American society are afflicted. The essential characteristic of American society, the book maintains, is hopeless self-division; America is divided into camps—social, ideological, and economic. The March on the Pentagon clearly revealed, to Mailer, the violent conflicts at the heart of the American republic; it also suggested that in the rebellious spirit of the marchers might be found the first evidence of the salvation that, as Mailer had indicated in *The Deer Park*, comes only through growth. Thus Mailer sees the March on the Pentagon as a social rite of passage, an elevation of cultural awareness to a higher level.

Toward the end of "Book One" Mailer thinks of the current crisis in which America is enmeshed. The passage, which describes the end of the long day of the March, is worthy of close consideration, for it epitomizes Mailer's sense that modern society is insane and schizophrenic and that its sickness issues in violence:

> Mailer had been going on for years about the disease of America, its oncoming totalitarianism, its oppressiveness, its smog—he had written so much about the disease he had grown bored with his own voice, weary of his own petulance; the war in Vietnam offered therefore the grim pleasure of confirming his ideas. The disease he had written about existed now in open air . . .
>
> He came at last to the saddest conclusion of them all for it was beyond the war in Vietnam. He had come to decide that the center of America might be insane. The country had been living with a controlled, even fiercely controlled, schizophrenia which had been deepening with the years. Perhaps the point had now been passed. . . . The average American, striving to do his duty, drove further each day in the opposite direction—into working for the absolute computer of the corporation. Yes and no, 1 and 0. Every day the average American drove himself further into schizophrenia; the average American believed in two opposites more profoundly apart than any previous schism in the Christian soul. . . . [These opposites] had brought the country to a state of suppressed schizophrenia so deep that the foul brutalities of the war in Vietnam were the only temporary cure possible for the condition—since the expression of brutality offers definite if temporary relief to the schizophrenic. . . . America needed the war. It would need a war so long as technology expanded on every road of communication, and the cities and corporations spread like cancer; the good Christian Americans needed the war or they would lose their Christ.   (188–189)

What Mailer must confront and evaluate is the "irredeemable madness of America" (151). We recall D.J.'s perception that "the center of things was insane": here, in *The Armies of the Night*, Mailer "had come to decide that the center of America might be insane" (188).

This insanity is the result of the split, in the social fabric and the lives of individuals, between desires and actions, illusions and realities, bodies and souls. Mailer records his constant premonition that "the two halves of America were not coming together, and when they failed to touch all of history might be lost in the divide" (157–158). This feeling carries the mark of the tragic, a sense of inevitable destruction, for the split in America may never be healed: "or was it simply impossible—had the two worlds of America drifted irretrievably apart?" (158).

As he had previously used cancer, Mailer uses schizophrenia as a rhetorical metaphor for the illness that besets society and modern men.[11] He sees America torn apart by the antithetical forces present in its populace and structured into its institutions. Though he had always believed that struggle between opposing forces is the condition of existence, he also had affirmed a need for a synthesis between opposing forces to resolve, if only temporarily, the struggle at the core of all existence. What he is claiming here is that in contemporary America there seems little possibility of synthesis, and that the dynamics of dialectical process have deteriorated into unresolvable antitheses. Opposites may no longer be reconciled; what appears to lie ahead is the effort of each half of a divided society to destroy the other, an effort that will possibly result in the destruction of both.

Mailer finds evidence for this diagnosis in his "growing sense of apocalypse in American life" (224), for "the expression of brutality offers a definite if temporary relief to the schizophrenic" (188). Throughout his fiction there is a recurrent pattern of unfulfillment which is eventually resolved in violence: Croft takes out his sexual frustrations in war; Rojack is driven to murder by repressed hostility for his wife, and D.J. enlists in the war in Vietnam because his family and society offer him no possibility of achieving manhood or the satisfaction of his deepest needs. The only release from such libidinal repression is an orgy of destructive violence:

> technology had driven insanity out of the wind and out of the attic, and out of all the lost primitive places: one had to find it now wherever fever, force, and machines could come together, in Vegas, at the track, in pro foot-

> ball, race riots for the Negro, suburban orgies—none of
> it was enough—one had to find it in Vietnam; that was
> where the small town had gone to get its kicks.   (153)

Neither the fear of an impending apocalypse nor a sense of a
schizoid America, divided and plunging toward that apocalypse,
is new to Mailer's work. The apocalyptic vision had been present
since the political fantasies of General Cummings and a sense of
global cataclysm forms the historical backdrop against which all
of Mailer's dramas are played out. Similarly, a sense of division
has marked all of his fiction and prose. The actual attribution of
schizophrenia, however, does not come forward until late: in
Mailer's analysis of modern society into two types, Cannibals and
Christians, and in his use of a divided character as narrator and
protagonist of *Why Are We in Vietnam?* For D.J. is both rich,
Texan, and white, and poor, black, and a resident of the urban
ghetto of Harlem. D.J. stands for, among other things, Dr. Jekyll,
that archetype of the divided personality. Lest the reader fail to
catch the allusion, Mailer calls the protagonist's alter ego Mr.
(Tex) Hyde.

One could regard "The White Negro," and the fiction that follows it, as Mailer's attempt to embrace the violence and the self-
interest of the Cannibal in such a way as to renew the Christian
tradition and give it relevance to the modern era. In *Cannibals and
Christians* he created an elementary division, for both America and
the world, into those two camps of personalities. What is fearful in
this split is that both Cannibals and Christians, whatever their separate intents, promise only destruction, and with the world in the
hands of one or the other "we are approaching the time when an
apocalypse will pass through the night."

> From Lyndon Johnson to Mao Tse-tung, we are all Chris-
> tians. We believe man is good if given a chance, we
> believe man is open to discussion, we believe science
> is the salvation of ill, we believe death is the end of dis-
> cussion; ergo we believe nothing is so worthwhile as
> human life. We think no one should go hungry. So forth.
> What characterizes Christians is that most of them are
> not Christian and have no interest left in Christ. What
> characterizes the Cannibals is that most of them are born
> Christian, think of Jesus as Love, and get an erection
> from the thought of whippings, blood, burning crosses,

burning bodies, and screams in mass graves. Whereas
their counterpart, the Christians—the ones who are not
Christian but whom we choose to call Christian—are
utterly opposed to the destruction of all human life and
succeed within themselves in starting all the wars of
our time, since every war since the Second World War
has been initiated by liberals or Communists; these Christians also succeed by their faith in science to poison the
nourishment we eat and the waters of the sea, to alter
the genetics of our beasts, and to break the food chains
of nature.   (*C&C*, 4)

In Mailer's fiction and also in his nonfiction we can observe his
struggle to reconcile these two antithetical archetypes. He is firmly
committed to a positive and optimistic view of the potentialities of
men; but he is also aware of the stale rhetoric of the Christian, a
rhetoric both outmoded and inappropriate to the central human
preoccupation with life, death, and individual fulfillment.

To a large extent, Mailer sees the Cannibals and Christians in
America divided along class lines. He finds an American "working
class finally alienated from any remote interest or attention in the
process of work itself" (87), the situation Marx had anticipated
as the final product of the capitalist state. But the middle class is
still more greatly alienated; the members of the middle class are
alienated not only from work but also from their own consciousness, which they experience as something alien and impersonal. The
middle class, and particularly its children, are estranged from "all
the good simple nitty-gritty American joys of the working class"
(258). In the terms we used in examining Mailer's earlier work,
they are living inauthentic lives, protected from the violence and
risk of death that hold the only promise of a restoration of authenticity. The middle class stands frightened before the power and
violence of the working class; there seems no possibility for reconciliation. Mailer's thesis is that if the two classes cannot be reconciled, if they move ever farther apart, then the human aspirations and ideals of the middle class will atrophy for want of the
vitality and force that only authentic experience, which the working class has, can bring.

The split in America which Mailer discusses in this book, as well
as in *Cannibals and Christians*, has many dimensions. Another is
that division between good and evil which Mailer chronicled in

"The White Negro" and *An American Dream*. This dichotomy is the basis of Mailer's approach to the first Patterson-Liston fight, an approach developed in the essay "Ten Thousand Words a Minute" (*PP*, 213–267). The essay documents "The battle of good and evil, that curious battle where decision is rare and never clear" (*PP*, 243). In it Mailer resolves, at least temporarily, the dichotomy between the pacific Christian and the destruction-oriented Cannibal. He recognizes that "violence may be an indispensable element of life" (*PP*, 246). He believes that boxing mirrors the human condition, which sometimes requires "some half-human way to kill a little in order not to deaden at all" (*PP*, 247). But neither the Cannibal nor the Christian, the Evil nor the Good, is willing to accept Mailer's contention that some violence is sometimes a necessary adjunct to human life. Thus the gap between the liberal and the fascist (for that is what Mailer's categories of Christian and Cannibal seem to boil down to) is ever widening.

Mailer sees other splits in American life: young against old, male against female, haves against have-nots, white against black. But the central conflict has always revolved about the unfathomed schism between the individual and society. His obsession with the tyranny of the state and the needs of the individual has grown tiring even to Mailer: "For years he had been writing about the nature of totalitarianism" (117), but by now he "had grown bored with his own voice" (188). *The Armies of the Night* is, nevertheless, another recognition of the power and destructiveness of social institutions and the state, of the "governmental military-industrial complex" (94), which he calls "corporation land" (62) and "technology land" (15). His concern with the corporation and its pernicious influence follows the stance he adopted in *Why Are We in Vietnam?* As Norman Mailer and his fellow marchers confront the government and its military extension at the Pentagon, Mailer gives a detailed picture of the power behind the corporate establishment.

One thing he discovers is that this power is rooted in technology. Mailer is not himself opposed to technology; his essays on city planning and architecture make this clear. What he fears greatly is that technology is not being used for the achievement of human ends, that it becomes an end in itself and the judge of what ends are to be achieved.

Precisely because technology has offered so many ways of furthering human security and prosperity, men (especially those whom

Mailer terms Christians) have come to accept the language and logic of technology as an ethical order, and not solely as a practical one. What frightens Mailer is that decisions are made because they represent technological possibilities or because previous technology demands them. What formerly were human decisions, made on the basis of right or wrong, emotion or rational thought, are now made by unconcerned technocrats who are only doing their job, or filling a niche in the technocratic ecology. Technicians make all our decisions, be they about the war in Vietnam, the planning of cities, or the future of the economy. The Christians, those who hope to better human life, have most unfortunately concluded, from the fact that technology can abet human progress, that technology *is* human progress.

> Liberal academics had no root of a real war with technology land itself, no, in all likelihood, they were the natural managers of that future air-conditioned vault where the last of human life would still exist.   (15)

> The Ruminant was by now convinced that technology land was the real capitalist bastion, and the mediocre middle-class middle-aged masses of the Left were—we have visited this station already—the first real champions of technology land: they could not conceive of a revolution without hospitals, lawyers, mass meetings, and leaflets to pass out at the polls.   (96)

Liberals have accepted a logic and ethics from technology, and this makes them unsuited to deal with the immense human problems with which society must cope. They fail to see that the mentality that "took the taste and crust out of bread and wrapped the remains in wax paper, was at the far extension of this same process, the same mentality which was out in Asia escalating, defoliating, orientating" (62).

Mailer felt that the March on the Pentagon was noteworthy because it was a symbolic and an actual confrontation between the spirit of individuality he admired and the totalitarianism of that corporate and technological establishment he had so often warned against. "Yes, he was more than a visitor, he was in the land of the enemy now, he would get to see their faces" (131). The two halves of the American psyche had emerged from the depths of the subconscious[12] and now the two must consciously face each other, the protestors must face the forces of order, the Christians must meet the Cannibals. The divisions Mailer emphasizes in contemporary American society and those he senses in himself epitomize his contention that our century reduces "all life to its ultimate alternatives" (*AM*, 357).

In Mailer's first novel there is a growing note of discord which arises from the simultaneous recognitions that society is ill and needs a cure, and that at present no cure seems possible. Mailer's first novel, *The Naked and the Dead*, pointed toward the disintegration of American society and the bankruptcy of conventional liberal political solutions. *Barbary Shore* continued Mailer's indictment of modern America and, furthermore, tried to demonstrate that a Marxist stance was, although necessary, surely inappropriate to the contemporary political life of this country. The force behind that book was Mailer's view that only a socialist revolution could begin to attempt a solution to the crises of modern society, and that the failure of the Russian Revolution to spread and become world-wide in the early 1920's made a modern socialist revolution close to impossible in the United States.

With the failure of *Barbary Shore* to discover a viable political alternative to those operative in modern life, the discordant strain became a sour note that made all Mailer's later fiction seem unresolved. He continually presented a searing vision of a disintegrating society stifled by totalitarianism, manipulated by corporations, and ripped apart by its own conflicting desires. In this milieu of disintegration and suffocation he focused on certain individual men, and either watched them go down to defeat, like Charley Eitel and D.J., or, at best, hold their own in the destructive clutches of society, like Rojack and O'Shaugnessy. Both of these two latter protagonists protected their spirits from annihilation by virtue of their courage, willingness to grow, and independence, but both achieved at best a stalemate: they failed to change the world that oppressed them. The omnipresent discordant note resulted from Mailer's intense belief that modern men are oppressed by society, and from his failure to suggest a politics or course of action which could eliminate or lessen that oppression.

Earlier it was noted that Mailer regards himself as a "Left Conservative." As a leftist he ascribes the sickness and inauthenticity of modern life to social institutions and their influence. But he emphatically dissociates himself from the "liberal" tradition of American politics, which seeks to overcome institutional oppression by liberalizing and enlarging, through massive and pervasive governmental involvement, the institutions responsible for much of the oppression. Mailer sees large institutions as the enemy, and, as has already been made clear, he grudgingly prefers nihilism to totalitarianism. His conservatism is an outgrowth of his commitment to the individual.[13]

There are characters in Mailer's works who achieve a sort of victory. But for Lovett, O'Shaugnessy, and Rojack, the characters who come closest to heroism and victory, any triumph is ironic. Their victory consists of their survival—physical and spiritual—in a hostile environment. All three recognize the oppression of society (although the pervasiveness of this awareness diminishes for the protagonist in each succeeding novel), but none of them is able, in any way, to do anything about eradicating this oppression. In Mailer's martial universe, his protagonists, unlike Hemingway's, cannot achieve "a separate peace." All they manage is survival and the growth requisite to facing the wars about them for yet another day or month. Small wonder, then, that irony is the dominant mode of the novels.

But it is a tragic irony. For beneath the surface events of the novels there is an intense desire on Mailer's part to go beyond the inferno, to move out of sickness and into health, to escape from alienation into coherence. The world that Mailer portrays in his novels is not the world he wants to live in but the world he believes modern men are condemned to live in. More than most of his contemporaries, Mailer refuses to ignore the disgusting and debasing and dehumanizing aspects of the urban, technological, and bureaucratic society that is becoming increasingly synonymous with modern American life. But to recognize such dehumanizing aspects is not enough; the society that debases must be altered, and the life of individual human beings in that society redeemed.

So, owing to the unwanted tension in his work between the need and the reality, it became necessary for Mailer to return to the political. Unless his protagonists can engage in social, not just individual, wars, society will have scant hope of change, the corporations will never be beaten back, and encroaching totalitarianism will never be halted. In one sense *The Armies of the Night* is a return to the political vision Mailer had entertained—and abandoned—in *Barbary Shore*. At the end of that novel Lovett went out alone into the night. The next three novels trace the paths of individuals like Lovett—Eitel, O'Shaugnessy, Rojack, and D.J.—

who seek what Lovett seeks, survival. Lovett's political mission was to survive so he could keep uncaptured the "little object" that would one day redeem mankind. Lovett must go out into an alien, hostile, and corrupt society; the next three novels explore the courses of action open to any man who wishes to both survive and, in surviving as an authentic man, keep alive some small hope for the future.

Yet, as Mailer realized in *Barbary Shore*, the only real hope for the betterment or even continuation of human existence is for the individual to integrate himself and his actions into socially meaningful action. And the only socially meaningful action is the socialist revolution. Lovett realizes this need for the integration of the individual and society, but he also sees that there is no present possibility for meaningful social engagement. The failure of the socialist revolution to become international is a reality, and the next such revolution is a long way off. In the interim one can only wait and protect one's courage, integrity, and hope.

In *The Armies of the Night*, for the first time, Mailer sees a possibility that the long hiatus between revolutions may be drawing to a close, and that the breath of a new age may again be upon America. There is hope for the future once again, and Mailer discovers and succors this hope, real and symbolic, in the March on the Pentagon. Having struggled for fifteen years to keep alive a hope for man by keeping alive the possibility to be a man (for this, after all, was the function of his glorification of the primitive and even bestial qualities in the hipster and in Rojack), Mailer recognizes the opportunity to shift the emphasis in his writing. He had consistently urged a return to primitivism, violence, and confrontation in order to protect contemporary men from the tragic consequence of alienation and inauthenticity. Now, he feels, the authentic man can emerge from the night into which he disappeared[14] and work for the revolution. It is significant that almost all of Mailer's actions in the novel, with the exception of the various acts of observation of himself and others, are directed toward urging people to enlist in the coming struggle against the powers of government, industry, and the entrenched elite. His drunken speech at the Ambassador Theater, his judicious and modest words at the Justice Department, his arrest, and his statement as he is released from jail are all meant to urge his fellows to enlist in the fight against "corporation land."

Mailer sees the March on the Pentagon as a potential turning point in the history of America and, indeed, the world, "that first major battle of a war which may go on for twenty years; let us even consider there is one interesting chance (one in a thousand) that in fifty years the day may loom in our history as large as the ghosts of the Union dead" (88). It offers the possibility of what he calls a rite of passage; it promises a transcendence of the sordidness of American life in the postwar era. This turning point is a moment of growth in the life of an individual; in a society it is usually a period of revolution or radical change. Mailer still believes in the truth of his oft-expressed dictum that one must "grow or pay more for remaining the same." This holds for societies as well as individuals. The Washington March allows Mailer to observe America at a critical point: growth, on the one hand, may lead to a better, more human society; refusal to grow, on the other, will undoubtably lead to stagnation and hasten the impending totalitarianism.

Growth has been critical in all of his novels. Each has focused on one man, or (in *The Naked and the Dead*) on a group, for a short period in which he undergoes intense emotional and ideational activity. Each novel focuses on an intense period of potential growth; each is concerned with the difficulty of growing, of ably performing the rite of passage. Two, *The Deer Park* and *Why Are We in Vietnam?*, examine as well the disastrous results of failing to grow, of "paying more for remaining the same." The novel-history before us examines not only the period when the individual (Mailer himself) grows, but also the agonizing moments as the American republic stretches, strains, and tries, as a society, to grow into new levels of awareness and activity.

What is important here—because it represents a change in Mailer's view of America and the plight of modern men, and because it forms the nuclear perception of the novel without which the other observations cannot cohere—is that the turning point, the moment of growth, is a societal one. The whole of western civilization, perhaps the whole of western culture, can be changed by the actions and events that began in Washington, D.C., in connection with the March on the Pentagon. In jail, Mailer recalls one of his own lines, one very close to his heart: " 'The essence of spirit was to choose that alternative which did not better your position but made it worse.' Mailer was quoting himself, but not with pleasure, for he was getting ready to go against his own maxims" (194). We examined the central role this maxim plays in *The Deer Park* and in the philosophy of the hipster. Now, for the first time, Mailer finds it not only applicable but relevant to the American situation. A war is breaking out between the separate halves of America's divided nature; Mailer isolates the moment before the first battle, as the massed troops of peace encircle the reflecting pool between the Lincoln and Washington memorials, and the massed militia of the totalitarian state—MP's, troops, police, and federal marshals—await the forces of peace before the five heavy flanks of the Pentagon.

And when the war does begin, the language Mailer uses to describe it is familiar to his readers, for he uses the same words and figures of speech to describe the protagonist in this book, America, that he used to describe the individual protagonists in his previous fiction. That exciting, unknown, and dangerous period of growth which Mailer had examined for various individuals is suddenly upon the United States:

> the air between New York and Washington was orgiastic
> with the breath of release, some promise of peace and
> new war seemed riding the phosphorescent wake of this
> second and last day's siege of the Pentagon, as if the
> country was opening into more and more of the resonance
> of these two days, more that was good, more that was
> bad. (214)

As with the individual, so with America: only by moving from the certainty of the past into the uncertainty of the present can growth be achieved. Growth holds the promise of a better existence, but it can also lead to a worse; it is the only way to life, but it can also lead to death. The metaphor Mailer frames for America on the brink of social change is the same one he uses in all his fiction for that exploration of the self which is at the center of growth: the metaphor of going out (or within) alone into the night: "the American Revolution must climb uphill blindfolded in the long Capitalist night" (67).[15]

The process of social growth is what Mailer calls a rite of passage: "the country had been founded on a rite of passage. . . . they were forever different in the morning than they had been before the night, which is the meaning of a rite of passage" (280). It is a rite analogous to both birth and death, for

> one has voyaged through a channel of shipwreck and

> temptation, and so some of the vices carried from an-
> other nether world into life itself (on the day of one's
> birth) may have departed, or fled, or quit; some part of
> the man has been born again, and is better.   (280-281)

Mailer finds two such rites in the course of the March. The first
is when the marchers cross the bridge over the Potomac, irretrievably committing themselves to confrontation with the enemy, "the
land of the warmakers" (281). The second, less public, more
meaningful, is the long night on the steps of the Pentagon (or in
jail), when the protesters must engage in the first protracted
struggle against the government. For it is one thing to start a battle
and another to decide to see it through. At the end of each rite, the
participants begin to realize the enormity of the struggle and its
possible outcome; they face the fact that henceforth they are
enemies in the heart of the land they had always believed theirs.

As Mailer's belief in growth indicates, there is no way to avoid
a rite of passage. When growth is called for, one must respond,
either by embracing the opportunity or by shunning it: "There are
negative rites of passage as well. Men learn in a negative rite to
give up the best things they were born with, and forever" (284).

The rite of passage is the only hope, Mailer believes, for an
America that is becoming increasingly divided. It holds promise of
growth, new direction, and perhaps coherence. In order to understand this rite, Mailer tells us, we must understand what the country
must grow out of, how this growth is to be effected, and what the
role of individual men is in the process of social change. This last
returns to Mailer's constant concern with how men react to their
environment, how they survive and grow. And this time the protagonist he examines is himself.

The corporate and military establishment is the constant object
of Mailer's concerns and fears, along with the advanced technology
and complex media which serve to mystify the majority of Americans about the totalitarianism that is impending. But until he wrote
The Armies of the Night, he had no sense of a viable strategy for
opposing them, and even less of a political force that might avail
itself of such a strategy. Liberalism died with Hearn; the Left,
already defeated and in hiding, expired with McLeod. In Mailer's
two previous extended attempts at political journalism—"Superman
Comes to the Supermarket" (*PP*, 27–61), which recounted the
events surrounding the Kennedy nomination in 1960, and "In the

Red Light: A History of the Republican Convention in 1964"
(*C&C*, 6–45)—he discounted the American political process. He
rejected the Democratic Party in the first, although he held out the
hope that John Kennedy, since his appeal was based on his style
rather than on substantive issues, might conceivably preside over
some strange existential change in the American body politic. The
bulk of *The Presidential Papers*, however, expresses Mailer's dis-
appointment that Kennedy failed to embrace these existential possibilities. His article on the Republican Convention is interesting in
that it emphasizes how unconservative the Goldwater-conservative-
Republican movement really was.

Mailer's writing is always shadowed by political despair. *The
Armies of the Night*, for instance, is filled with references to the
inadequacy of any possible political solution suggested by the existent elements of the political process. He finds the Old Left, like
the liberals, subject to the same excesses as its eternal opponent,
corporation land: a dependence upon technology and bureaucracy:

> Just as a study of foreign policy usually succeeds in de-
> pressing any lover of democratic process because foreign
> policy is encapsulated and therefore self-governing, so
> political life on the American Left tends to have an inner
> development which bears little relation to subtle changes
> in the external political context. (221)

The Old Left, in its struggle against alienation, became alienated;
the effort to change society only resulted in its losing touch with
society. Worse of all, the Old Left and its sometime allies, the
liberals, had, through token opposition and concurrence, only
strengthened what they claimed to oppose. "And the Left had been
until this year the secret unwitting accomplice of every great increase in the power of the technicians, bureaucrats, and labor
leaders who ran the governmental military-industrial complex of
super-technology land" (94). But the March on the Pentagon her-
alded, at least to Mailer, the advent of a New Left, one implacably
opposed to the "governmental military-industrial complex of super-
technology land," and whose methods held hope of eventual success. Deliberations over the planning of the March had seen the
drive and impetus "pass from the Old Left and the peace groups
to the New Left and the youth groups" (224). For several reasons
Mailer finds this New Left novel and exciting: it is existential, it
recognizes the power of art and imagination, especially in politics,

and it grows not out of ideology or platitudes but out of the malaise of American life, which he had been decrying for over two decades.

Mailer's commitment to an amalgam of existentialism and politics suffuses all of his nonfictional prose. His second book of prose writing, *The Presidential Papers*, has as its aim an attempt to involve Kennedy in existential politics. It is often difficult to determine exactly what Mailer means by the phrase; the most general and applicable interpretation is that he is calling for political and social action which grows out of the exigencies of the present, which is rooted in the actualities of American life. As such, it is the antithesis of conventional American politics, which has as its end the maintainance of certain structures (the political process itself, the two-party system, the capitalist economy) rather than the alleviation of social ills and a responsiveness to the electorate and social problems.

The New Left evidently rejected this commitment in favor of less defined and more socially relevant goals. Although to some extent it can be traced to a visionary political program—the "Port Huron Statement" of 1960—it was primarily a movement that developed in response to the pressing exigencies of the sixties. The New Left grew out of the civil rights and antiwar movements; it did not create them. The actions of the young and the minorities shaped the direction the movement was to take. To this we might compare the conventional political process, which formulates social policy on the basis not of existent social conditions, but of political needs. Strategy determines actions—not the reverse, as Mailer claims for the New Left—and political priorities determine strategy. Mailer stresses the example of Castro in Cuba as a major factor in the development of the New Left: "what seemed significant here, was the idea of a revolution which preceded ideology; the New Left had obviously adopted the idea for this March" (88). The new politics is founded upon a commitment to growth, despite its unknown and unpredictable results—a view of growth which matches Mailer's own: "The aesthetic of the New Left now therefore began with the notion that the authority could not comprehend nor contain nor finally manage to control any political action whose end was unknown" (88).

The New Left has incorporated existential principles because "The idea behind these ideas was then obviously that the future of the revolution existed in the nerves and cells of the people who created it and lived with it, rather than in the sanctity of the original idea" (88). But this belief in grounding politics in the lives and actions of people has an important implication. If "you created the revolution first and learned from it, learned of what your revolution might consist and where it might go out of the intimate truth of the way it presented itself to your experience" (87), then your experience becomes of central importance. Politics becomes one of the implications—albeit an immensely important one—of the way in which a person lives his life. Life style is prior to political content: "one's idea of a better existence would be found or not found in the context of the revolution" (105). And so, in *The Armies of the Night*, Mailer realizes that the most important political characteristic of Dick Harris, a young black involved in the ceremony of returning draft cards to the Department of Justice, is his élan, which is rooted not in his ideology but in his immediate political experience. The most significant aspect of the March, then, is its symbolic aspect: in choosing to march, marching, facing the assembled guardians of law and order, and resisting their authority, the New Left has made "revolution" a meaningful term to itself in the context of the American experience. By actively confronting government and society, even if their actions are effective only symbolically, its adherents have become resisters and revolutionaries.

Furthermore, this recognition of the importance of life style is a reconciliation of the division between art and life. Art is relevant because it is a way of *making* one's life. Significantly, Mailer discusses the relation between truth and his writing style directly after he discusses the political import of the creative modes of dress he observes on the steps of the Justice Department. And the central actions of the March—the exorcism of the Pentagon and the confrontation with the troops, often accomplished by inserting flowers in the barrels of the rifles the soldiers are carrying—are both symbolic and actual, art and real life. The March is theater in the streets; it is also, according to Mailer, a possible beginning of a new revolution.

This new American life also holds promise, in Mailer's opinion, because it grows directly out of the malaise of American life. The youths who surround Mailer are "mad middle-class children" (34) who have grown up in the heart of technology land. They were born into, and grew up in, "a dead de-animalized middle class," which has chosen the "principle that American was right, America was might" (280), rather than confronting the mysteries of existence. Because of their parents' rigid principles, views, and values, these children rejected authority and tried to find salvation in mystery, in the unknown. Thus they turned to a belief "in LSD, in witches, in tribal knowledge, in orgy, in revolution. . . . Their radicalism was in their hate for authority" (86). They share Mailer's revulsion at the deadening approach of totalitarianism; they share as well his belief in mystery and excess as the only possible routes to authentic existence in modern society.

When Mailer describes Jerry Rubin's political vision, he is giving us a slightly distorted picture of himself, of his own belief in chaos and growth, in the place of spirit in the war of existence, and in the magical and mystical (267). Mailer also diagnoses Rubin as an extraordinary romantic, a diagnosis which, as we found in "The White Negro," is applicable to Mailer himself. This romantic belief in the possibilities within man, in growth, and in the things of the spirit is also shared by the amorphous collection of youth which we call the New Left:

> An extraordinary multiplication of the romantic, but it was not Rubin's apocalyptic vision alone—it had been seen before by men so vastly different (but for the consonants of their names) as Castro, Cortes, and Christ—it was the collective vision now of the drug-illuminated and revolutionary young of the American middle-class. (267)

But if the rise of the New Left signals a change in the quality and nature of life in America, it is paralleled by a change in Mailer. Believing for the first time in twenty years (since his youthful and optimistic efforts in behalf of Henry Wallace and the Progressive Party in 1948) that America hovers on the brink of transition, and that he has allies who will also struggle to check the descent into totalitarian control, Mailer involves himself in the political scene. And his involvement, his *engagement*, leads to changes in his outlook, his feelings, and even his character.

Because Mailer recognizes that the March is important to America symbolically and actually, he decides to engage the enemy. No longer just criticizing, he will march into "the eye of the oppressor, greedy stingy dumb valve of the worst Wasp heart, chalice and anus of corporation land, smug, enclosed, morally blind Pentagon" (114). The immediate result of his decision to engage the enemy is "the thundering justification . . . to his legitimate . . .

sentiment of pride in himself" (114). He realizes that this is a
turning point for himself, a personal rite of passage; he is about to
cross "some divide in his own mind wider than the Potomac"
(113). He decides (to use the slogan for the March) to "Confront
the Warmakers," on their own ground. And so he has a keen sense
that he is more worthy than he was, that he has indeed grown in
the rite of passage he has begun: "the sense of danger to the front,
sense of danger to the rear—he was in fact in love with himself
for having less fear than he had thought he might have—he knew
suddenly then he had less fear now than when he was a young
man; in some part of himself at least, he had grown" (113).

As a result of his engagement and the bravery which led to and
supported his resistance, Mailer finds that his radical role is becoming significant: "He felt as if he were being confirmed. (After
twenty years of radical opinions, he was finally under arrest for a
real cause)" (138). At the start of the book Mailer presents himself as a serious man turned buffoon, a dedicated man who is so
alienated from both himself and others that he appears to them,
and to himself, as a clown and a *poseur*. But the March has been
a rite of passage for him, and he feels, for the first time, in joint
with the political role he has been playing for twenty years. The
description of himself which follows his description of the feeling
of confirmation is revealing because it describes both his former
alienation and his present sense of mental and physical integration:

> He felt his own age, forty-four, felt it as if he were finally
> one age, not seven, felt as if he were a solid embodiment
> of bone, muscle, flesh, and vested substance, rather than
> the will, heart, mind, and sentiment to be a man, as if
> he had arrived, as if this picayune arrest had been his
> Rubicon.   (138)

He believes he has been transformed, through his actions in joining the March and seeking arrest, from a man who wishes to one
who acts, from a dreamer separated from actuality to a man whose
life is consistent with his sentiments.

All of Mailer's novels deal with the affairs of men who feel like
strangers in their own society, who sense that they are cut off from
their selves. In *The Armies of the Night*, for the first time, Mailer
discovers the alternative to alienation, a sense of coherence and
wholeness. When the events of the March are finally over and he
is in prison, he feels "a sense of cohering in himself which he sup-
posed the opposite of those more familiar states of alienation he

could always describe so well" (163). What the March on the Pentagon has done is to allow Mailer to reenter the political arena. No longer must he be a Jeremiah, wailing at the wretched and horrifying excesses of America; he can now play an active role in a struggle to free American society of its most obnoxious and destructive facets. It is important to note that his efforts here—as opposed to his efforts in behalf of Henry Wallace in 1948 or his abortive attempt to run for Mayor of New York in the early sixties —can redeem him because there is a hope of success. His earlier political actions were all totally symbolic, acts of resistance rather than revolution. But now the thought of a successful social revolution and his demonstrated willingness to commit himself to it have replaced his alienation with a sense of coherence.

The coherence that Mailer experiences receives public expression as he is released from the jail at Occoquan. He faces the media, reporters, and his faithful film-makers and delivers a short speech:

> Today is Sunday, and while I am not a Christian, I happen to be married to one. And there are times when I think the loveliest thing about my dear wife is her unspoken love for Jesus Christ. Some of us were at the Pentagon yesterday, and we were arrested in order to make our symbolic protest of the war in Vietnam, and most of us served these very short sentences, but they are a harbinger of what will come next, for if the war doesn't end next year, why then a few of us will probably have to take longer sentences. Because we must. You see, dear fellow Americans, it is Sunday, and we are burning the body and blood of Christ in Vietnam. Yes, we are burning him there, and as we do, we destroy the foundation of this Republic, which is its love and trust in Christ.   (214)

Not only is Mailer's use of Christian imagery new, but also the quiet and resolved tone in which he speaks. The difference between this short speech and his drunken antics on the stage of the Ambassador Theater, which is our introduction to the book, is overwhelming. The reason for this difference is that Mailer has moved out of his alienation and into a sense of coherence—the feeling that body and mind, wish and reality, individual and society, mesh together in a harmonious whole—and this feeling precludes the need for Mailer to constantly affirm his identity. Where his self is no longer fractured and his different aspects are no longer alien to each other, he does not have to make the continual assertions which Keats called the "egotistical sublime." For the first time he need not resort to the romantic and existential assertion of the self, for he has discovered the sense of identity he has labored so hard to create. "Standing on the grass, he felt one suspicion of a whole man closer to that freedom from dread which occupied the inner drama of his years, yes, one image closer than when he had come to Washington four days ago" (213–214).

One result of his new-found coherence is a change of attitude toward violence, always one of the central concerns of his life and work. He is still violent; even after his arrest, he squares off with the "Nazi" (141) who is incarcerated on the same prison-bound bus as he. But now this violence is tempered with love, as his speech upon his release from Occoquan makes clear. He says he feels and comprehends the spirit of Christ, one which he understands as the wellspring of compassion and brotherly love. This development is not altogether unanticipated; in *An American Dream* Rojack's decision to accept the complexities of love with Cherry reveals, to him and to the reader, the possibility for fulfillment and peace. But Rojack later proves that he is not quite ready to carry the burden of love, and so he loses both Cherry and his possibility for fulfillment.

Here, in *The Armies of the Night*, we see a protagonist who tempers his violence with love. As Mailer explores the impending social struggle, he abandons some of the heavy emphasis on individual violence which had marked his earlier work. The coming revolution will require not only bravery and commitment but also two new qualities, loyalty and brotherhood. As Mailer merges the needs of the individual into the needs of a prerevolutionary society, his feeling of alienation is mitigated by a new-found sense of coherence.

Although the first part of the novel, which focuses on Mailer, concludes with an affirmation of compassion, the effect of the work as a whole is the need for violence. Mailer sees himself as a member, often a general, of an army, and the basic metaphor of the book is a military one, of two armies facing each other, one young and alienated, the other uniformed and in the service of corporation land. The title of the book is taken from the closing lines of one of Matthew Arnold's best known poems:

> And we are here as on a darkling plain
> Swept with confused alarms of struggle and flight,
> Where ignorant armies clash by night.

Arnold's poem emphasizes the ironic vision that informs the book, for "Dover Beach" balances the wish for a world "so various, so beautiful, so new" with the harsh reality expressed in the military metaphor above. Mailer's discovery of coherence is balanced by his sense of battle, of growing division. Thus he ends "Part One" with an affirmation of love and compassion, and ends "Part Two" with a short passage—"The Metaphor Delivered" (see below, page 193)—which intensifies the war imagery of Arnold's poem and the novel itself in order to suggest that violence and division may protend either destruction or birth.

A sense of division—one could call it ambivalence or schizophrenia—permeates the novel, thematically, in its tone and its formal construction. The tone of the novel is a result of the amalgam of feeling, introspection, analysis, and explicit comparison which Mailer offers the reader. He describes the plethora of reactions—emotional, logical, physical, metaphorical—that are caused by the events of the March, thereby recreating some of the division and confusion we associate with "real experience." Nothing is rendered in isolation; every experience is embedded in a continuum of thoughts and events which precede and follow it, so that significance is not so much intrinsic as relational. Mailer works at achieving not only a picture of an event but also a recreation of the workings of the "primary imagination," which Coleridge maintained were inseparable from the direct perception of experience. We, as readers, learn about both the March on the Pentagon and Mailer himself.

This combination of the objective and the subjective, the historical and the symbolic, the factual and the imaginative sets the book apart from either the novel or most contemporary journalism. It leads Mailer to entitle one of its sections "History as a Novel" and the other "The Novel as History." Through the continuous infusion of his ego and his imaginative insights, the factual nature of reportage is modulated into an esthetic whole which resembles, in its dedication to the creation of a world (as opposed to the description of a world), the literary works we are accustomed to call novels. On the other hand, *The Armies of the Night*, grounded in actual events, also resembles a history.

The book honors two principles at the heart of the historical method. First, Mailer writes about actual events, which are socially and historically verifiable. Second, he subscribes to the assumption that he, as historian, must be factually inclusive. While the journalist attempts to convey only the most topically relevant facts, the historian feels a larger responsibility: to convey all the details and information which might conceivably be relevant to an understanding of the events; and the historian feels a need to arrive at an understanding of events which is not confined merely to topical significance. Though Mailer most certainly does not include everything related to the Pentagon March, he does try, particularly in "Book Two," to account for its genesis, to recount the major incidents, and to reveal the immediate aftermath. He is, in addition, writing two sorts of history: "Book Two" is akin to the history we find in most history books, written history seen from the viewpoint of the historian, who appears above and beyond his material, marshalling data into its most understandable form. "Book One," however, is more like oral history or memoir: it recounts events from the perspective of the actor and is in itself history and the source material for future history. The comparison to oral history is particularly apt because Mailer is focusing on himself as participant, an actor (but not necessarily *the* actor, as in a memoir) whose individual recollection of his experience conveys much that cannot be found in official or documentary descriptions of the event.

The novelist's perspective is also central to the book. Though Mailer swears allegiance to facts, he is even more concerned with the ambience, personal and social, which imparts significance to those facts. Mailer is using the facts of the mind to uncover the truth of the heart or, in less literary terms, the psyche. Consequently, while he will not offer false data, he is especially concerned with recounting the aspects of human history which are not verifiable, the emotions, moods, and symbolic overtones that provide color, intensity, and depth to experience. His primary allegiance is to the imagination, and he brings all the novelist's imaginative gifts to his historian's task. Mailer does more than present persons, he creates characters—Robert Lowell, Commissioner Scaife. He does more than describe settings, he creates them. His history is not only chronological, at least in each part, it has also an upward emotional curve which resembles a plot. And he does not remove the historian in order to give the illusion of objectivity; rather, he uses himself as narrator, and emphasizes the creative and imaginative function of the narrator. He is attempting to do, from a more subjective orientation, what Edmund Wilson did in *To the Finland Station*: bring to the craft of history the devices, methods, skills, and imaginative vision of the novelist.

This division between the historical and fictional aspects of the work reflects, of course, the division Mailer sees in America and in himself. In *The Armies of the Night* he achieves a remarkable consonance of content and formal qualities. America is schizophrenic, Mailer is divided, and his recreation of these divisions will utilize a form and method that are themselves divided. So Mailer's novel is divided into two parts, and each part, furthermore, is an amalgam, yoked by a dialectical tension, of two styles and formal approaches, those of Mailer the novelist and Mailer the historian.

One of the hallmarks of twentieth-century literature has been fragmentation. As explorers of chaos and confusion, modern artists have utilized discontinuity, both formally and stylistically, to recreate their experience of the modern world. Mailer departs from this tradition. His division is one of opposites, which are in dialectical relationship to each other. God and the Devil, good and evil, the individual and society—all exist in a necessary bilateral relationship. And this overarching relationship, this dialectic, encompasses both diversity and unity. Thus Mailer's use of a style and structure that are divided is a reflection of the reality he is describing and creating. Form and content mirror each other. In the book the historical and fictional aspects are sometimes at odds with one another, yet that they are yoked together coherently, in one volume, is esthetic justification for believing in the possibility of that coherence which Mailer claims he discovers at the end of the March on the Pentagon. The content of the book—the historical aspects, the events that actually occurred—provides an impetus toward the divided form of the book; the esthetic elements—style and form— make that content credible. Though most modern writers begin with a search for wholeness and discover fragmentation, Mailer begins with divisions which, through dialectical confrontation, are eventually united into a coherent whole.

This dialectical unification takes place within the psyche of the protagonist, Norman Mailer. The insights into society and his own experience become, in the crucible of Mailer's psyche, acts of affirmation of the self. His order becomes the order of the universe. His analysis of the Pentagon March is not characterized by what Keats called "negative capability," the capacity of the artist to remove himself from what he creates in such a way as to ensure that the characters and actions proceed according to their own internal logic; rather, it is one of the foremost examples of what Keats called the "egotistical sublime," the creation of an esthetic world dominated by the needs and emotions of its maker.

It is this romantic and egotistical affirmation that is perhaps at the core of Mailer's popularity. There is no doubt that he is a modern culture hero, that many individuals and certain American subcultures find in his character and writing something worthy of admiration, adulation, and imitation. A large part of this reaction is owing to Mailer's egotistical assertions: Mailer, to many, seems accurate in his assessment of American society as devoid of the satisfactions which men require for personal fulfillment; corporation land seems more frightening than utopian in its possibilities. And his recognition, throughout his fiction and nonfiction alike, that modern men can no longer depend upon the values and reactions of the past in coping with their environment and are presently at a loss to forge new values and patterns of behavior strikes very closely to the core of modern experience. In a crisis of values, when the past seems inadequate and the present confused, when all order either has broken down or threatens to break down, the affirmation of one's ego becomes a significant and courageous act. What stimulates many, it appears to me, is not Mailer's ideology or even the frequent excellence of his prose, but the public act of assertion he so often makes in his writings and in his life. Because many of his readers are faced with a simultaneous loss of belief and a fear of impending totalitarianism, they find his egotism little short of sublime.

Thus, although Mailer moves to some extent beyond egotism and the need to constantly reassert himself, *The Armies of the Night* is based primarily on the strident self-assertion he ultimately seems to transcend. The book is meaningful to the reader because Mailer's egotistic self-assertion offers a slender refuge to the many readers who feel themselves mired in the modern condition Mailer attempts to describe, a condition of alienation, self-division, and atrophy of the will. In addition, his transcendence of this condition, his movement from alienation to coherence, offers a real hope that his way of existential self-affirmation may ultimately lead others to a personal integration of their own fractured psyches.

This, then, is a novel that may give hope. All of Mailer's earlier novels were hopeful only in that they rejected hopelessness in the world they portrayed. But *The Armies of the Night* offers evidence of the possibility that America may yet become "a new world brave and tender, artful and wild" (228). The earlier works were marked by tragic irony, but this novel's ironic vision is colored by the comic. The principle of disintegration, *spargamos*, dominated the social world Mailer portrays in his writings. But while the earlier works despair at this disintegration, in *The Armies of the Night* Mailer finds it hopeful. The brave new world he hoped for and which seemed far distant in *Barbary Shore* is now once again within possibility. The March on the Pentagon is, he feels, a turning point, a rite of passage. It is this hopefulness that makes the novel comic; it involves *anagnorisis*, the recognition at the heart of comedy and tragedy. But whereas tragic *anagnorisis* involves the recognition of the limits and boundaries of human possibility and existence, "the archetypal theme of comedy" involves the "recognition of a new-born society rising in triumph around a still somewhat mysterious hero and his bride."[16]

This phrase describes *The Armies of the Night*. Mailer recognizes that the March is a possible first stirring of a new society. "Book One" ends with his celebration of his present marriage. The marriage symbolizes for Norman Mailer, who is a "simple of a hero," love and compassion, unity and wholeness.

Yet our mysterious hero ends his work with a mysterious metaphor. Although he is hopeful, he recognizes that his hope must coexist with despair, and that even the resolution he seeks appears in the guise of division. The final passage, which conjoins images of combat, passage, and birth, is as ambiguous as he believes the American situation to be. Nevertheless, the metaphor concludes with a recognition of impending birth, and this, both in terms of the metaphor and in the light of Mailer's philosophy of growth, is ground for hope.

THE METAPHOR DELIVERED

Whole crisis of Christianity in America that the military heroes were on one side, and the unnamed saints on the other! Let the bugle blow. The death of America rides in on the smog. America—the land where a new kind of man was born from the idea that God was present in every man not only as compassion but as power, and so the country belonged to the people; for the will of the people—if the locks of their life could be given the art to turn— was then the will of God. Great and dangerous idea! If the locks did not turn, then the will of the people was the will of the Devil. Who by now could know where was what? Liars controlled the locks.

Brood on that country who expresses our will. She is America, once a beauty of magnificence unparalleled, now a beauty with a leprous skin. She is heavy with child—no one knows if legitimate— and languishes in a dungeon whose walls are never seen. Now the first contractions of her fearsome labor begin—it will go on: no doctor exists to tell the hour. It is only known that false labor is not likely on her now, no, she will probably give birth, and to what?—the most fearsome totalitarianism the world has ever known? or can she, poor giant, tormented lovely girl, deliver a babe of a new world brave and tender, artful and wild? Rush to the locks. God writhes in his bonds. Rush to the locks. Deliver us from our curse. For we must end on the road to that mystery where courage, death, and the dream of love give promise of sleep. (288)

Chapter VIII

Epilogue

Mailer wrote *The Armies of the Night* at the age of 43, at the height of his literary powers. All expectations were that he would refine his craft and move ever closer toward producing the overwhelming masterpiece, the Great American Novel, which he has so persistently announced would be forthcoming. The seven ensuing years, however, have seen no further novels; he has continued to mine, in a variety of costumes and with a variety of equipment, the lodes and veins and pockets of twentieth-century America. *Advertisements for Myself* and *The Armies of the Night* were, it turns out, the signposts for the direction of Mailer's work in the late 60's and early 70's.

He has published frequently. *Miami and the Siege of Chicago* appeared in late 1968, and both it and *The Armies of the Night* were nominated for National Book Awards in that year. The following year he described the first landing on the moon, in *Of a Fire on the Moon*. In 1971 *The Prisoner of Sex* appeared in the midst of growing interest in women's liberation; with it, he confirmed his reputation as one of the most controversial figures in American cultural life. A collection of writings, *Existential Errands*, appeared in 1972, as did an assessment of the Presidential campaign, *St. George and the Godfather*. In 1973 the picture book *Marilyn* appeared with great fanfare and with ninety thousand words by Mailer.[1] During this period shorter works were published: an essay on film coupled with the script of *Maidstone*, a report on the heavyweight championship bout between Muhammed Ali and Joe Frazier, a booklet accompanying a record on bullfighting, and an assessment of the phenomenon of graffiti art.

In all of these works Mailer displays his dazzling verbal virtuosity. There is no one writing in America who can turn as compelling a metaphor as he; no one can weld as powerful and individuated a prose as he. Used to fusing the disparate pieces of his psyche together in unique ways, he can uncover correspondences in, and reveal insights into, contemporary American life that are staggering in their suggestiveness and exciting in their intellectual promise. There is little question that his verbal talents continue unabated.

But there is question about the quality of his *oeuvre*. Is Mailer, who showed such great promise as a novelist, now content to be merely the finest journalist of his time? Or, is the "merely" in the previous question an indication that the questioner does not comprehend the changing imperatives and nature of fiction? Is journalism as elevated a pursuit as fiction? Does Mailer's new journalism, energized autobiography, autobiographical fiction—whatever we choose to call it—become ever more revealing, sharper, more exciting; or is it becoming repetitive? Such are the questions with which any reader of his work during most of the last decade must grapple.

To begin to answer them we must reconsider Mailer's earlier work, for the currents that first set him off propel him still, and his view of human existence has major implications for all his work. A major thesis of Mailer's writings, fiction and nonfiction, is that the individual in the contemporary world is constantly in danger of being overwhelmed and destroyed by the social environment he inhabits. This hostile social structure is sometimes in the foreground of his novels, as in *The Naked and the Dead*; sometimes it is the backdrop against which an individual seeks to work out his destiny, as with Rojack in *An American Dream*. But in all of them society is alienating and it is totalitarian, or becoming so; it is seen to be destructive to the very values that individuals must have in order to survive.

In the face of this hostile situation, Mailer develops a sense that modern men must strive to endure. Endurance—sometimes physical endurance but most often endurance of a self able to hope and to keep alive the possibility of a larger and more satisfying life in the future—is a major strand in the fiction. Goldstein and Ridges, Sergius O'Shaugnessy, the hipster, Rojack, D.J., and Mailer himself all try to live into tomorrow without giving up either their lives or all their beliefs in the potentiality of human existence.

Because society is so hostile, Mailer is committed to developing our social structures and mores into forms that will succor rather than destroy the benign aspects of human life. This commitment is clear in the first two novels and in *The Armies of the Night*; in the intervening works the struggle for survival of the individual is so important, and the thought of changing society so far beyond the range of possibility, that Mailer focuses on the difficulties of survival. But even when the need for social change is not explicit, the social origins of many of the problems of his protagonists underscore the necessity for social change.

In *The Deer Park* Mailer first emphasizes the absolute necessity for growth. Conceiving of life as struggle between good and evil, integration and disintegration, and predominantly between life and death, he sees each moment as representing the possibility for either growth and new life or stagnation and the slide toward spiritual and physical death. In a dynamic universe inaction represents stasis and can only increase alienation and hasten death. So Mailer compounds, in "The White Negro" and *An American Dream*, an ethic of growth and courage. One must continually search for the possibilities inherent in the moment, embrace those possibilities, and ride them into the future, when new choices will appear.

Only in this way, he believes, can one achieve that authenticity which is so rare in our media-dominated, bureaucratic, technological culture. Authenticity is the result of intense self-exploration, "exploring the rebellious imperatives of the self" which he counseled in "The White Negro." Here his admiration for violence, so problematical for him in his early novels, becomes a necessary part of his view of the human condition. Only through violence, through a personal wrenching away from the totalitarian state and from social norms of behavior, can an individual begin to confront what is within him. This is exacerbated by Mailer's understanding that much of that within us is violent, and to accept ourselves we must refuse to pretend that such violence is not at the core of our being. Entering deep within our selves, he maintains, is a way of plunging into our collective human past, and any explorer of the self will find himself confronting primitive urges and desires, magic, and a primordial dread. Thus, if we are to be authentic, and Mailer conceives of no higher goal for human existence, we must resist totalitarian society, endure, grow continually, and explore the deepest recesses of our psyches with courage and the willingness to accept whatever riches we may find there, however frightening or disorienting they may be.

In everything he has written since *The Armies of the Night*, he has struck these chords again and again. It is clear that he has developed a mature and reasonably coherent *Weltanschauung*, which is the basis of those explorations of society and culture he continues to make. Insofar as that world-view has value, Mailer's continuing work is exciting and significant.

But the reverse is also true. Insofar as Mailer's developed viewpoint has limitations and insufficiencies, the work he bases on it multiplies those insufficiencies. Despite the brilliance of his prose, the keen eye and clear mind he brings to his writing, and occasional passages that stand with any American writing of any period, his more recent work is not totally satisfying.

The prime reason is that Mailer's subject has become boring. Reading Mailer's *Of a Fire on the Moon* or *The Prisoner of Sex*, for instance, is at times a tedious chore. What Mailer is up against is in the end the central problem of romanticism: ultimately, the ego reveals its limitations. Earlier, we applied Keats's judgment of Wordsworth as a poet of "the egotistical sublime" to Mailer. Like Wordsworth's, Mailer's writing is often sublime, and for that we ignore his egotism; even more, since there is a necessary relationship between the sublimity of his writing and his egotistical persona, we celebrate the egotism as well as the excellence of the prose. But ultimately reduction of the world to the self appears as a reduction of the world, a shrinking of possibilities, a denial of the autonomy of others. There is not only Norman Mailer's way of experiencing the world, there is also mine. And all his emphasis on divisions in the self will not rescue him from his readers' growing sense that Mailer is not coextensive with themselves. The recognitions that bind the reader to the writer begin to break down; marvelous similarities and insights pall as they are continually reencountered, and the reader's attention turns more and more toward differences between himself and the romantic author. In addition, and here is where Mailer's abandonment of the novel is crucial, the romantic writer, caught up in his own subjective sensibility, is often incapable of sustaining that "negative capability" which Keats opposed to "the egotistical sublime." Negative capability, as Keats described it, is that exercise of imaginative projection and introjection which allows a writer to create other consciousnesses, which seem to operate following their own internal motivations, and whose validity seems independent of the specific consciousness of their author. And this ability, in his subjective new journalism, Mailer often seems to lack.

He has made a heroic attempt to deal with these romantic dilemmas. He has written about events largely outside himself, hoping that the exploration of a shared reality (of the political process, a prize fight, the globally observed landing on the moon), even though approached through his own subjective experience, would mitigate the effects of his egotism. Also, and perhaps more important, he stresses the division within himself (and within America, within the astronauts, within Marilyn Monroe) in order to project a self that is somehow not single, isolated, bound by its own experience. If one's experience is myriad, he says, is not one's self a myriad of selves? And then cannot each of us be any and all of us? Overwhelmed by such a strategy, many readers feel the answer is yes. But the problem is that this strategy—emphasizing division, revealing the self as but a basket into which are deposited the separate pieces of self—eventually becomes less effective. For in time the reader discovers that that self he is perceiving is, like a basket, limited, and the divisions within are divisions of an entity: Norman Mailer.

The core of the problem may be that there was great interest in discovering who Norman Mailer was, how he became what he was, what he lacked, what he had to struggle with. But now we know, and Mailer does not interest us as much. Indeed, one gets the sense that Mailer does not interest himself as much. In *The Armies of the Night* he declared that he was growing "bored with his own voice." It is significant that he has not repeated that suspicion, as if he realizes that the cutting edge of the observation is now pointed at too vital a nerve.

There is, then, a threefold difficulty he encounters as he continues to write subjectively approached nonfiction. The first is involved with the problems that arise from the romantic concern with the self. Wordsworth, after all, wrote acceptable but unexciting poetry in his older years. *The Prelude* exhausted his theme; he had himself to write about, and after he had done that, after he had plumbed himself as deeply as he was able, he wrote topical poems and lightweight verse. It may be that the "egotistical sublime" is a limited genre.

A second difficulty also arises from what has been one of Mailer's strengths. There has always been a heady excitement about his prose, for he is the one contemporary writer who has seemed willing to confront the problems of our own day in the context of the events and institutions of our day. There is something stirring about a writer who can take a contemporary event, such as an antiwar march or a political campaign, and use that socially shared reality as the subject of a work that seems to transcend the boundaries of the contemporary. Mailer has, time and again, tapped the power that accrues to a writer who deals with what it is to be human within the confines of contemporary culture and experience. But an unfortunate underside to his efforts is beginning to emerge: the modern world is perhaps as boring and lifeless as Mailer has always suggested it might become. And, worse, the speeded-up pace to history which Mailer recognized as a major psychological problem in "The White Negro" continually transforms what is topical today into what is banal or boring or superfluous tomorrow. In an age of future shock we seek the topical as the only firm support for our psyches, yet change occurs at so rapid a rate that we no sooner suppose we have found a support than cultural change renders it obsolete.

The third difficulty is, in many ways, intrinsic to Norman Mailer. One of the essential underpinnings of his view of human reality is that men must change continually or they will stagnate and die. Mailer judges his characters by the attempts they make to keep changing, and he insists that he holds the same standard up for himself. Certainly the passion with which he has committed himself to the necessity of change, and his willingness to judge others by their willingness to embrace growth, impel the reader to judge Mailer by his own standard. And the harsh facts are that Mailer has not changed or grown much in the past six or seven years. He has been content to repeat his successes of the past, those of subjective reportage, and often (as in his analyses of the political conventions of 1968 and 1972, or in his dramatic reporting on the Ali-Frazier fight) he has just imitated prior successes. The Mailer who said he wrote *Barbary Shore* rather than write a sequel to his first novel called "The Naked and the Dead Go to Japan" seems a figure of the past, and Mailer, in his middle age, bears an uncomfortable resemblance to Charley Eitel, who sold his artistic talents and integrity for success.

Whatever his talents as a journalist, he needs the novel. Even if he wishes to continue exploring the interstice where fiction and history, or reportage, or biography, meet, he must plunge into fiction, with all the risks that implies for him, or lose the excitement that is a hallmark of his style. One wonders—and here the judgment is perhaps unfair and certain to strike to the heart of

Mailer's vanity—if he has become afraid of the risks of fiction. Since his first two novels, every one of Mailer's works, fiction or nonfiction, has been written at top speed (so that he could avoid confronting himself in the activity he was engaged in?) or under the influence of stimulants or drugs of some sort, or, what has become his normal pattern, under the external pressure of a deadline. Sitting down to write a novel, to write it as well as he can, seems at present beyond Mailer's psychological capabilities. Yet if he is to be the extraordinary figure in American letters which he wishes to be, he has to turn once again to that frightening blank page that must be filled with the verbal outlines of his imaginative world.

There is great hope that Mailer will turn to fiction once again. He may be enjoying the fruits of his earlier efforts now, but the needs of his psyche should eventually propel him to make new efforts. Whether he realizes that growth, for him, must involve rejecting parts of the world-view he has so painstakingly built up in order to try new postures, views, and insights is something we will not know until he makes the attempt to change once again. For a man who has written six novels, all different from one another in many significant ways, moving on to a seventh could mean the rediscovery of one of his most important qualities, his readiness to explore, to plunge into new worlds, to describe experience at the ever-changing boundaries of human consciousness.

The finest writing Mailer has done since *The Armies of the Night* appears, somewhat surprisingly, in his biographical essay, *Marilyn*. Amidst all the furor the book occasioned, with its lush photography, its expensive price, its preposterous conclusion, its idiosyncratic analysis of the appeal and performance of America's most charismatic film star, the book's great strength was largely overlooked. Mailer recreates, from the usually turgid biographical sources, Marilyn Monroe's childhood and youth, and it is a virtuoso performance.

Despite the ire he has provoked from liberated women who find his pronouncements about sexuality and his characterizations of women repellent, his portrait of Marilyn's early years emerges as a most sensitive recreation of the psychic forces that could conceivably have impelled the later development of a strange and complex woman. There is a paucity of detail concerning her early years as Norma Jean Baker, and Mailer at times must deal with what he labels "factoids" (public relations truths which, whatever their factual basis, are minted in the brassy coin of a press agent's deviousness), yet he describes her formative years with what appears to be uncanny insight. He approaches his biographical task with all of his novelist's skills. By focusing on the madness that plagued her mother and grandmother, on her early fantasy (or did it actually happen?) of suffocation, on the moral and psychological ambience of the families with whom she lived, he limns an astonishing depth to the woman who was later to become the prototype of the dumb blonde. Once again he makes use of projection, describing the woman as an analogue to himself: artist, half-mad, irremediably split into two, or two hundred, selves; Marilyn has huge ambition, great sensitivity, and a continually uncharted liaison with the deep secrets of human existence. Despite the analogue, however, Marilyn is not Mailer in this biography, but a complex person in her own right. The first twelve years of her life, as he describes them, are filled with portent and possible clues to the riddles and secrets of her personality. In his characterization he reveals not only a sensitivity to childhood experiences which is exciting in and of itself, but also a clear indication that he still retains the capability of creating enormously powerful and complex characters who are not simply extensions of Norman Mailer.

His skills as a novelist have accounted for many of the finest portions of his writing of the last eight years: his shrewd and precise characterization of politicians, technocrats, astronauts; his unerring sense of place and mood, be it Chicago during a convention or a Texas suburb prior to a moon shot. But only here, in *Marilyn*, does one forget, temporarily, Norman Mailer. Perhaps the sensation of being smothered does not explain the later insomnia of Marilyn Monroe, but it does explain the "Marilyn" who is the protagonist of this strange amalgam of biography and fiction.

As Mailer realizes, only the imaginative grasp of a novelist can fathom those mysteries which transformed Norma Jean into Marilyn Monroe, the cinematic image; and only the novelist can transform Marilyn, the image, back into the complex of suffering, understanding, and flesh which first projected forth that image:

> It is possible there is no instrument more ready to capture the elusive quality of her nature than a novel. Set a thief to catch a thief, and put an artist on an artist. Could the solution be nothing less vainglorious than a novel of Marilyn Monroe? Written in the form of a biography? (*Marilyn*, 20)

But the "novel" of Marilyn Monroe falls apart. The subject becomes increasingly tedious, as Mailer mixes factuality with fantasies incubated by his egotistic needs (to demean Arthur Miller, his competitor in art and for Marilyn's love; to tie together Marilyn, suicide, and Bobby Kennedy in a grand Mailerian synthesis). Yet, largely owing to the exploration of the psyche of the girl-child, Norma Jean, the portrait of Marilyn Monroe as an individuated and self-motivated person dominates the biography.

There is hope that Mailer will write another fine novel, perhaps even one that surpasses previous efforts. *Marilyn* reveals an understanding of the growth of the human psyche and a sensitivity to the complexities of womanhood, which Mailer had never demonstrated before. This, conjoined with his insights into the nature of society and the struggle of individuals who must cope with their personal and social existences, and with his splendid prose and sense of verbal mood and balance, may yet enable Norman Mailer to become the outstanding novelist of our age.

Notes

I: *The Naked and the Dead*

1. New York: Rinehart, 1948. Page references are to this edition.

2. In a discussion with Harvey Breit, Mailer said: " 'Actually—a funny thing—the biggest influence on *Naked* was *Moby Dick*.' Had he known while writing it? Mr. Mailer nodded. 'I was sure everyone would know. I had Ahab in it, and I suppose the mountain was Moby Dick.' " The interview, dated June 3, 1951, is reprinted in Breit, *The Writer Observed* (Cleveland: World, 1956), 199–201.

3. Emile Zola, "The Experimental Novel" in *Documents of Modern Literary Realism,* ed. George J. Becker (Princeton: Princeton University Press, 1953), 174.

4. "Norman Mailer: The Embattled Vision," *Partisan Review,* 23 (1959), 374.

5. That a writer urges, by means of naturalism, a view of a deterministic universe and then finds heroism in one who rebels against circumstance and a deterministic universe is not so strange. Malcolm Cowley sees rebellion as the major stance of most naturalistic writers. See "A Natural History of American Naturalism" in Becker, 438.

6. Cowley, 439.

7. Dreiser, in Cowley, 439.

8. Cowley, 432.

9. Podhoretz, 377.

10. Ibid., 377.

11. Ibid., 377.

II: *Barbary Shore*

1. *Barbary Shore* (1951; rpt. New York: New American Library, 1951). Page references are to this edition. Most of the reviews were either mixed or negative. See, for instance, Charles J. Rolo's mixed review in "Reader's Choice," *Atlantic Monthly,* 187 (1951), 82–83, or Irving Howe's negative review, "Some Political Novels," *Nation,* 172 (June 26, 1951), 568–569, or Maxwell Geismar's mixed review, "Frustration, Neuroses and History," *Saturday Review,* (May 26, 1951), 15–16.

2. This is the sole reference to "barbary" in the novel. Mailer elucidated the title in an interview with Harvey Breit: "I may as well tell you what the title of the new book means. It has a double meaning. 'Barbary', for me, is

a very rich word. One of the meanings is barbarism and the other, not in the Oxford dictionary, has romantic connotations. You think of the exotic, of pirates, or romantic things." Breit (see above, Chap. 1, note 1), p. 200.

3. In the social production of their means of existence men enter into definite, necessary relations that are independent of their will, productive relationships that correspond to a definite stage of development of their material productive forces. Karl Marx, "Preface to a Contribution to the Karl Marx Critique of Political Economy," in *Marx's Concept of Man,* ed. Erich Fromm (New York: Frederick Ungar, 1967), 217.

4. Leon Trotsky, "Three Concepts of the Russian Revolution" (from *Stalin,* 1941), in *The Basic Writings of Trotsky,* ed. Irving Howe (New York: Random House, 1963), 140. It should be noted that Jean Malaquais, a French Trotskyist who was a friend of Mailer's, had an important influence on Mailer.

III: *The Deer Park*

1. New York: Putnam's, 1955. Page references are to this edition. The title of the novel refers to the Deer Park, a hedonistic resort for the nobility during the reign of Louis XV. It was, as the quotation from Mouffle d'Anger-ville which precedes the novel attests, a place of decadence and debauchery. Whether Mailer was aware of the other Deer Park—in which the Buddha meditated and was enlightened by his realization of the origin of human suffering—is unclear.

2. The comparison is especially apt, since Mailer's epigraph, "Please do not understand me too quickly," comes from Gide.

3. Ernest Hemingway, *In Our Time* (New York: Scribner's, 1931), 81.

4. *AM,* "Advertisements for Myself on the Way Out: Prologue to a Long Novel," 512–532.

5. Mailer had considerable difficulty publishing *The Deer Park* because several sexual passages were offensive to the publisher who had originally planned to bring out the novel. After a legal confrontation and rejections from six other publishers, Putnam's agreed to issue it. Mailer, however, de-cided he had to revise sections of the work, even as the galley proofs were coming in. During this period he increased the importance of Faye. When an interviewer asked, "How did Marion Faye emerge?" Mailer responded, "The book needed something which wasn't in the first draft, some sort of evil genius. One felt a dark pressure there in the inner horizon of the book" (*C&C,* "The Art of Fiction," 212–213).

6. The concept of authentic existence will be examined in the next two chapters; it is comparable, and in some ways identical, to Heidegger's con-ception of authenticity.

7. References to Hemingway abound in Mailer's nonfiction. See for instance, *AM,* 311–313; *PP,* 104–105; *C&C,* 156–159.

8. Ernest Hemingway, *Death in the Afternoon* (New York: Scribner's, 1950), 213.

9. *The Great Gatsby* (New York: Scribner's, 1953), 4. "And so with the sunshine and the great bursts of leaves growing on the trees, just as things grow in fast movies . . ."

10. *Norman Mailer* (New York: Viking Press, 1972).

11. *The Deer Park: A Play* (New York: Dial, 1967), 190.

12. *Anatomy of Criticism* (Princeton, N.J.: Princeton University Press, 1957), 192.

13. Frye, 41–42.

14. In "The Time of Her Time" (*AM*, 478–503), Mailer's most explicit treatment of sex, the protagonist is once again O'Shaugnessy, now a bull-fighting teacher in Greenwich Village.

IV: *The White Negro*

1. *Dissent*, 4 (Summer 1967), reprinted in *AM*, 337–358. Page references in this chapter refer to the essay as reprinted.

2. Strange though it may seem, Mailer never adequately defines the hipster. In "Hipster and Beatnik" (*AM*, 372–375), he attempts to delineate the difference between the two: the hipster is anti-intellectual, in search of physical experience (quintessentially the orgasm), and directed toward violence. The beatnik is none of these. Mailer's inability to define the hipster may indicate that he is more concerned with pursuing his own vision than accurately describing the hip subculture.

3. His focus on the peculiar nature of the postwar world is similar to that of Camus in the essay "Neither Victim nor Executioner," 1946; trans. Dwight MacDonald in *Seeds of Liberation,* ed. Paul Goodman (New York: Braziller, 1964), 25–43. In this essay Camus states his belief that contemporary men face existential problems which arise out of the recent experience of the Second World War, and in particular the power of and reaction to Hitler in Germany. The basic problem, according to Camus, is how to face the modern threat of totalitarianism without embracing either the inhumanity of the tyrant or the docility and resignation of the tyrannized. Although this has always been a problem for men living in society, Camus finds, as does Mailer, that the modern experience makes the dilemma unique. He sees the rise of French existentialism as a concomitant of the experiences of the Occupation and Resistance.

4. Indeed, the havoc wreaked by the plague seems far greater than the havoc of the atomic age, so far; cf. DeFoe's *Journal of the Plague Year* and the German *Simplicissimus.*

5. Besides Mailer and Camus, one could mention the psychologists Rollo May and Erich Fromm, the philosophers Hannah Arendt and Herbert Marcuse, and the scientist Albert Einstein as sophisticated observers who believe

human consciousness has necessarily changed since the events of the last war. It seems to me even stronger corroboration that this change of consciousness can be found in the often overwhelming mass concern with the thought of atomic death. The enormous popularity of books like *On The Beach* and *Seven Days in May* and films like *Dr. Strangelove* indicate a public concern with the threat posed by the atomic bomb. More convincing yet is Johnson's successful campaign for reelection in 1964 in a campaign based primarily on the question "Whose finger do you want on the atomic button?"

6. Morse Peckham, *Beyond the Tragic Vision* (New York: Braziller, 1962), 33–84. In the discussion that follows and throughout the chapter, I lean heavily on Professor Peckham's work for my understanding of the romantic sense of order, value, and identity.

7. *The Prelude*, especially Book XI, "France."

8. One thinks of Keats's reference to Wordsworth's poetry as "the egotistical sublime" (letter to Richard Woodhouse, October 27, 1818). His criticism of Wordsworth could well be directed against Mailer: "But, for the sake of a few fine imaginative or domestic passages, are we to be bullied into a certain Philosophy engendered in the whims of an Egotist? Every man has his speculations, but every man does not brood and peacock over them till he makes a false coinage and deceives himself. . . . Why should we kick against the Pricks, when we can walk on Roses? Why should we be owls, when we can be Eagles?" (letter to John Hamilton Reynolds, February 3, 1818). Yet despite these criticisms Keats could evidence a large appreciation for Wordsworth's poetry and some of the things it attempted to do.

9. One thinks of Wordsworth's great commitment to the ideals of the French Revolution. Enlightening too is the influence exerted on his thought by William Godwin, the anarchist philosopher. Mailer's espousal of anarchy in this essay is another similarity between the growth of his vision and that of Wordsworth.

10. Consider Wordsworth's depression in Books XI and XII of *The Prelude*, which deal with the impairment of imagination and taste; or the dejection resulting from the loss of feeling in Coleridge's "Dejection: An Ode."

11. *Being and Time*, trans. from the 7th ed. by Macquarrie and Robinson (New York: Harper, 1962), 307.

12. To some extent, the comparison with Heidegger breaks down after this point. Mailer will find in the hipster's search for orgasm—a primitive hedonism—a manifestation of authentic existence. Heidegger would call this search, because it has pleasure as its end, a manifestation of inauthentic existence. Mailer's concept of authenticity, differing from Heidegger's, involves not only "Being-towards-death" (Heidegger, 306) but also the "uncharted journey into the rebellious imperatives of the self" (*AM*, 339). This phrase is Mailer's best definition of the requirements for authentic existence.

13. References to these two figures are frequent in his essays. See, for example, the concluding passages of "The White Negro" and those of his reply to Jean Malaquais' criticism of it.

14. Marx describes human needs, and their repression, in his *Economic and Philosophic Manuscripts.*

15. Mailer rewrote the opening sentences of *The Interpretation of Dreams* and *Das Kapital* in order to show the close relationship between Marx and Freud. Both selections deal with the conflict between individual desires and social needs and show how the former desires (or needs) are thwarted (*AM,* Sources—A Riddle in Psychical Economy, 438–439).

16. From his *Journals,* December 1840. Reprinted in *Selections from Ralph Waldo Emerson,* ed. Stephen Whicher (New York: Houghton Mifflin, 1960), 146.

17. *Selections,* 177.

18. Ibid., 178.

19. Lindner's study of the criminal psychopath is *Rebel Without a Cause* (1944; rpt. New York: Grove, 1944).

20. In addition to sublimation, Freud mentions absorption and renunciation of instinctual drives as the foundations of cultural evolution. He does question, however, whether renunciation is possible, suggesting it might be as yet unsuccessful sublimation. See Freud's *Civilization and Its Discontents,* trans. James Strachey (New York: Norton, 1961).

21. Recent studies on schizophrenia in R. D. Laing's *The Politics of Experience* (New York: Ballantine, 1967), offer a detailed and supported elaboration of the general hypothesis Mailer makes here.

22. "The Development of Orgasm Theory," in *Selected Writings* (New York: Farrar, Straus & Cudahy, 1961), 48–49.

23. Ibid., 51.

24. Several important points of Reich's Orgasm Theory should be mentioned. Reich was a well-respected psychoanalyst; his theories about character armor made important contributions to the psychoanalytic canon. Second, his views on orgasm, while they took Freud's theories as their ground, were rejected by Freud. Third, his later theories about orgone energy met with very little approval. Fourth, Reich's theory presents a position very close to the general misconception of Freudian theory, that sex is the basis of all illness and, indeed, all things human. (This is a descriptive statement; I undertake no value judgment of the misapprehension.) I find Reich stimulating and often insightful; his analysis of orgasm is sound, but his connection between orgasm and neurosis is simplistic and erroneous. Mailer finds more in Reich than I do. Indeed, the seminal idea of "The White Negro"—that a social revolution may develop out of sexual rebellion—is thoroughly Reichian.

25. See Freud's *Civilization and Its Discontents.* For a complete discussion

of the social conflicts that are generated by repression, see Herbert Marcuse, *Eros and Civilization: A Philosophical Inquiry into Freud* (New York: Random House, 1955).

26. *Soul on Ice* (New York: McGraw-Hill, 1968).

27. "The Black Boy Looks at the White Boy: Norman Mailer," *Esquire*, 55, no. 5 (1961), 102–106.

28. The mechanism of this process is discussed in Marcuse, *Eros*. If society limits the natural "polymorphous perversity" of the child, and channels all libidinal energy into productive paths, either social or sexual (i.e., genital, productive sex), then sexual activity in our society can be seen as a sublimated form of libidinal energy. This, of course, raises an important question: is not the hipster then adapting to the dictates of society in his search for orgasm? Is not the hipster, rather than rebelling, following a path prescribed by the very society he claims to be rebelling against? The question is a difficult one for Mailer. His best possible defense is that the mania with which the hipster seeks his sexual fulfillment causes him to move beyond the pale of the socially desirable into the explosive forces that Freud mentions (quoted below).

29. Sigmund Freud, *A General Introduction to Psychoanalysis,* trans. Joan Riviere (1924; rpt. New York: Washington Square Press, 1966), 27.

30. "Self-Reliance," *Selections,* 149.

31. "The American Scholar," *Selections,* 68.

32. The logic is that if society becomes psychopathic and returns to its "infantile dilemmas," it may have another chance to choose between socialism and totalitarianism, the choice Mailer believes it had in the first two decades of this century.

33. Lindner, p. 16. Jean Malaquais makes a similar assertion in his response to "The White Negro" (rpt. *AM*, 359–362). He says, "Hip is but another name for lumpen, and lumpen make excellent conformists and the best potential hangmen for 'order's' sake" (*AM,* Malaquais, 360).

34. Mailer here ignores Lindner's conclusion that "psychopathy is, in essence, a prolongation of infantile patterns. . . . The random behavior betrayed in typically psychopathic nomadism, the inability to marshal the requisite determination for the achievement of specific goals of a socially acceptable order—these reflect . . . the purposeless conduct of a very young child" (Lindner, 3). How is the hipster, the philosophical psychopath, ever to organize or work for social ends when the very root of his being, the impetus behind all his actions, is his antisocial nature, which refuses to achieve any goals?

V: *An American Dream*

1. January–August 1964.

2. New York: Dial, 1965. Subsequent references are to this edition.

3. Mailer's most complete portrait of a hipster is in his short essay "Hipster and Beatnik: A Footnote to 'The White Negro' " (*AM*, 372–375). The fact that Rojack is not a hipster according to these standards seems to reinforce my point that Mailer admires the hipster not so much for what he is but for his style and some of the values which he holds and which guide his actions.

4. In the following analysis and throughout the chapter, "mode of perception" is used to refer to a manner of interpreting sensory experience. "Perception" is clarified by this definition from Webster's Third: "physical sensation as interpreted in the light of experience: the integration of sensory impressions of events in the external world by a conscious organism especially as a function of non-conscious expectations derived from past experience and serving as a basis for or as verified by further meaningful motivated action."

5. Edward Burnett Tylor, *Primitive Culture,* Vol. 1, (1871: rpt. as *The Origins of Culture,* New York: Harper, 1958), 115–116.

6. Sir James G. Frazer, *The Golden Bough* (abr. ed. New York: Macmillan, 1950).

7. *Totem and Taboo: Resemblances between the Psychic Lives of Savages and Neurotics,* trans. A. A. Brill (1918; rpt. New York: Random House, 1946), 118–119.

8. For Rojack, the moon is more than a symbol; it is a physical force, and it functions as such throughout the novel. It is inconceivable that Rojack could have performed any of the actions of the novel if the moon were not full. He regards it as an essential component of his actions, and this belief is essential to his motivation.

9. In *Totem and Taboo* Freud suggested that the thought processes of neurotics were similar to those of primitive peoples. He claimed that the hallmarks of primitive thinking are a dependence upon totem and taboo—respectively, upon a magical animism and "Negative magic" (Frazer's description of taboo).

10. Freud, *Totem.* According to Freud, almost all emotions are ambivalent. In the two cases he deals with, the neurotic and the primitive, the outstanding characteristic of their emotions and ritual acts is this ambivalence.

11. "This book has an existential grasp of the nature of reality" (*PP,* 5).

12. H. J. Blackham, *Six Existentialist Thinkers* (New York: Macmillan, 1952), 92–96.

13. Several years earlier, on November 21, 1960, Mailer stabbed his second wife, Adele, in the abdomen and back. She was rushed to the hospital, where her condition was listed as critical. Only after extensive questioning by the police would she admit that her wound was not accidental; she told the police that Mailer suddenly walked up to her and stabbed her with something resembling a pen-knife (*New York Times,* November 22, 1960, 25). A police doctor's report found him "both homicidal and suicidal," and he was committed to Bellevue for observation. Mailer appealed to the

judge who committed him: "It's important for me not to be sent to a mental hospital, because my work in the future will be considered that of a disordered mind. My pride is that I can explore areas of experience other men are afraid of. I insist I am sane" (*New York Times,* November 23, 1960, 26). He was subsequently found sane; his wife refused to sign a complaint against him; the charge of stabbing was referred to a grand jury despite her refusal; he was indicted for felonious assault and pleaded not guilty; he admitted the stabbing; he was put on probation and finally got a suspended sentence with his probation continued.

14. Kate Millett's *Sexual Politics* (Garden City, N.Y.: Doubleday, 1970) explores Mailer's sexual politics in great detail.

15. *The Short Stories of Ernest Hemingway* (New York: Modern Library, 1942), 477–481.

16. By breaking a taboo Kelly risks magical retribution. But he also gambles that breaking the taboo will associate him with the magical powers which support the taboo, and give him diabolic powers. Breaking taboos is the path to the powers of sorcery.

17. Ernest Hemingway, *A Farewell to Arms* (1929; rpt. New York: Scribner's, 1953), 258–259.

18. An interesting aspect of this ambiguity is the fact that Barney Oswald Kelly is named after Mailer's father (*Advertisements for Myself* was dedicated "to my father ISAAC BARNETT (Barney) MAILER") and Lee Harvey Oswald, the assassin of Jack Kennedy, who appears on page one of the novel.

19. The novel is reminiscent of *The Scarlet Letter*. In Hawthorne's novel, too, the subject seems not so much evil as the effect of what may be evil on the human psyche. It is interesting to compare the two works. Rojack is analogous to Hester Prynne and his murder to her adultery, for both break social laws out of a need to "trust the authority of your senses": for both, the antisocial act leads to disgrace (see the chapter entitled "A Catenary of Manners" for Rojack's dismissal from society) and also a renewal for Hester, symbolized by Pearl, and for Rojack, by his affair with Cherry. Deirdre is very similar to Pearl; combining the innocence of a child and the amoral wisdom that can go along with such innocence, she seems both the child and the incarnation of the wisdom of the ages. There is much of Dimmesdale in Rojack, and much of Chillingsworth in Kelly. In addition, both novels are romances; each flirts with allegory and, in so doing, runs a considerable risk that readers will find the characters unreal.

20. Leo Bersani suggests that Mailer's central concern in *An American Dream* is to show how Rojack increasingly uses his imagination to recreate his world. In his view the elements of magic and dreams in the novel are evidence of Rojack's efforts to revitalize his psychic existence. Rojack is an archetypal artist, who "discovers richness in himself instead of fearing it as an ominous signal from mysterious, external powers." The novel is not about

what happened to Rojack but how Rojack transforms what happened to him into a richly imaginative work of art. "The Interpretation of Dreams," *Partisan Review*, 32, no. 4 (Fall 1965), 603–608.

VI: *Why Are We in Vietnam?*

1. New York: G. P. Putnam's Sons, 1967. Page references are to this edition.

2. Richard Poirier suggests a different view. He finds D. J.'s many roles and voices a reflection of Mailer's concern with the dialectical nature of reality and the struggles that exist within the psyche. "In this work D.J. functions as Mailer has done in others: as the theorist of multiple identity." Poirier sees Mailer's most significant achievement as his recognition that his one self is actually many selves, and that all should receive expression in his writing. *Norman Mailer* (New York: The Viking Press, 1972), 129. Mailer supports Poirier's observation when he quotes Virginia Woolf in *Marilyn*: "A biography is considered complete if it merely accounts for six or seven selves, whereas a person may well have as many as one thousand" (18). Despite the validity of Poirier's insight into Mailer's sense of "multiple identity," his praise of D.J. takes Mailer's intention as his accomplishment. I maintain that whatever Norman Mailer intended when he created D.J.'s multiple voices, he did not succeed in creating a believable voice.

3. Roger Ramsey, in "Current and Recurrent: The Vietnam Novel," *Modern Fiction Studies,* 17 (1971), 415–431, suggests that Konrad Lorenz, Robert Ardrey and other contemporary cultural anthropologists are the source of Mailer's belief that violence is a necessary aspect of human, and natural, life. He further suggests, with sharp judgment, that their thinking tends to be reductive and is therefore reductive in Mailer as well.

4. Mailer believes that cancer is the prototypical sickness of the modern era. His metaphor is apt: cancer, unlike other illnesses, is dangerous not because it destroys body cells but because it involves the unordered and unusual rapid multiplication of its own cells. The metaphor, when applied to modern American society, underlines the proliferation of discovery and technological achievement, the rapid increases in population, and the expansion of big government which are characteristic of modern postindustrial societies, and emphasizes the potential dangers of rampant and undirected progress: "Well, it has been the continuing obsession of this writer that the world is entering a time of plague. And the continuing metaphor for the obsession—a most disagreeable metaphor—has been cancer. The argument is old by now: its first assumption is that cancer is a disease different from other diseases, an ultimate disease against which all other diseases are in design to protect us" (*C&C,* 2). At times, unfortunately, Mailer takes the metaphor as reality and sounds like a crackpot rather than an imaginative

thinker, as for instance in "Metaphysics of the Belly" in *C&C*, 262–299.

5. It is interesting to note that Mailer's apparent insecurity about his masculinity and fear of castration, revealed clearly in *An American Dream*, is here indicated by the imagery he uses to describe God. The primordial beast is a sort of castrating female principle whose main features are a cave (womb), defended by a giant jaw and huge teeth (for castration), and an intrinsic allure.

6. This primitive ceremony also represents the brotherly pact to resist the authority of the father—an ironic ceremony in that it signals an end to brotherhood and an incipient fatherhood, as the participants move to supplant the father and his place in the world. D.J. returns from the hunt having rejected his father. The rejection culminates in D.J.'s enlistment in Vietnam, which can be seen as a gesture that he is now ready to play the role of father in American culture.

7. It should be remembered that Mailer's ubiquitous use of obscenity is also an assertion of his and D.J.'s manhood. The use of obscenity often serves in our society as a passport into the world of adult male society.

8. The basis for much of this discussion is Freud's concept of the polymorphous perverse and Marcuse's extended analysis of this and other Freudian concepts in *Eros and Civilization*.

VII: *The Armies of the Night*

1. *The Armies of the Night: History as a Novel, The Novel as History* (New York: New American Library, 1968). The book is a revision of two earlier pieces: "The Steps of the Pentagon," *Harper's* 236 (March 1968), 47–142, and "The Battle of the Pentagon," *Commentary* 45 (April 1968), 33–57. Page references are to the NAL edition.

2. Mailer's subtitle to *The Armies of the Night* classifies it as both novel and history. It resembles the novel in that it attempts the creation of a personal universe and stresses imaginative insight over historical fact. It resembles a history in that it takes contemporary historical phenomena as its subject and attempts to be both accurate and complete in dealing with these phenomena.

3. *The Prelude* (1850), "Book One."

4. Ibid., ll. 636–643.

5. Mailer can also be compared to Byron. His continual public self-assertion, his efforts to create a powerful cultural persona for himself, are in the Byronic tradition. Byron's persona was a dominant cultural force in nineteenth-century Europe; in many ways Mailer seeks to emulate him, hoping in the process to achieve Byron's immense influence and cultural and historical importance.

6. This, of course, is a seeming rejection of Mailer's celebration of the

hipster, and his search for an apocalyptic orgasm. It is, in fact, a powerful confirmation of his divided character. Ambivalence, for him, is not always vital enough. He constantly embraces one extreme or the other, or, as in this instance, both extremes at once.

7. Recounted in *Miami and the Siege of Chicago: An Informal History of the Republican and Democratic Conventions of 1968* (New York: New American Library, 1968).

8. Mailer's campaign is documented and described in *Running against the Machine: The Mailer-Breslin Campaign,* ed. Peter Manso (Garden City, New York: Doubleday, 1969).

9. The flexibility of the New Left, to be discussed below, is relevant to an understanding of both the March on the Pentagon and this book on it. The commitment to both social change and individual freedom is evident in the concept of "participatory democracy" (cf. "The Port Huron Statement" of SDS), which formed the nexus out of which the New Left grew.

10. "So far, about morals, I know only that what is moral is what you feel good after and what is immoral is what you feel bad after." *Death in the Afternoon* (New York: Scribner's, 1932), 4.

11. It should be noted that Mailer uses primarily the most common meaning of schizophrenia—split personality—as the foundation for his metaphor. Schizophrenia is actually a complicated mental state of which a split personality is only one possible manifestation.

12. One recalls that *An American Dream* is indeed a dream, and that *Why Are We in Vietnam?*, the narrative of disc jockey D.J., is Mailer's attempt to capture the collective unconscious of America, and in particular, the subconscious and unconscious fantasies that made Vietnam necessary.

13. This importance of the individual is in many ways a Romantic conception. Concern for the plight and freedom of the individual is at the very core of the liberal humanism which Mailer believes he is fleeing. Neither Marx and Engels, with their "dictatorship of the proletariat," nor Edmund Burke (that leading conservative thinker whom Mailer quotes widely and prominently in his essay on the 1964 Republican Convention—"In the Red Light: A History of the Republican Convention in 1964," *C&C,* 6–45) with his emphasis on the importance of traditional modes of governance and behavior, would be satisfying to Mailer in most questions pertaining to the individual. Rather, he is closer to Emerson or Thoreau, both Romantic humanists.

14. As do Lovett and O'Shaugnessy; Rojack disappears into the jungle.

15. This is Mailer's most important metaphor for describing the struggle of the individual against society and himself. The platoon in *The Naked and The Dead* makes its first spiritual and physical journey, a futile one, in the night as it carries the field artillery through jungle mud; Hearn's final night is a night of decision as he faces himself and his future and decides to resign his commission. In *The Deer Park* O'Shaugnessy wrestles with his soul in the

night following the visit from the two investigators from the Committee. In *An American Dream* all the significant episodes of Rojack's odyssey take place as he, alone, confronts the night and the missions he must accomplish in the night. D.J. and Tex set out into the wilderness alone, a trial that culminates as darkness falls and they face the wild Arctic night. The most important parallel to *The Armies of the Night* is to be found in the allegory of *Barbary Shore,* in which almost all the action takes place at night, and which ends with Mike Lovett running out alone into the night, trying to save the "little object" from destruction in the long capitalist night that impends.

16. Northrop Frye, *Anatomy of Criticism,* 192.

VIII: *Epilogue*

1. *Miami and the Siege of Chicago: An Informal History of the Republican and Democratic Conventions of 1968* (New York: New American Library, 1968), first published as "Miami Beach and Chicago," *Harper's* (November 1968), 49–130. *Of a Fire on the Moon* (Boston: Little, Brown, 1970), first published as "A Fire on the Moon" in three installments in *Life,* August 29, 1969; November 14, 1969; January 9, 1970. *The Prisoner of Sex* (Boston: Little, Brown, 1971), first published in *Harper's* (March 1971), 41–92. *Existential Errands* (Boston: Little, Brown, 1972). *St. George and the Godfather* (New York: New American Library, 1972). *Marilyn: A Biography* (New York: Grosset & Dunlap, 1973).

Index